At the End of the Storm

*The remarkable story of Liverpool FC's
greatest ever league title triumph – 1946/47*

by Gary Shaw and Mark Platt

First published in November 2009 by Gary Shaw

ISBN 978-0-9557283-1-0

Printed in Great Britain by the MPG Books Group,
Bodmin and King's Lynn

Published privately by
Gary Shaw

Contents

Preface

Although not universally known until 1956 - and not adopted by the Kop as its unofficial anthem until the 1960s - *You'll Never Walk Alone* contains a phrase which we deemed more than suitable as the title for this study into, arguably, Liverpool's greatest ever title triumph. At the end of the storm that was the Second World War, Liverpool emerged as the surprise package of the season to win the title - without even playing. The season had been extended until June as the weather - the worst ever recorded - wet and windy and full of rain, hail, snow and storms - caused havoc with the fixture list. In both respects, there could be no more apt title.

Research for the book commenced a long time ago but only in the past two and a half years did we first meet, discuss and eventually decide that it was a project worth investing time, money and - not too little - effort!

As passionate Liverpool supporters with a keen interest in the history of the club we always knew the story was a good one so, once the decision was made to go ahead with it, we took to the role of researchers easily enough - visiting libraries, scouring obscure publications and talking to as many people as possible who lived though this period at every opportunity to, hopefully, provide not only an entertaining and enjoyable read but also a solid piece of social history. All quotations are taken from these sources.

The story also counters the argument - one given exclusively by opposition supporters - that Liverpool's history only started with the arrival of Bill Shankly back in 1959. It didn't. The team of 1946/47 proved that nothing was impossible. They won the league against the odds through commitment, teamwork, discipline, belief and ability - with a little bit of luck thrown in along the way. What Championship winning side doesn't need all of them - even today?

Football has changed almost beyond belief since the post-war period. Many would say it is virtually unrecognisable, but as you will hopefully find, there is also a lot that remains the same. Football is still a simple game. Good teams require good players, good managers, committed fans and brave chairmen. Nothing would give us greater pleasure than for the current Liverpool side to emulate the achievements of the original 'Crazy Gang'. If their story can act as an inspiration to future generations of Reds then all our hard work will have been worthwhile.

Gary Shaw & Mark Platt - November 2009

Acknowledgements

We cannot fail to acknowledge the contribution made by so many in helping us confirm facts, figures and footballing knowledge throughout our research, as well as obtaining rare and previously unseen photographs. In particular we would like to thank Charlie Ashcroft, Albert Stubbins, Stan Palk and Laurie Hughes, who were all at one time interviewed by ourselves. They provided their time and memories with the good grace we have come to expect from their generation. Sadly, during the course of writing this book, Stan Palk and fellow title winner Ray Lambert passed away. Our condolences to their families.

Similarly, we extend our heartfelt thanks to the rest of the 1946/47 squad - who sadly we never had the chance to meet - as without their effort, energy and endeavour over 60 years ago, we would simply have no story to tell. Our thanks also to all the families and friends of the Liverpool team of 1946/47 we have met and talked to over the course of our research. We hope this is a fitting tribute to your loved ones who gave thousands of Liverpool fans the most precious of footballing memories.

Our thanks also go to Liverpool FC Museum Curator Stephen Done for providing and allowing us access to the Liverpool FC archive, as well as providing an excellent foreword for what is clearly - like ourselves - a subject very close to his heart; Adrian Killen and Barry Devonside for providing rare photographs and memorabilia; Eric Doig for his statistical knowledge; Arnie Baldursson from lfchistory.net - an excellent resource for every Liverpool fan; Colin Jose for his help with the team's pre-season tour of America and Canada; Tony Barrett; Dan Nicolson; David Wotherspoon at Marine FC for providing information and a photograph of Len Carney; Dave Hewitson; Paul Sullivan; Mark Forshaw; Getty; Terry Lindsay for his many stories of this title winning side; and Frank Beardwood for his memories of that great season when he was just 14 years old - young and innocent and red!

Our thanks also to the local journalists of the time; *Ranger, Contact, Stork* and Ernest (*Bee*) and Leslie Edwards. Your words have entertained us, guided us and kept us company over the past two and a half years.

Last but definitely not least, special mention must also be given to our respective families. The many late nights and constant talk of Stubbins, Balmer, Nivvy *et al* are over at last. Roll on the next one!

Whilst every effort has been taken to ensure that all information is correct, some factual errors may occur. We only hope this does not detract from your enjoyment of the book. Likewise, whilst every care has been taken to ensure all photographs used have been done so correctly, if any institution feels thay may have an issue over use of a particular photograph, please do not hesitate to contact us.

Gary Shaw & Mark Platt - November 2009

Foreword

I have always been fascinated by Liverpool's 1946/47 season. My late father often told me of how, when he was a teenager, he and his family were holidaying in New Brighton in the summer of 1947 and paid a visit to some, now long-lost, relatives off Scotland Road. As a treat, he and his brother were taken for a walk around the perimeter of Anfield - there was no museum or guided tour at the tatty old ground in those days - to look at the home of the very first post-war English League Champions; the team who had seen off the forces of Manchester United - then managed by a young ex-Liverpool player named Matt Busby, the mighty Wolverhampton Wanderers - led by great Stan Cullis, and a Stanley Matthews' inspired Stoke City, to clinch the title by just one point!

My father could still recall some of their names;- Billy Liddell, Cyril Done (another distant relative) and Albert Stubbins. This was especially significant when you consider that, at the time, he was living in a small town in Shropshire, without the benefit of TV and with only the occasional crackly radio broadcast or the back pages of wafer thin newspapers to keep him informed. They clearly made an impact.

I found a photograph of this historic team - taken in September 1946, just as the longest season in English football records was gathering pace – and was immediately struck by the feeling that these men came from a different age, a different time, almost a different world from what we know now.

There were no player's agents; few - if any - owned a car; many lodged in 'digs' or rented club-provided houses. There were no lucrative boot deals, discussions on image rights or advertising contracts. Their kit is ragged, faded, darned and mis-matched. Their socks are rumpled around their ankles, not because of youthful rebellion, but because they were so old they no longer held up on their own. For this was Britain in 1946, a country gripped by a vicious 'austerity' that is a far cry from the one it is claimed we are experiencing in 2009.

Such privation was the lingering after-shock of the Second World War that had ended just 15 months before the season started. Fuel, food and clothes, almost everything, was severely rationed. If a player wanted a new shirt, he had to use his own valuable clothing coupons as the club was often in the same situation - low on everything except optimism. Unsurprisingly, many elected to soldier on in the same tired and worn kit they had always worn. Everyone, irrespective of class or income, ate the same restricted diet.

Yet these men managed to win Liverpool's fifth league championship. One player, the great Billy Liddell, became such a talisman that the club was dubbed 'Liddelpool', whilst Albert 'the Burning Stub' Stubbins came in to add much-needed firepower up front, quickly becoming a Kop hero and eventually being immortalised on the cover of The Beatles' 'Sergeant Pepper's Lonely Hearts Club Band'. Bob Paisley - not long out of the Army where he had seen action in Italy and North Africa - and then just one of a number of promising young footballers at Anfield, and who had waited since August 1939 to get on the team sheet, commenced his incomparable relationship with the club; first as a solid and highly rated left-half and then becoming the most successful football manager of the 20th Century.

These were true footballing heroes of the classic mould. Humble men who played for the honour and the sheer joy of the game. Who slogged it out through the worst winter in living memory and were still there ten months later, kicking a competitive ball at the start of June - in one of the hottest summers. Experience and youth - the ideal mix. All gave the greatest performances of their careers. It truly was a classic season. A great season. And one that I believe rates amongst the very best of the 18 Championships our great Club has known. This book tells their story. It is a story worth telling.

Stephen Done
Curator
Liverpool FC Museum

A rarely seen team photo of the Liverpool squad from July 1946. Yet to be demobbed a host of team-members are missing, there is no goalkeeper in the picture and the poor state of the club's kit due to war-time shortages can be clearly seen. Back row (left to right) Bob Priday, Phil Taylor, Harry Eastham, Eddie Spicer, Bill Jones, Bob Paisley, Len Carney. Front row (l to r) Berry Niewenhuys, Cyril Done, Bill McConnell (Chairman), Willie Fagan (captain), Jackie Balmer.

Introduction

"No supermarkets, no motorways, no teabags, no sliced bread, no frozen foods, no flavoured crisps, no lager,…no Pill, no trainers, no hoodies…Abortion illegal, homosexual relationships illegal, suicide illegal, capital punishment legal…Heavy coins, heavy shoes, heavy suitcases, heavy tweed coats, heavy leather footballs…Meat rationed, butter rationed, lard rationed, margarine rationed, sugar rationed, tea rationed, cheese rationed, jam rationed, eggs rationed, sweets rationed, soap rationed, clothes rationed."

David Kynaston, Austerity Britain 1945-51, p. 19

The war in Europe ended on 8 May 1945. Those few people who found time amidst the celebrations to spare a thought for football did so knowing that the practicalities of immediate post-war Britain made a return to 'normal' football - with no regional leagues, no guest players and no promotion/relegation - impossible. Tens of thousands of men were still waging war in the Far East; hundreds of professional footballers were still serving in the Pacific and in Europe; thousands more would not be demobbed for a year at least. There were still 338,000 POWs in Britain, some of whom were drafted in to help save the harvest of July 1946, ravaged as it was by some of the worst storms seen for decades – a portent of what was to come barely six months later.

Travelling to away games was still out of the question. Fuel was short and rationed – only essential travel was allowed. Playing Portsmouth away just wasn't essential enough. Football equipment was also hard to find. Football boots especially were scarce. Welsh international Ivor Powell returned home from India with no footwear. His club, QPR, duly asked for fans with a spare pair – size 6, 7 or 8 – to drop them off at the ground. Even Dennis Compton, poster boy for a generation of players who were the last to be capped regularly by England at both football and cricket, played against Scotland in a pair of boots borrowed from the son of Arsenal's assistant manager.

Clothing, and by definition football kits, were also rationed – purchasable only by coupon. When Southend played Everton in the Cup they found their shirts clashed with the visitors. Enroute to Goodison for the second leg they stopped off at Aston Villa to borrow the Midlander's kit as they had no spare. Even Manchester United were forced to ask for assistance from fans – one of many clubs who pleaded for spare coupons with which they could buy new shirts, shorts and socks.

Balls too, were precious commodities. Liverpool's directors told their players not to kick them in alleyways or on the road so as to give them some degree of longevity as replacements, although cheap, were not well made. In the closing minutes of the 1946 FA Cup Final between Derby and Charlton, the ball burst after a typically hard shot by Derby's robust centre forward Jack Stamps. The same thing happened in a league game five days later between the two sides. One also burst in the 1947 final between Charlton and Burnley.

The chronic housing shortage also affected clubs. Middlesbrough's England captain George Hardwick had guested for Chelsea during the war but when asked about a move to the Londoner's one thing was uppermost in his thoughts, "What about a house?" he enquired. Crystal Palace manager George Irwin shared his home with four or five players who could not find a flat in London. Watford feared they would be without a team as they could not provide housing. They bought building plots to house their married players, as did Charlton – who spent £9,000 on seven houses for theirs. "If you can get me houses for players...I can get you the best team in the world!" said non-league Colchester United Chairman Ted Fenton. He was probably half right.

Squatting was common and widespread - September 1946 marking its highpoint. It was estimated that around 50,000 people were squatting at this time. In the same month six families moved into empty temporary Army housing in West Derby – some with young children. All were arrested and evicted within a week. Without an adequate water supply cases of dysentery rose alarmingly. The proposed Liverpool Corporation's new housing developments at Speke and Kirkby couldn't come quick enough but a severe shortage of bricks, due to too few factories and too few people to work in them, merely prolonged the wait. With hindsight the decision by Liverpool's directors to purchase six houses in a newly built street in the Liverpool suburbs was a masterstroke. Food and clothes' rationing, fuel and housing shortages. For the football authorities as well as the fans, it was clear that they and the clubs needed time to regroup.

League football finally resumed in August 1945, albeit on the already well-known regional basis to limit non-essential travel. The top two divisions were split into North and South – the river Trent being the dividing line, whilst the Third Division was split into five smaller regional groups. There was no promotion or relegation and guest players were still permitted. Despite these temporary league limitations, the FA Cup resumed in all its glory. Almost. Ties were to be decided over two legs. In both competitions it was clear that fans - who attended in unprecedented numbers - demanded as swift a return to normality as possible.

Interest in football was only intensified by the arrival of Dinamo Moscow in November 1945. The Russian side's short and controversial tour lasted 33 days. During this time they played just four matches, winning two and drawing two, scoring 19 goals and conceding nine. The four games, at Stamford Bridge, Ninian Park, White Hart Lane and Ibrox, were watched by almost 270,000 spectators.

If the visitor's tactical approach, their emphasis on diet and scientific preparation, and even their warm-up before the game – an innovation that was unheard of at the time – was not universally adopted by English teams immediately, the interest the tour generated showed how popular football was in the hearts and minds of the English football fan. Few could talk of anything else for weeks after Dinamo's departure. The 'proper' season couldn't come soon enough.

As war-damage, neglect and a lack of both money and materials for improvements took its toll, many grounds were in a state of disrepair. With attendances at some as high as 60, 70 and 80,000 it was perhaps inevitable that handling and controlling such huge crowds would cause problems. With police reluctant to release men to control an estimated 85,000 fans at a second-leg FA Cup tie at Burnden Park in March 1946 – constables were guarding stockpiles of food in the Burnden Stand to prevent looting – crush barriers collapsed and 33 people died. All the casualties were located within a ten-square metre space near a corner flag. Over 500 were injured. Severe restrictions were placed on attendance levels at football grounds immediately - ironically causing even more queuing problems the following season.

Despite this tragic incident, the return of the FA Cup went some way to restoring football to some sort of pre-war 'normality'. More players returned from overseas. More were demobbed. New kit was found, new balls bought and new signings were made – one of the most notable at managerial level where Manchester United unveiled former Liverpool captain Matt Busby as their new man in charge.

Other clubs eyed the large number of prolific goalscorers in war-time football and wondered which ones were worth gambling on. Even if they did, what could the clubs offer? Most players were on little more than a skilled man. Maximum and minimum wages were set by the Football League - the increase of which the Players' Union demanded throughout this, and subsequent seasons. It was not a friendly dispute.

Providing a house would almost guarantee a player's arrival - no matter who the club was, as could another job, training courses or the promise of a foreign tour - preferably to a country where food rationing was unknown as the one thing everyone was short of throughout this period was food. Almost everything was rationed and no-one was immune. In the House of Commons the only meat on the menu at one time was whale or seal steak. So worried that their hosts would not have an adequate supply Bolton Wanderers took their own food whenever they went to an away game. Nowhere was a footballer's poor diet more vividly illustrated than when a club hosted a foreign team or travelled abroad. Wolves toured Sweden prior to the start of the 1946/47 season and their players noted that, "there was as much meat in one meal as in a week in England." On his first England trip to Ireland, Manchester United half-back Henry Cockburn exclaimed, "What food we had in Dublin! Chicken, eggs and lashings of wonderful ice cream." By contrast, British housewives queued up for meat – rabbit if they could get it, and some hadn't bought or even seen a banana for nearly six years.

In the midst of these food shortages, Liverpool's trip to the USA for their own pre-season tour was both a brilliant tactical plan – enabling the players, both new and old, to regain comradeship and confidence with a series of easy matches (10 games and 10 wins in just over a month together) - and a desire to ensure they were properly fed and well-looked after in the New York state and Canadian sunshine. Every player came back having put on weight, some by as much as half a stone.

Nationally, the summer of 1946 saw bread rationing extended to include cakes and other, "puddings," and the minimum size of some types of loaves was reduced. Bakers duly threatened a national strike. Sugar, chocolate and clothes rationing remained. Soap rations had also recently been cut and there was still a shortage of bricks. It was clear that rebuilding the country, both figuratively and literally, was going to be a slow process. Ominously, for builders and footballers alike, the typically unreliable British weather brought both a heatwave and the worst flooding for decades - "cloud bursts, winds of hurricane force and 1½ inch hailstones." In July. It would remain as volatile and unpredictable throughout the coming winter.

Locally, post-war shortages in a host of other, less essential goods, was highlighted in the case of the ship's greaser who pleaded guilty to bringing stockings and combs into Liverpool from Montreal in order to sell on the black market. He was fined £100. Ten tons of sugar was stolen from Liverpool docks - to sell to ice-cream makers in Blackpool. The court case would rumble on throughout the year. Fiery meetings were held in Council chambers, where the lack of local bricks remained one of the main topics of conversation. The city's bomb damaged areas would remain so for another 20 years.

The last week of August also saw another 'war' tragedy. An inquest was opened in Liverpool into the sinking of the Dock Board tender *Denham* which had blown up at New Brighton the previous month. It was found that the ship had hit a German mine that had been dropped during the 1941 blitz and remained undiscovered ever since. Eight crewmen perished in the blast.

Despite such stark reminders of the recent conflict however, the sporting arena at least was returning to normal. In July, Liverpool winger Berry Niewenhuys' great friend Bobby Locke shot a record equalling 69 in the first round of the British Golf Championship at the Old Course. The following day Hindhead's Dai Rees bettered the South African's score by two strokes. In cricket, India were in the middle of their tour of England - a match against Lancashire at Liverpool's Aigburth cricket ground was arranged, but the weather saw it cancelled.

Amidst this semi-chaos, football fans up and down the country prepared for their first game of 'proper' football for over six years as many do today; talking with their friends and family about their side's prospects for the coming season; discussing new signings - or the lack of the same; how they would like their team to play; who they should sell and where they would meet afterwards - to have the same conversations all over again. Football was back at last. Whoever won the title would go down in history - winners of the first post-war league Championship. Liverpool were not expected to be this side.

Gary Shaw - November 2009

Who's Who

Before the story of Liverpool's most remarkable title triumph is told, it is important to first put into context the club's standing in the game at this time. Champions of England on four previous occasions – 1901, 1906, 1922 and 1923 – Liverpool were undoubtedly a big club but a host of others commanded more respect. Aston Villa (6), Sunderland (6), Arsenal (5) and Everton (5) could all boast more titles, while Newcastle and Sheffield Wednesday were level with the Reds on four championships apiece. The fact they were also yet to get their hands on that most coveted of trophies, the FA Cup, meant that in terms of English footballing aristocracy the Reds were looked upon as under-achievers at best, and second-rate at worst
.

With every passing year Liverpool's once proud reputation was diminishing. Indeed, prior to the outbreak of war in 1939, they had endured the bleakest period in their history. Regular flirtations with relegation and 16 years without any silverware had plunged the Red half of Merseyside into a state of despondency. Seemingly surrounded by mediocrity, Liverpool supporters could only look with envy at their neighbours across Stanley Park. Since the Reds' last title win Everton, with three titles and one FA Cup, had gained the upper hand on Merseyside. The Blues had also won the last championship before the war in 1938/39 and, as title holders and with the new season looming, they were deemed to be a sure bet to finish above their city rivals once again.

As a club Liverpool had done all they could for the war effort but they were now counting the cost of the conflict. Back in 1939 the team were among the first to offer themselves for conscription, setting an example for others to follow by joining the Armed Forces en masse, but no-one knew then that it would be another six years before life, both social and sporting, would return to 'normal'.

By the time peace was declared many Liverpool players were past their prime - or so we were led to believe. The Reds' squad was certainly an ageing one, top heavy with men approaching their thirties and a host of promising pre-war youngsters - as yet untested in 'proper' football - now in their mid-twenties. Others, like goalkeeper Arthur Riley, were now simply beyond reasonable playing age and had retired. Former captain Tom Cooper, although he too would have been too old to carry on playing, had been killed in a motorcycle accident while serving in the Military Police in December 1940, and inspirational half-back Matt Busby had left to embark on a career in management and his journey to legend status with Manchester United.

With no exciting new signings added to the ranks, supporters were claiming the club lacked ambition and of the players that remained, not much was expected. It was the start of the season however, and everyone started with a clean slate. Here, in alphabetical order, were the men upon whose shoulders Liverpudlian hopes for the first post-war Football League campaign of 1946/47 were carried.

Charlie Ashcroft
Born: Chorley, 3 July 1926   *Position: Goalkeeper*

Spotted by Liverpool scout Bob Morris playing for his local side Eccleston Juniors Charlie initially joined Liverpool on a part-time basis in December 1943. Standing at over six foot two he was particularly adept with high crosses. During the war he worked at his local gasworks until, aged 19, he was offered a professional contract by the Reds. Made his debut in a Football League North fixture at home to Sheffield United in March 1946 and went on to figure in five of that season's last 11 games. One of the younger members of the squad Charlie was considered to be the second-choice goalkeeper behind Cyril Sidlow when the season started.

John 'Jack' Balmer
Born: Liverpool, 6 February 1916   *Position: Inside-forward*

The nephew of former Everton full-back brothers, William and Bob Balmer, young Jack followed in their footballing footsteps. A former pupil at Liverpool Collegiate, his prolific schoolboy scoring form brought him to the attention of the Goodison club and it was they he initially joined as an amateur - while still working as a joiner in his father's building business. The early signs were promising and after breaking into the Blues' reserve team it wasn't long before the well-educated boy West Derby boy was being spoken about as a possible long-term successor to the great Dixie Dean. Frustrated by lack of first-team opportunities however, he soon switched allegiances to the Red side of Stanley Park while a teenager and Everton's loss was to be Liverpool's gain.

It was May 1935 when Balmer signed in at Anfield for the first time. Within four months he was making his debut in a 0-1 defeat away to Leeds United, taking the 'place of legendary Reds forward Gordon Hodgson in the process. In December that year Jack netted his first goal for the club, a late winner in a home victory over Preston, then established himself as a regular the following season. As a forward who possessed pace and skill in equal abundance, he was forever on the lookout for goalscoring opportunities and loved to try his luck from distance. Despite his slender frame he also packed a powerful shot but wasn't so keen on the more physical aspects of the game, a fact – together with his apparent middle-class upbringing – that unfortunately ensured the Anfield crowd never fully took him to their hearts. As a result he did consider the option of moving on - Arsenal enquired after him prior to the war - but he was persuaded to stay.

In the two seasons prior to the declaration of war, Balmer hit double figures in the scoring stakes and such was his form England recognition was seemingly heading his way. Army duties meant he appeared only sporadically for the Reds during the hostilities but, as well as turning out as a guest player for Brighton and Newcastle, he won his one and only England cap in a wartime international versus Wales at Wrexham. Demobbed early, Jackie returned on a regular basis in 1945/46 and was quickly hitting the back of the net once again. His balding head and Alastair Sim style moustache disguised the fact that he had only recently turned 30 but with the Football League set to resume his experience was considered vital.

Tom Bush
Born: Hodnet, 22 February 1914   *Position: Half-back*

The longest-serving player on the club's books at this time, Bush was a 19-year old amateur when he signed from Shrewsbury on a free transfer in March 1933. He was just starting to establish himself as a first team regular, with 69 appearances under his belt, when war broke out. Made his debut nine months after arriving, in a 1-1 draw at home to Wolves, but his second appearance just two days later saw the Reds concede nine in an emphatic defeat away to Newcastle and it was not until midway through the 1936/37 campaign that Tom enjoyed another run in the side. He figured prominently over the next two seasons and netted his first goal, almost straight from the kick-off in a 3-2 win at Roker Park. Served with the Liverpool Kings Regiment and was commissioned to the Kings Own Scottish Borders during the war but managed to continue with his football by guesting for Brighton, Leeds and Fulham as well making a further 33 wartime appearances for Liverpool.

Len Carney
Born: Liverpool, 30 May 1915   *Position: Inside-forward*

Blonde-haired Len Carney Brave was an amateur player who first represented the club in November 1939. From the Childwall area of the city Len was very academic-minded and attended the same school as Jack Balmer. Came to Liverpool's attention while playing for the Collegiate Old Boys and made his debut in a 1-0 home win over Manchester United. Just a month later, against New Brighton, he scored his first goal and in total netted an impressive 15 goals in 33 wartime appearances for the Reds. Also served with the Queens Own Regiment in the Middle East and Italy during the war and won the Military Cross at Monte Cassino.

Cyril Done
Born: Bootle, 21 October 1920   *Position:Centre/Inside-forward*

Another product of the local junior scene where he starred for Bootle Boys' Brigade, Done's, "prowess and promise," was spotted by George Kay during a close-season trial with the Reds in 1937 and he holds the distinction of scoring the last Liverpool goal before war was declared in 1939. It came as an 18-year old on his senior debut at home to Chelsea in September that year, the winner in a 1-0 home win that was unfortunately then expunged from the record books the following day thanks to the intervention of Adolf Hitler. It was to be seven years before he next got the chance to play in the Football League but in the meantime he set about blitzing opposition defences in the regional wartime competitions.

Six foot tall and weighing 13 stone, Cyril was a strong, bustling type of forward whose burly frame made him a handful for opposing defenders. After battling back from appendicitis Done went on to hit a remarkable 148 goals in just 137 first team appearances between 1939 and 1946, more than any other Liverpool player during this time, and even missed 18 months after badly breaking his leg against Manchester City in 1944. His tally included 14 goals against Everton. Cyril cored 37 in the Football League North title-winning season of 1942/43 and a goal in the final of the following year's two-legged Lancashire Cup Final triumph over Bolton.

Lethal with his left foot and capable of playing either through the centre or just inside, Done was a firm favourite with the fans and one of the games most feared marksman. With normal service about to resume and his best years - supposedly - lost to the war, Cyril was desperate to prove himself on the big stage again.

John Easdale
Born: Dumbarton, 16 January 1919   *Position: Centre-half*

Signed from Scottish junior club Alexandria in February 1937, Easdale had to bide his time in the reserves and didn't figure in the senior side until the first wartime season of 1939/40. His debut came in a 3-0 away win at Stockport County when he took the place of Matt Busby. Played a further two games during that campaign but it was not until early in 1945/46 that he featured again, deputising mainly for Laurie Hughes.

Henry (Harry) Eastham

Born: Blackpool, 30 June 1916   *Position: Forward*

Following in the footsteps of his father and elder brother in becoming a professional footballer, Eastham came through the youth system at Blackpool but failed to make a senior appearance for his hometown club and was signed by Liverpool in February 1936. Two-footed and with great individual technique, he was capable of playing in all forward positions but was perhaps at his best as an outside-right. Played a starring role on his Reds debut in 2-0 home win over a then powerful Arsenal and, three weeks later, netted his first goal in a 5-2 victory away to Manchester United. But despite establishing himself as a prominent member of the first team during that 1936/37 campaign Eastham lost his place the following season and made only a further handful of appearances before competitive football was suspended in September 1939. Represented the Reds just 11 times during the war and guested for a host of other clubs, including, among others Leeds, Newcastle and Southport.

Willie Fagan

Born: Musselburgh, 20 February 1917   *Position: Inside-forward*

As a boy he, "craved to be a famous opera singer," but it was at football that red-headed Fagan hit the high notes. A former miner, Willie first showed promise in his native Scotland as a teenager with Celtic's reserve team. He moved south to join Preston - where he played alongside Bill Shankly - as a 19-year old in October 1936 for a fee of just under £7,000 and helped them reach the FA Cup Final later that season. Unfortunately, North End lost 3-1 to Sunderland and within six months Fagan had moved on to Liverpool.

He was the second signing of George Kay's managerial reign at Anfield and it cost the Reds a then joint club record £8,000 to acquire his services. A strong, hardworking and exceptionally skilful inside-forward, who could also operate in the centre, Willie went straight into the team and quickly set about repaying that fee as, just a week after his debut at home to Leicester, he opened his scoring account in a 3-2 win away at Sunderland. Soon established himself as a regular in the Liverpool side of the immediate pre-war years, during which time he also made a name for himself as a frequent goalscorer, thanks both to his uncanny knack of drifting unnoticed into the opposition box, and the effectiveness of his powerful toe-end shot, which he spent hours perfecting on the training ground.

The Scot had few equals when it came to bringing a ball under control and was renowned for both his deceiving body-swerve and film-star style facial expressions. Served in the RAF throughout the war but continued to turn out for the Reds whenever he could and netted 66 times in 104 wartime appearances as well guesting for Aldershot, Leicester, Northampton, Newcastle, Chelsea, Millwall Reading and Crystal Palace. Represented Scotland in the 1945 international against England at Villa Park - alongside Liverpool team-mates Billy Liddell and Matt Busby - and was held in such high esteem at Anfield that he inherited the captain's armband in the wake of Busby's departure to United.

Jim Harley
Born: Fife, 21 February 1917   *Position: Full-back*

Strong, rugged, and tough in the tackle, Jim Harley was an uncompromising defender who's most notable asset was undoubtedly his pace. Born and bred in Scotland, he first come to the attention of Liverpool scouts as a youngster playing for his local team in Fife - Hearts of Beath - and was signed in April 1934. His debut came in a 5-0 home win over West Brom in September the following year and although only 18 his sound defensive attributes, including superb positional defence, were clear for all to see. Went back to learn his trade in the reserves for a couple of years and during this time famously won the renowned Powderhall Sprint up in his homeland. Skipped training to compete in the race – which he entered under the pseudonym A B Mitchell – and as a result was fined by the club but it did his long-term prospects no harm and by 1937/38 he was a regular in the first team.

Predominantly a right-back, he could also play on the left and, recognised as one of the hardest players of the time, not many opposing wingers got the better of him. Was sent-off - a rare event at the time - against Chelsea on 2 September 1939 but never served the suspension due to the outbreak of war the following day. A Royal Navy commando for the duration of the conflict he still managed to pull on the red shirt at least a couple of times a season during this time and also represented his country.

Was mentioned in despatches for bravery in the Dieppe raid and also saw action at Dunkirk on a destroyer that made several cross-Channel trips. Classed among the veterans of the team upon his full-time return to Anfield, but another with lots of lost time to make up for.

Laurie Hughes
Born: Liverpool, 2 March 1924   *Position: Centre-half*

A born and bred Scouser, who had lived just off Everton Road before relocating to Waterloo during the war, Laurie Hughes was a player who originally slipped through the Liverpool scouting net. Despite being one of the star players in the Liverpool Boys team of the time, Anfield officials deemed him too small to even invite him for a trial and Hughes ended up at Tranmere. When a late growth spurt eventually saw him shoot up to six foot tall Liverpool realised their error and rectified it by signing him on amateur terms in February 1943.

A classy centre-half with outstanding heading ability and great positional sense, Hughes was also a supreme reader of the game and certainly possessed more brains than brawn. He made impressive progress through the ranks and was an almost ever-present during the last three seasons before the resumption of the Football League. Made his official debut away to Chester in the third round of the FA Cup in January 1946 and although one of the youngest players on the clubs books heading into the first post-war league season he was one who many looked upon with high hopes for the future.

Bill Jones
Born: Whaley Bridge, 13 May 1921   *Position: Utility*

Initially joined the Reds as a 17-year-old forward in September 1938 from Derbyshire amateur outfit Hayfield St Mathews, but like many of his generation Bill had a long wait for his official Liverpool debut. In between his 16 wartime appearances for Liverpool he also turned out as a guest for York, Leeds and Reading, playing alongside such greats as Matt Busby, Frank Swift and Joe Mercer.

Marked his first senior appearance for the Reds with a goal in a 5-2 home win over Sheffield United in February 1942 and went on to fill various positions in the team between then and 1946, hence the tag 'utility' player. Quiet and unassuming off the pitch;

Jones was unquestionably committed to the cause on it and, without fuss, would do whatever was asked of him if it benefitted the team. Powerfully built with a bold streak to match, he could head, pass and tackle, and had few flaws in his game.

Bill's versatility was not just confined to football. He was also a keen cricketer and golfer - adept at both - while his bravery in the army won him a Military Medal after he rescued a wounded comrade during the Allied crossing of the Rhine. It was typical of the man and, not surprisingly, he was a hugely popular member of the Liverpool dressing room.

George Kaye
Born: Liverpool, 19 April 1919   *Position: Right-half*

A regular member of the Reds' team during the war, Kaye's record of 170 appearances was bettered only by keeper Alf Hobson who could boast two more. A native of the city, he signed for the club in 1940, turning professional the following year and made his debut in a 5-2 home win over Bury in March 1941. A virtual ever-present from there on in, he missed just two matches during the 1942/43 Football League North title-winning campaign and also found the time to guest for Bradford City, but he faced fierce competition for a first-team place once all the regulars returned after the war.

Ray Lambert
Born: Bagillt, 18 July 1922   *Position: Left-back*

The then youngest-ever player to be signed by a League club - Ray was just 13 years and 189 days old when he joined Liverpool as an amateur in July 1936. He'd made a name for himself playing for Flint Schools and, having been alerted to his potential, the Reds moved swiftly to secure his services and head off rumoured interest from Arsenal. It was as a member of the Anfield ground-staff that his talent was carefully nurtured and so impressed where watching officials by the progress he was making that he was taken on the pre-season tour of Sweden in 1939. He signed professional forms around the same time but with Britain at war just two months later Ray was forced to wait until January 1946 - an FA Cup tie against Chester - before making his first senior appearance for the club.

Prior to this he had featured in over 100 wartime matches for the Reds, the first of which came away to Wrexham in 1939. Represented Wales in four wartime internationals against England and also guested for Reading while stationed in Southern England with the RAF. Dubbed old before his time because of a rapidly receding hairline, the stocky Welshman looked anything but past it on the pitch where his blistering pace and tough tackling were among his main attributes. Was also two-footed and could play in either full-back position.

Billy Liddell
Born:Townhill, 10 January 1922   *Position: Outside-left*

One of the most exciting wingers of his generation, it was on the broad shoulders of flying Scotsman Billy Liddell that Liverpudlians were pinning their hopes as the 1946/47 season loomed. Strong, fast and skilful, Billy would have no doubt been a star already had it not been for the six years of combat. It was after being tipped off by Matt Busby that the club's scout in Scotland went to take a look at the then raw 16-year old winger plying his trade for local amateur outfit Lochgelly Violet. Almost immediately he was signed up in a deal worth just £200 and during the summer of 1938 Liddell moved south.

He turned professional the following year but just as he was beginning to settle into his new life on Merseyside war was declared and his official debut for the club was to be delayed for six years. It was in a Western Division match at home to Crewe Alexandra on New Year's Day 1940 that he made his unofficial bow in a red shirt and he celebrated by getting his name on the scoresheet in a 7-3 win. In total Liddell scored 82 goals in 152 wartime appearances for Liverpool and, when able to get leave from his post as a RAF Navigator, guested for Chelsea, Linfield, Cambridge Town, Toronto Scottish and Dunfermline, as well as representing his country on eight occasions.

A quiet, modest and studious young man, he combined his footballing duties with his role at the club accountants Simon Jude and West and therefore trained only twice a week. It was testimony to his natural athleticism however, and the fact that he didn't drink or smoke, that he was just as fit as those who trained full-time. Although naturally right-footed and originally a right-winger, it was on the left that he predominantly played and his ability to either beat a man out wide or crack in a shot from anywhere on the pitch marked him down as one of the team's most promising young players.

Tommy McLeod
Born: Musselburgh, 26 December 1920   *Position: Inside-left*

Recommended to the club by Daily Post journalist Leslie Edwards - who saw him playing for the Army in Germany - Tommy McLeod was invited for a trial at Anfield and, after making an immediate impression in a run-out with the reserves, was offered a professional contract in October 1945. Began his career with a junior club in Edinburgh and was reported to pack a powerful shot. Had not yet made his first team bow in a red shirt but deemed to be one of the more promising players in the second string.

Berry (Nivvy) Nieuwenhuys
Born: Kroonstad (South Africa), 5 November 1911   *Position: Outside-right*

With his 35th birthday fast approaching veteran South African Berry Nieuwenhuys, or Nivvy as he was christened by fans who had trouble pronouncing his surname, was the oldest player on Liverpool's books going into first post-war Football League season. Joined the Reds 13 years previous - back in September 1933 - following in the wake of arguably the most esteemed Anfield Springbok Gordon Hodgson, with whom he linked well during his early years at the club. Signed from South African outfit Germiston Callies, he was thrown in for his first-team debut after just five outings for the reserves and in only his second senior appearance netted as Everton were beaten 3-2 in front of Kop.

A colourful character, who played the game with a smile on his face, Nivvy lit up Anfield during the dark days of the 1930s and became a real favourite with supporters. Tall and slim with a loping stride, his pace could be deceptive and his inventive wing play added a new dimension to the Liverpool attack. A fine header of the ball, he also possessed a potent right-foot shot.

Such was the high regard in which he was held a football writer of the time rated him, "as being without superior, and I am not excluding Stanley Matthews. He is much more the direct and effective player; a goal-getter and a goal-provider." Top scorer for the Reds in 1938/39, a season in which was also awarded a benefit match by the club that drew a crowd of 13,000 to Anfield for a game against Everton and earned him £658. A non-smoking teetotaller, his other great sporting love was golf and he was well-respected member of the local West Derby club. During the war he served as a Physical Training instructor in the RAF, helping train Czech fighter pilots - for which he was awarded the Czech Medal of Merit - while also turning out as a guest for Arsenal and West Ham. Also managed to clock up another 136 appearances in the red shirt, scoring 63 goals in the process and winning a Lancashire Cup medal in 1944.

Bob Paisley

Born:Hetton-le-Hole, 23 January 1919   *Position: Left-half*

A young Bob Paisley shrugged aside the bitter disappointment of being rejected by his boyhood favourites Sunderland to win the FA Amateur Cup with Bishop Auckland in 1939. A life-changing move to Liverpool followed almost immediately. Bob arrived on Merseyside full of hope and expectation but his new career unfortunately stalled before it had the chance to get going.

Managed just two reserve outings before normal football was suspended and it was to be in a Western Division fixture at Old Trafford in March 1940 that he made his senior bow for the Reds. It was not the most auspicious of starts but it got better and despite only making 58 wartime appearances for his new club Bob showed he had what it takes to be a vital member of the squad.

During the war Bob was drafted into the Royal Artillery, serving as a gunner in Montgomery's 'Desert Rats', with whom he saw plenty of action in North Africa and Italy between 1941 and 1945. Although a touch on the small side, his stocky build meant he could more than look after himself out on the pitch and with his tenacious tackling he took no prisoners. An indefatigable spirit and dogged determination combined with his boundless reserves of energy helped endear him to the crowd from day one, while he also possessed in his armoury a secret weapon – a deadly long-range throw-in. In the final Football League North season of 1945/46 he played in over half the games and made his long-awaited official debut in a FA Cup tie away to Chester the same season.

Stan Palk

Born: Liverpool, 28 October 1921   *Position: Inside-forward*

A boyhood Liverpool fan, Stan Palk achieved his dreaming of signing for the Reds after a former team-mate at South Liverpool recommended him to Anfield director Mr Martindale. A trial was promptly arranged and Palk suitably impressed watching boss George Kay. Made his debut in May 1940 during a 4-3 home win over Stockport County and the following year netted his first Liverpool goal in a 2-0 defeat of Bury.

An intelligent and creative footballer, Palk showed plenty of early promise, scoring 14 goals in 62 wartime appearances, including a memorable strike against Everton in the Liverpool Senior Cup. Missed out on the Reds' Football League North title triumph of 1942/43 but played a part in their Lancashire Cup triumph the following season. In 1944 he was called up by the Navy and shipped to Mombassa for two years but on returning to these shores immediately reported back to Anfield and pledged his support to Liverpool's inaugural post-war title bid.

Bob Priday
Born: Cape Town (South Africa), 29 March 1925   *Position: Winger*

The latest in a long line of South Africans at Anfield, flame-haired Bob Priday joined up with compatriot Nivvy at the club in December 1945. He'd played the majority of his football back home in his native Cape Town and Transvaal, and it was thanks to Liverpool's contacts in that part of the world that they were tipped off about his potential first. Travelled to England on a liner and was met by a delegation of Liverpool officials at Southampton docks who quickly tied up a deal.

Quick, skilful and incisive, Bob was a tricky winger with a lethal shot. Made his debut three days before Christmas the year he signed and registered his first goal on Christmas Day in a 5-2 home win against Barnsley. Did his long-term prospects at the club no harm with a further three goals during that final wartime season of 1945/46, during which time he made a total of 12 appearances. Mainly operated on the left-wing but could function with equal effect as an outside-right and was seen as a more than able deputy for either fellow South African Nivvy or Billy Liddell.

Bernard (Barney) Ramsden
Born: Sheffield, 8 November 1917   *Position: Left-back*

A solid and commanding full-back, proud Yorkshireman Barney Ramsden was just 16 when, in March 1935, George Patterson signed him for Liverpool from his local amateur club in Sheffield. Under the watchful eye of the Anfield coaching staff his talent developed for two years in the reserves. It was Patterson's successor, George Kay, who handed Barney his first-team debut on the opening day of the 1937/38 season. Unfortunately, it was an afternoon to forget as Liverpool suffered a 6-1 drubbing at Stamford Bridge but, undeterred, the youngster kept working at his game and by the start of 1939/49 had established himself as a regular in the number three shirt, forming a quietly effective full-back partnership with Jim Harley.

The start of hostilities interrupted his progress and over the course of the next six years he made just 33 more appearances for the Reds but also played as a guest for Brighton, Leeds United and York City. Hard in both the tackle and shot, wavy-haired Ramsden was a thoroughly dependable member of the squad and renowned among the players for his operatic vocal prowess. On the long coach journeys to away games he would often keep his team-mates entertained, with Yorkshire folk song 'Ilkley Moor', sung at the top of his voice, being a particular favourite.

Cyril Sidlow

Born: Colwyn Bay, 26 November 1915   *Position: Goalkeeper*

Liverpool's most recent acquisition, Cyril Sidlow was signed from Wolves for £4,000 in February 1946 and pitched immediately into the side that was then competing in the Football League North. Signed by Chairman Bill McConnell with the following season very much in mind, it required what was then a record fee for a goalkeeper to get him. Hailing from North Wales and a carpenter by trade, Sidlow started his professional career relatively late and turned out for several local Welsh clubs, including Llandudno and Colwyn Bay, before joining Wolves for just £100 in May 1937 after being spotted by Molineux boss Major Frank Buckley. Made just four Football League appearances for Wolves but memorably kept goal in their record all-time win. Featured a lot more during the war, when not serving in the Duke of Wellington's Regiment, and was in the team that beat a Sunderland side - including Albert Stubbins - in the two-legged Football League War Cup Final of 1942. Also appeared as a guest for Notts County, Wrexham, Darlington, Burnley and Hartlepool United.

Won several wartime international caps but became unsettled at club level when Bert Williams emerged to take his place as Wolves' number one. When not playing football he was also a keen all-round cricketer who had played for Denbighshire. Cyril stood tall at just over six foot and while never one to make an eye-catching save when a simple one could do the job just the same, he was renowned for his quick reading of the game and became one of the first keepers to throw the ball out rather than simply launch it upfield with his boot.

Was 31 by the time he joined the Reds and continued to live in the Midlands, training with Wolves during the week and only meeting up with his new team-mates on a matchday, but after just nine appearances in the 1945/46 campaign Sidlow was considered first choice between the sticks at Liverpool.

Eddie Spicer

Born: Liverpool, 20 September 1922   *Position: Half-back*

A schoolboy footballer of some repute, Eddie Spicer represented England aged just 14 and captained Liverpool schools to victory in the English Shield shortly before joining the Reds as an amateur in September 1937. Turned professional in 1939 but signed up with the Royal Marines - aged just 17 - at the advent of hostilities. Worked his way up to Lieutenant level and personally captured a German NCO who it later transpired was an international footballer. Later wounded in action but decorated for his bravery and recovered to resume his football career with the Reds, for whom he clocked up 54 wartime appearances.

First appeared on the Liverpool team-sheet in an 8-3 victory at home to Tranmere Rovers in May 1940. Played in the half-back line on that occasion and while that was considered to be his more natural position he was also capable of operating on either flank as a full-back. A tenacious tackler with a powerful shot, "steady Eddie," was not averse to anything flashy but could be relied to get his job done efficiently and effectively. Made his competitive debut in a fourth round FA Cup tie at home to Bolton in January 1946 and, at just 23, was pushing for a regular first team place come the start of the 1946/47 season.

Phil Taylor

Born: Bristol, 18 September 1917   *Position: Right-half*

In Phil Taylor, Liverpool had a worthy successor to the great Matt Busby. "A gem of Busbian worth," was the description given to him by one local newspaper and there's no doubt his presence at the club helped softened the blow of Busby's departure.

It was as an inside-right however, that Taylor signed for the Reds as an 18-year old in March 1935. A teenage footballing prodigy who had captained England schoolboys, he joined the ground-staff at local side Bristol Rovers when only 14 and turned professional three years later. It wasn't long before his precocious talents attracted the attention of most leading clubs and Liverpool pulled off a major coup to pip two of the biggest at the time - Arsenal and Sunderland - to his signature in a deal that cost £5,000 and saw Ted Harthill move in the opposite direction.

Phil arrived in March 1936 and within two was marking debut by scoring a last-minute goal that rescued a point in a 2-2 draw away to Derby County. The majority of his pre-war football at Anfield was played in the forward line but an injury to Busby gave him a chance at wing-half and it was in this position that he was to excel. Soon being hailed as a player of supreme elegance, oozing class and professionalism, he was the natural heir to Busby's half-back throne.

Another fine cricketer, Taylor even made a first-class appearance for Gloucestershire in 1938. A typical English gentleman, he was always immaculately turned out and proved to be a fine ambassador for the club. Was one of the first Liverpool players to sign up for the Territorial Army just before the outbreak of war and later served in the 9th King's Regiment, guarding the viaducts on the Liverpool to London train line. He was just four appearances short of 100 for the Reds during the war and also guested for Leeds, Newcastle and most of all Brighton.

A clever footballer who believed the game should be played on the floor, one of his key assets was the ability to deliver a precision pass to his forwards. With League football about to resume the now 29-year old was at the peak of his game and with Busby gone the stage was there for him to prove to a wider audience just what a quality player he was.

William Watkinson
Born: Prescot, 22 March 1922   *Position: Outside-right*

Signed from his hometown club Prescot Cables in February 1946, Bill Watkinson started life at Liverpool in the reserves but was viewed very much as a player with the potential to challenge for a first team place. Given his broad-shouldered physique it was perhaps no surprise that he started out at Prescot in 1939 as a centre-forward but he was much more than a burly striker. Strong, reasonably quick and possessing a good right-footed shot it was as an outside-right that he made an early impression in the Anfield second string and, at the start of the 1946/47 season, he was pushing for a senior start amid stiff competition.

George Kay - Manager

Born in Manchester a year before the formation of Liverpool FC on 21 September 1891, Kay started out in football as a player with his local amateur club Eccles before embarking on a professional career that took him briefly to Bolton and then across the Irish Sea to Distillery, where he became the first Englishman to skipper an Irish League side.

The First World War halted his progress and he was to suffer shell-shock during combat on the Western Front, but when football resumed he joined West Ham and rose through the ranks to captain them in the famous 'White Horse' FA Cup Final of the 1923, the first to be played at Wembley.

After falling ill while on a pre-season tour of Spain three years later he decided to hang up his boots, although he did come out of retirement to play two games for Stockport in 1927. Aged 38 he decided to try his hand at management, initially learning the ropes in the lower leagues, stepping up from player-coach to boss at Kenilworth Road in Division Three South and, three seasons later, moving up to Division Two when he took charge of Southampton.

The end of the 1930/31 season was approaching when Kay arrived at The Dell and his ambition was to take them up into the top-flight for the first time. Unfortunately, in the five years he was on the South Coast he was unable to achieve a higher position than mid-table but, according to the authors of Saints – A Complete Record, George;

"was tremendously enthusiastic and he worked hard throughout his stay at The Dell, using up a considerable amount of nervous energy at every match. He 'played' every kick and his body would visibly vibrate to the stresses and strains on the playing field."

Although his managerial track record may not have been great, Kay was a well-respected figure within the game and it was well known that severe financial problems and the continual sale of the club's best players had prevented him from fulfilling his true potential at The Dell. To illustrate this the Southampton Board resigned en masse in June 1936. The new Board asked Kay to resign in order to cut costs but, although he refused, the writing was on the wall and two months later he had no hesitation in accepting Liverpool's offer to become their new manager.

Under his Anfield predecessor George Patterson, the Reds were in decline and had only escaped relegation the previous season by three points. With Phil Taylor, Berry Nieuwenhuys and Jack Balmer already at the club however, along with established Kop favourites Tom Cooper, 'Tiny' Bradshaw, Jimmy McDougall, Matt Busby and Alf Hanson, Kay set about the task of turning around their fortunes but his first campaign in the hot-seat saw them fare only marginally better - this time avoiding the drop by three points again but finishing one place higher.

Matt Busby recalled that Kay, "worked like a Trojan to put things right," and during the two seasons prior to the war, as new faces such as Willie Fagan, Harry Eastham, Barney Ramsden and Jim Harley were introduced, Liverpool's form gradually improved, with successive 11th place finishes. Under Kay's stewardship the outlook was looking a lot brighter at Anfield. Youngsters like Billy Liddell and Bob Paisley were added to the ranks but with the clouds of war closing in, it would be a long time before Kay's new team was able to take shape.

Always on the lookout for different ways in which he could get the best out of his players he once risked the wrath of the dressing by banning them from playing cricket, a hugely popular pastime with many of them at the time, but, such was the regard in which he was held his decision was excepted without fuss. Renowned for his deep thinking and shrewd tactical nous, Kay was regarded as a man who ate, slept and lived for football, and his dedication to the Liverpool cause continued unabated throughout the six years of conflict. Never one to tear a strip off his team if they'd suffered an off day or criticise them in the press he was a keen reader of books about psychology and a supreme motivator of men. To the outside world he may have come across as dour authoritarian figure but Kay could always count on the full respect of his players, one of whom - Cyril Done - later described him as, "the Bill Shankly of his day." There can be no greater compliment.

Bill McConnell – Chairman

A caterer who ran a string of dockside cafes 'Billy Mac', as he was commonly known, was a lifelong Liverpool fan who had been following their fortunes since the turn of the century. Came from a large family in the south end of the city and all but one of his brothers were red-hot Liverpudlians. Went away to sea as a young man but returned to set up in the catering business and joined the club's Board of directors in February 1929. A hugely popular figure in all walks of life, it was he who was credited with keeping the dockers fed during the dark days of the blitz, while he commanded the utmost respect at every club throughout the country. An inspirational and forward thinking leader,

McConnell was elected Chairman in 1944 and, never afraid to spend big if he thought it would improve the side, under his guidance Liverpool had reportedly, "never been in safer hands."

Albert Shelley – Trainer

Born in Romsey, Hampshire, in August 1899, Albert Shelley was part of the Southampton team that first entered the Football League in the early 1920s. A right-half, he was to stay with the Saints for the remainder of his playing career, winning a Third Division South championship medal in 1922, and after hanging up his boots immediately joined the coaching staff at The Dell. Later worked under boss George Kay and when Kay came to Liverpool in 1936 he brought his tried and trusted trainer Shelley with him.

Jimmy Seddon – Trainer

Enjoyed an illustrious playing career with Bolton Wanderers, with whom he won three FA Cup winners medals – including one in 1923 against George Kay's West Ham. Also collected six international caps for England and after retiring as a player coached in Holland before joining the backroom staff at Anfield.

Beginner's guide to 1946 football

There were two points for a win, one for a draw.
The FA Cup had no limits to the number of replays it took to decide a tie.
There was no League Cup, no European Cup no UEFA Cup.
No substitutions were allowed - except by prior arrangement in internationals.
England internationals were few - the only competition they took part in was the annual Home Countries Championship - together with Scotland, Wales and Northern Ireland.
No club had undersoil heating. Or floodlights. Midweek afternoon games were a regular occurrence although frowned upon by the Government who feared - quite rightly - industrial absenteeism on a large scale at these times.

Players' occupied a distinctive position on the pitch and were described both by their perceived roles - back, half-back and forward - and their area of the field - left, right, centre. Thus the centre-half was in the middle of a defensive line of three. Half-backs and inside-forwards were midfield players.

The teams that started the Football League in 1946 were placed in exactly the same divisions as they had been at the start of the aborted season of 1939/40.

Liverpool played in red shirts, white shorts and red and white hooped socks.

The first day of league football - Saturday August 31 - was the last day of the Nuremberg War Trials.

At the End of the Storm

*The remarkable story of Liverpool FC's
greatest ever league title triumph – 1946/47*

by Gary Shaw and Mark Platt

Most of the Liverpool party on board the Queen Mary enroute to the pre-season tour of North America.
Manager George Kay and director G Richards are absent.
Fourth row left to right; Joe Seddon, Barney Ramsden, Bob Priday, Jack Balmer.
Third row; Bob Paisley, Laurie Hughes, Berry 'Nivvy' Nievenhuys, Phil Taylor, Harry Eastham, Tom Bush.
Second row; Cyril Sidlow, Jim Harley, Willie Fagan, Eddie Spicer, Albert Shelley (trainer), Bill Jones, Cyril Done.
Front row; R K Milne, Bill McConnell (Chairman), Captain of the Queen Mary, S R Williams and J H Troop.

Chapter One
Born in the USA

"Liverpool came to the States for a crack at our teams and our vitamins. It was a clean sweep. The Britons swept all ten of their matches and, like Jack Spratt and his wife, they also swept the platter clean. Not only was there a perceptible gain in strength on the playing field, but the squad averaged a gain in weight of seven pounds a man."

The New York Times

It was on a diet of giant t-bone steaks, pancakes with maple syrup and freshly squeezed orange juice that Liverpool's quest to win the inaugural post-war Football League title began. The new season was still more than four months away but the Reds stole a significant march on their rivals by escaping the bleak austerity of food-rationed Britain and setting off on a ground-breaking tour of the United States and Canada.

The tour was the brainchild of Chairman Bill McConnell, who had visited the States on official catering business 12 months before and who was well aware of the nutritional benefits that could be gained by leading the team on such a trip. Concerned about the effects post-war rationing was having on Liverpool's malnourished looking players, the popular Chairman extolled the virtues of a pre-season trip across the Atlantic to manager George Kay and explained it would be the perfect preparation for the club's return to competitive league action.

Kay was quickly won over by the idea and plans were drawn up for a tour that was to go down in Anfield folklore as one of the most memorable and inspirational the club has ever embarked upon. Compared to modern continental jaunts it was an expedition of mammoth proportions - a round-trip well in excess of 5,000 miles, encompassing eight weeks away from home, eight different cities and ten historic matches.

The squad left Anfield on Friday 3 May 1946, just four days after completing their Football League North campaign with a 1-0 defeat away to Bolton, a result that brought an impressive eight-game unbeaten run to an end and confirmed a disappointing finishing position of 11th. It was a low note on which to finish the season, but the prospect of being the first English club for over a decade to visit America was the cause of much excitement for press and fans alike and the players' every step was followed with eagle-eyed interest on both sides of the Atlantic. "Liverpool go as ambassadors of English football," was the proud declaration of the Liverpool Echo on the day the squad departed, "they realise their responsibilities, and they go with every confidence that they will do well."

The party that left Liverpool on the first leg of the journey contained 16 players - Fagan (captain), Sidlow, Seddon, Harley, Ramsden, Spicer, Bush, Hughes, Paisley, Taylor, Nieuwenhuys, Balmer, Jones, Eastham, Priday and Done – manager George Kay, trainer Albert Shelley, Chairman Bill McConnell and four other directors. Among the notable absentees were Billy Liddell, who had been unable to secure his release from the RAF, and Ray Lambert, who had been selected to travel with the RAF team on their less glamorous tour of Scandinavia.

Enjoying dinner on board the Queen Mary en-route to North America.
From l to r; Manager George Kay, directors R K Milne, G Richards, S R Williams (Vice-President) and Director J H Troop.

As he led his fellow footballing pioneers onto the coach outside Anfield ahead of the long drive to Southampton for the six-day voyage 'across the pond', captain Willie Fagan told waiting reporters that, "the boys are all looking forward to the tour, and I think we will do well."

Eddie Spicer just made the squad after being demobbed from the Marines on the day of departure, whilst Sidlow's inclusion came about only after some subterfuge by both Liverpool and the Army. Wales had selected Liverpool's new signing for a game against Northern Ireland in Cardiff but, having gained special leave from the Army to go on tour with Liverpool only, the Welsh FA received no answer to their repeated and, as kick-off approached, increasingly desperate calls for his whereabouts to player, club and unit alike. It was only when the touring party was an hour out of Southampton that Liverpool finally confirmed Sidlow's inclusion to the international selectors, "explaining that he was only released on condition secrecy was maintained until the Queen Mary had sailed."

Once aboard the luxurious Cunard White Star Liner, Liverpool were treated like royalty, with the ship's newsletter proudly stating, "we are honoured to have such personalities among us." Already it was an eye-opening experience for all involved. It was to get even better.

J H Troop and Bill McConnell enjoy a game of Quoits on the deck of the Queen Mary.

On arrival in New York the players and officials, the vast majority setting foot on American soil for the first time, received a tremendous reception and it was to set the tone for an unforgettable six-week stay State-side. Feted wherever they went, the lavish hospitality on offer throughout could only have been dreamt of back home and the players understandably lapped it up, as George Kay explained in a letter he sent back to Echo correspondent *Ranger*.

"The terrific hospitality we are receiving is the only thing likely to beat us. You can get all the dishes anybody could possibly desire in the eating places and naturally we are taking advantage of the opportunity. All the party are now in good shape but the heat is so terrific that you get free and involuntary Turkish baths in the hotels, which still have he central heating on. Fortunately there is a swimming pool in our hotel, where the players spend most of their little spare time which the day's full programme leaves them."

As well as maintaining their fitness in readiness for the forthcoming tour, and the season ahead, it was also hoped - by their hosts at least - that Liverpool's appearance would also help, "put soccer on a solid footing as a major sport in the United States."

The Liverpool players enjoy lunch with their hosts at the team hotel in New

The fact that soccer, when compared to baseball, American football, basketball and ice-hockey, is still viewed as a poor relation in the average American sports' fans consciousness, may suggest that Liverpool's trip wasn't entirely successful in achieving this particular goal, but the tour generated a level of interest in the game that would not be repeated until the New York Cosmos-inspired NASL boom of the mid-1970s. During the course of their stay Liverpool more than repaid their hosts' kindness with a series of exceptional performances that both captivated American sports' lovers and left them begging for more.

The only dark cloud of the tour was the sad news from England that forced Tom Bush to fly home after the third game. Bush's nine-month old daughter was seriously ill in hospital with gastric enteritis and, following a call from his anguished wife after the match, he immediately caught a flight back to Britain. Sadly, young Christine eventually lost her brave fight for life and, although deeply saddened by events, Bush's team-mates vowed to play on in her honour.

The action got underway in New York on May 12 and a bumper crowd at the Triborough Stadium on Randalls Island saw Jack Balmer net the first goal in a 3-1 success for the Reds. Balmer added another and Fagan scored the third as Liverpool outplayed the locals, who had goalkeeper Gene Olaf to thank for ensuring the scoreline remained respectable.

The local newspaper reported that Olaf, a top-rated keeper who many felt could have gone to the 1950 World Cup but instead chose a career in the police force, made a total of 32 saves during the match, many of which were spectacular. He was the first, but by no means the last opposition goalkeeper to be kept busy by the visitors during their stay.

Although poor quality, an idea of the size of the venue and the 20,000 crowd at The Triborough Stadium for Liverpool's first game of the tour can be seen here.

The Liverpool squad prior to their first game of the tour v The New York All Stars at the Triborough Stadium, Randalls Island. Tom Bush, to the right of captain Willie Fagan (holding ball), would later receive news that his nine-month old daughter was seriously ill. He returned home immediately but tragically, the baby girl died just a few days later.

With no local reporters having travelled across the Atlantic to cover the tour, newspapers back home had to rely on the goodwill of those in, or with, the team for regular updates on how the Reds were faring. Berry Nieuwenhuys was in regular contact with Evening Express correspondent *Pilot* and he wrote that, "the Americans have made a rapid advancement in football and in our first game they gave us plenty of trouble for the first half. Later we ran them off their feet on a small ground, which earlier on had cramped us a little." The attendance of 20,000 was, "the largest crowd to see a soccer game here in years," and so lucrative were the receipts generated that it was believed the cost of Liverpool's entire tour was covered by this opening game alone.

Action from Liverpool's opening game v The New York All Stars.
Above: Bill Jones challenges the All Stars keeper whilst Willie Fagan looks on.
Below: Jackie Balmer (left) awaits a tackle by Phil Taylor.
A slightly sanded base or pitcher's mound can clearly be seen behind Balmer.

From New York it was on to Baltimore, via a swift sight-seeing tour of Washington, where among other places of interest the Liverpool party called in at the White

Jackie Balmer scores one of his four goals v the Baltimore Americans.

House and were shown the Capitol Building by a leading US Senator. Their opponents at the city's Municipal Stadium were the reigning America Soccer League champions, the Baltimore Americans, and it was a match significant for the fact it was played under floodlights. To such a forward thinking manager like George Kay the use of night lighting in football was an interesting concept;

"It was just like daylight; in fact, much clearer than a winter's day in England. What it would cost to install and the actual night charge for lighting I don't know, but there is no doubt that soccer games could easily be played at night under the lighting system we saw here."

Floodlit sporting events in the US, particularly baseball, were not unusual but it would be a few years before such an innovation became common practice in England - mainly due to the real threat of electricity cuts in the immediate post-war era, and another 11 years before they were installed at Anfield. It is therefore, the first known instance of Liverpool playing under lights.

LIVERPOOL REDS
OF ENGLAND
VS.

BALTIMORE AMERICANS
AMERICAN LEAGUE CHAMPIONS

The first international game in 15 years

BALTIMORE STADIUM

MAY 15, 1946 · 8:30 P. M.

JOINT AUSPICES OF

BALTIMORE SOCCER CLUB and BALTIMORE AMERICANS F. C.

WELCOME LIVERPOOL FOOTBALL TEAM

As an old football (soccer to you) player myself, it is a real privilege to welcome the Liverpool team to the United States, and most particularly to Baltimore.

Baltimore is indeed honored that the resumption of international games should be in our City and I hope that our Baltimore 'Americans' will continue to be soccer champions in the United States, and in the not too distant future will be making return matches.

John T. Menzies

President
The Crosse & Blackwell Co.

Programme for Liverpool's first game under floodlights.

Liverpool Echo cartoonist George Green wonders if the touring party will return with American accents!

7

Prior to the game local hopes were high that Baltimore's finest could put up a reasonable fight but, "the well-oiled Reds' combination encountered little trouble," and Liverpool romped to an emphatic 9-0 win. Their superior speed and staying power ensured they were never in danger of conceding. Balmer, "tallied four times against the Marylanders," taking his tour total to an impressive six in just two games. Done was also a hat-trick marksman, whilst Fagan netted a brace as the so-called, "Liverpool Reds," impressed watching journalists;

"the Reds could have 'jolly well' have let the locals use two teams and still would have had nothing to worry about. This is no reflection on the Baltimore team, which played its hardest but could not match the skill of the English team."

George Kay's own notes from the game v Baltimore.
Note the last reference to 'night lights'.

It was a performance that begged the American press to ask, "just how good is this Liverpool Football Club? That's the question in the minds of American Soccer fans today and little wonder." Fans back in New York however, remained convinced that, "American teams are on a par with the top British elevens," and so Liverpool's third game attracted yet another healthy crowd to Randalls Island - where the locals were desperate to see an American Soccer League All-Star side prove them right.

Co-managers Johnny Slaven and Jimmy McGuire were equally determined to show that the Yanks were more than a match for the touring Englishmen and it was widely expected that their team would provide the, "invaders," with their sternest test to date. There was much reason for the hosts to be confident. Several of the squad at their disposal had played against the Reds in the opening tour match a week previous and, "bolstered by the addition of outstanding men throughout the pro circuit," it was hoped they could at least put up a better fight.

However, "high-riding Liverpool continued its triumphant American tour," with a comfortable 5-0 victory and once again it was reported that only the, "brilliant goal-tending of lanky Gene Olaf...saved the Americans from a worse drubbing. Olaf repeated his performance of last week, making [a string of] brilliant saves." Done

Balmer, Done and Fagan (Priday extreme right) prepare to kick-off the third game of the tour.

hit his second hat-trick in as many games, Priday also got on the scoresheet and Balmer continued his rich vein of form in front of goal by adding another to his rapidly-increasing collection.

Liverpool had triumphed with ease over the best the All-Stars had to offer and, explaining the heavy loss when interviewed afterwards, American co-boss Jimmy McGuire said simply, "the British work at it and the Americans play at it." Back home the Echo was reporting that Liverpool, "are undoubtedly doing a grand job of work out in America, for they are showing they Yanks a thing or two, and are still unbeaten."

Cyril Done scores the first of his hat-trick against an American League Select at the Triborough Stadium.

Next port of call was a trip to one of the more renowned hot-beds of US soccer, Fall River in Massachusetts. It was here that Liverpool encountered their strongest opposition of the tour to date, and at venue where visiting foreign teams had traditionally never fared favourably. Back in 1906 the famous Corinthians club from Brazil, fresh from an 18-0 victory in New York, suffered a 3-0 loss here, while in 1928 Glasgow Rangers did well to claim a 0-0 draw.

Fall River's unique passion for the sport compared to other US cities was fuelled by its large immigrant population, especially those of Portuguese origin, and flags bearing the emblem of Portugal's foremost club Benfica were once a common sight along the city's main thoroughfare. Indeed, it was players of mainly Portuguese stock that formed the basis of the team to face Liverpool and while they may have been only of amateur status they certainly gave more than a good account of themselves.

Heavy rain on the day of the game forced it to be rescheduled for the following night when, "many out-of-town newspapermen," attracted by the presence of Liverpool and the temporary stands, constructed especially for this game, ensured the arena was near to capacity and the atmosphere inside the small stadium electric. 6, 387 - the, "largest soccer crowd in Fall River for many years," - turned out to catch a glimpse of Liverpool and they were rewarded with what George Kay later described as, "good, hearty, rough and tumble football with a good deal of all-in wrestling thrown-in."

Perhaps unsurprisingly, Balmer opened the scoring with his eighth goal of the tour a minute before half-time, and when Priday netted twice inside the opening 20 minutes of the second period another resounding win seemed on the cards. In a spirited fight-back however, Joe Chapiga and Ed Souza, one of the players who helped shame England at the 1950 World Cup, reduced the deficit to set-up a thrilling finale. After each of their goals the Fall River players reportedly, "flung their arms around each other and waltzed round the centre circle." According to George Kay, "it needed only a banjo to make it into a real hill-billy show."

The scene prior to Liverpool's game v a New England XI at Fall River - their toughest test of the tour to date.

Thankfully for Liverpool there was to be no more dancing and, although Sidlow was forced to make several good saves in the last few minutes, the Reds' winning run remained intact. It was a rare home defeat for the Fall River side and Kay admitted afterwards that it had been a hard scrap, "they were evidently waiting for us and were all set to lower our colours." In the opinion of Milt Miller, an American journalist covering the tour, it had been, "the first real threat to Liverpool's marked superiority," over any of their US opponents since the Red's arrival. Despite the competitiveness of this game, the contrast in standards couldn't have been greater when Liverpool rolled into Philadelphia for their next challenge just four days later.

By half-time at the Yellow Jacket Stadium the Reds had raced into a four-goal lead and not even the extreme narrowness of the pitch - it was calculated it was barely 40 yards wide - could stop them. After the break Liverpool treated the crowd to an exhibition of, "finesse, ball control, shooting, short passing and teamwork," before topping it off with another eight goals without reply.

Balmer squeezes between two defenders to score one of his three of Liverpool's 12 goals v Philadelphia.
Cyril Done, who netted four times in the same game, is the no. 9.

Philadelphia's Evening Bulletin newspaper reported that, "the ball was in the vicinity of the local goal 90 per cent of the time," and could not disguise the fact that the local Select XI had been totally, "outclassed," in an exhilarating demonstration of, "how the game is played in England." Although only a friendly, and taking into account the obvious poor standard of the opposition, to score 12 goals in any game was a remarkable feat. Indeed, at the time it was Liverpool's record winning score - until a San Fransisco side were beaten 14-0 on another tour of the States in the 1960s. Liverpool's goals in Philadelphia were scored by Done (4), Balmer (3), Taylor (2), Fagan (2) and Priday.

'England's Star Booters', as they were now widely referred to in the States, were attracting more and more column inches in the sports pages of the American press and even those who previously looked down their noses at soccer were starting to sit up and take notice.

From Philadelphia the Liverpool party travelled west to St Louis. Upon their arrival they were amused to find that their new found fame had got there before them. The visit was eagerly anticipated and ahead of the game the local St Louis Globe Democrat reported somewhat gushingly that;

> *"The Liverpool club is an aggregation which does not have a weak spot. It plays the old country system of fine short passing. What's more, each player knows what is expected of him and he'll be in the right spot at the right time."*

Once again, the sheer presence of Liverpool caused attendance records to be shattered. The 12,493 crowd was the largest, "ever to see a soccer contest in the history of the game in St Louis," and the Reds lived up to their blossoming reputation with another clinical performance at the Public Schools Stadium. Against an All-Stars team consisting of players from the local Municipal Soccer League who had been selected by a public vote, Liverpool were, "methodical and automatic in everything they did," with Fagan (2), Balmer, Done and Priday getting the goals in a 5-1 whipping of the excited hosts.

Art Garcia, captain of the St Louis All-Stars, and Willie Fagan (who netted two) exchange greetings prior to their game whilst British Consul A Stanley Fordham (left) and St Louis' Mayor A P Kaufmann look on.

Such was the professionalism shown by the Reds that American sports journalists were astounded to discover just how little the players earned compared to the average American sportsman - a comparison that was to be vented angrily on more than one occasion by the Players' Union during the coming English season, and a reason, in their eyes at least, for a long overdue increase in both the minimum and maximum wage. In a country where Detroit baseball star Hank Greenberg had recently signed a contract worth $60,000 a year, Kay told inquisitive reporters that a standard English footballers wage, "adds up to about 15 quid a week." Considering clubs like Liverpool were capable of attracting regular crowds of 50,000 it came as no surprise that the reaction was one of incredulity, but with a shrug of the shoulders Kay sidestepped any further probing by pointing out that it was, "still a lot better than working in the mines."

From an American perspective, Liverpool's on-field prowess had earned them superstar status but away from the pitch the players were far from living the high-life. Sleeping four to a room in most hotels they stayed at – eight to a room at one point in Brooklyn due to a severe room shortage – their daily allowance from the club stretched to just seven dollars and this included all their meals.

The tour was now past its halfway point, but despite a gruelling schedule that had saw them play six games in just over two weeks, and taking into account the hard season they had only recently completed, the Liverpool players were surprisingly showing no signs of tiredness. Indeed, it was quite the opposite. "You guys look pretty good after five years on short rations," was the reaction of one reporter when meeting the Liverpool squad for the first time, to which one of the players instantly replied, "since we went aboard the Queen Mary we've done nothing but eat!" It was clear for all to see that the players were benefitting from the volume and variety of un-rationed food at their disposal. So much so that it was reported in one US newspaper, "some experts figure that their unlimited activities with knife and fork over here have added 25 per cent to Liverpool efficiency."

Such an improvement stood them in good stead for their next challenge, played at what Berry Nieuwenhuys described as, "the Wembley of Chicago," - the hugely impressive Soldier Field Stadium. It was a far cry from the small, compact grounds they had played at in Fall River and St. Louis, and although the 7,000 crowd may have resembled, "a drop of water in a bucket," those who were there, "saw a display of soccer by the Liverpool FC that literally opened their eyes."

Action from before and during the match v Chicago Maroons at the impressive Soldier Field Stadium.

At times the Reds left the Chicago Maroons, "spellbound," especially with their terrific, "right-wing combination play." Eastham, Taylor, and Balmer inflicted much of the damage, with the latter two helping themselves to four goals apiece. Priday

13

scored the other in what was officially recorded as a 9-3 victory, although Herold Anderson, co-editor of the Chicago-based National Soccer News, was of the belief that, "without question, the left winger for the English squad [who would have been Nivvy] drilled one right through the net in the last ten minutes, which would make the count, Liverpool 10, Maroons 3."

Nivvy rated the Maroons as, "the poorest team we have played against to date. Our boys could have scored when and how they chose," but Anderson went on to describe how much a privilege it was seeing, "the great Liverpool outfit," and stated that the Reds, "were every bit as good as their record indicated."

Seven wins out of seven was a record George Kay and his players were immensely proud of and they were determined to maintain their winning run for the remainder of the tour. With three games to go they crossed the North American border to Canada, touching down in Toronto on Tuesday 4 June to another fabulous and extravagant welcome. A whole page in the Toronto Globe and Mail was dedicated to Liverpool's arrival and, with a red carpet literally rolled out for a team described as, "one of the best in the world," a sumptuous banquet was held in their honour.

One of the many dinners held in the Reds' honour during the ground-breaking tour.

Despite the welcome, no sooner had he stepped off the plane the ever-professional Kay was enquiring about the quality of the opposition Liverpool were next to face. "Having a splendid time this tour but of course soccer is paramount," he told a local reporter, before adding, "what kind of club have you got here?"

Manager George Kay shares either a joke or some amusing tactical knowledge with his players the evening before the game v Ulster United.

As was now the pre-match norm it was predicted locally that, "the toughest game on this side of the Atlantic probably faces them here," but, like all before them, the Ulster United team - one of the greatest sides in Canadian history according to North American soccer historian Colin Jose, and the 1946 National (Ontario and Quebec) champions - were no match for the goal-hungry Reds. The match report the following morning declared that, "perhaps the finer art of soccer was never better displayed in this country than was the case last night at Maple Leaf Stadium."

Toronto Star sports journalist, Lancashire-born Bill Entwistle presents Jackie Balmer with a rose the evening before the game v Ulster United at The Maple Leaf Stadium. Eddie Spicer looks on.

In front a capacity 13,759 crowd – the largest in Canada for two decades – Ontario President George Drew started the game then took his seat in the VIP section to watch Liverpool turn on the style in an 11-1 romp that left the locals searching for new superlatives to describe the manner of their victory. One enthralled observer summed it up - perhaps a little dramatically - by simply commenting, "they came, we saw and they conquered." In the Evening Express, Nivvy wrote, "although Ulster showed more method than any team we have met to date they could not stand the pace. Liverpool are playing as a team and that is where our success lies."

*Ontario President George Drew starts the game v Ulster United,
much to the amusement of Bill McConnell
and the bemusement of Cyril Sidlow.*

To put the goal-fest into perspective, Ulster United would lose only 4-2 to a powerful Manchester United side in Detroit in 1952.

Fagan (3), Priday (3), Balmer (2), Nieuwenhuys, Taylor and Done were the Liverpool scorers, while Harley put through his own net to give the home crowd something to cheer. Bob Paisley also made his first appearance of the tour in this game. In the eyes of the fans, "every one of the visitors was a star," and Balmer and Fagan were singled out for particular praise as, "as they supplied the brainwork of a forward line that lived up to all expectations." It was an occasion for all to savour and;

"a tribute to the splendid display of the Liverpudlians was the fact that few of the large crowd moved from their seats before the end of the contest. Soccer received a boost last night that will inspire local officials to bigger efforts to bring the game to the forefront."

*Bob Priday (extreme left) scores one of his three goals against Ulster United.
Together with a United defender and goalkeeper, Cyril Done and Willie Fagan watch
the 20-yard shot on its way into the goal.*

For the Liverpool players it was also a memorable evening in that they finally got their hands on a much sought after pair of nylon stockings they had promised to take home to their wives and girlfriends. Until now their search for these rarest of British goods had proved elusive but, once local officials heard of their quest, they made a surprise presentation to the team as they came out for the second-half.

Willie Fagan and the rest of the Liverpool squad receive the rarest of war-time goods - nylon stockings - from their hosts in Canada!

Together with a trip to Niagara Falls the following day, the Reds' stay in Toronto was the highlight of a brief but enjoyable stay in Canada before they flew to New Jersey for the penultimate game of the tour against Kearny Celtic, a team comprised of Irish and Scottish ex-pats. Before they flew back to America however, there was a sombre wreath-laying ceremony to be undertaken at Toronto City Hall. For many of the Liverpool players, most of whom would have played and trained with Tom Cooper - the former Red's captain who was killed in during the conflict - this was a stark reminder of just what dangers they themselves had faced barely two years previously.

Balmer, "the scoring wizard of the team," with 16 tour goals so far, was unavailable for the game against Kearny due to a sprained ankle, but even without him Liverpool cruised to a ninth straight success. The 3-1 scoreline suggests it was a much closer affair than in Toronto but although Kearny deserved credit for being the only team to hold Liverpool to a goalless 45 minutes, in sweltering conditions the Reds did just what they had to do to ensure victory. Goals from Fagan and Done (2) gave them a commanding first half lead and it was then a case of preserving their energy for the grand finale of the busy tour just two days later.

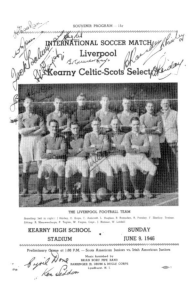

Rare signed programme for the game v Kearny Celtic.

Could the, "Liverpool booting artists," complete a clean sweep by making it ten wins out of ten? Standing in their way was the cream of the American Soccer League, another All-Star side selected from nine leading clubs and including Fabri Salcedo of the Brooklyn Hispanos, the League's leading scorer in 1945/46 and veteran Billy Gonsalves, a US

A final farewell to Canada from Chairman Billy Mac and the rest of the party.

soccer 'hall-of-famer' who had represented his country at the 1930 and 1934 World Cups and who is widely considered to be the greatest American player of all-time. Ebbets Fields, home of the famed Brooklyn Dodgers baseball team, was the venue and on a wet and stormy night;

> *"the local boys started like a house on fire and forced three quick corners, but just as it looked as if the Reds had finally met their match Willie Fagan picked up one of Priday's fine crosses to start the scoring parade."*

It remained a competitive contest until just before half-time, but then the floodgates opened. A further goal from Fagan and one apiece from Priday and Balmer put the outcome beyond doubt and the second half was exhibition stuff as Liverpool rounded off the tour with a ruthless flurry of goals from Done (4), Ramsden and Eastham. In reply Al Jennette, a refugee from the Brookhattan team, fired past Sidlow, just as he had done in the first game of the tour on Randalls Island a month earlier.

"The Yankee team made their last attempt to beat us and they thought this a possibility, until we started slamming them home," said Kay afterwards and the hosts could only look on in awe as the Reds ran up another impressive high-scoring

18

victory. 10-1 was a fitting way in which to record a remarkable tenth straight success and bring the curtain down on a tour that had seen 70 goals scored and just ten conceded.

The New York State Soccer News bulletin reflected on Liverpool's stay, describing it as, "one of the most successful soccer tours ever undertaken." Indeed, having, "displayed sportsmanship on and off the field above reproach," the men from Merseyside left a long-lasting impression on their hosts. So popular had they been, an official request was made for them to stay on for a further few weeks so that fixtures could be arranged against teams from Mexico and possibly Costa Rica but, with families to see and a new Football League season to prepare for, the invitation had to be politely declined - although Liverpool would return in 1948, 1953 and 1964. Before sailing home the appreciative Liverpool party held a farewell dinner to thank the tour organisers before heading back to a Britain ravaged by bad weather with an unblemished record, an enhanced reputation and the best wishes of every soccer-loving Yank ringing in their ears;

"For some this tour marked the first time in many years that they have witnessed an international soccer match. As for the newcomers who never attended an international game they will never forget Liverpool's display of masterful, fast exciting soccer. Yes – the entire tour created a tension of excitement on the outcome of every contest played by the invaders. 'Cheerio' Liverpool."

Esteemed British sports writer Frank Butler, then of the Daily Express added;

"Soccer will never compete against baseball or American Football in the United States but I am willing to wager that soccer will have many thousands more American enthusiasts following Liverpool's successful tour."

Laurie Hughes appears very much in control of things against the American League Select.

Manager, trainer and players (Tom Bush absent) enjoy their final dinner party.

It had been an unforgettable month. "I think we rather surprised the soccerites of USA by our superiority," reflected Kay, whilst for director James Troop it had been, "the best and happiest tour in 23 years." Chairman Bill McConnell also admitted it couldn't have gone any better. Prior to boarding the Queen Mary for the journey home he told US officials;

> *"I'm happy I convinced my colleagues to bring the team over here. While I understand we helped the cause of American soccer considerably, I'm happier to know our boys were ambassadors of goodwill, and helped to strengthen the friendship and international relations between our two countries."*

Billy Mac's decision had been fully justified in every sense. The foundations for a tilt at the inaugural post-war Football League title had been laid and, after six weeks spent feasting on the best culinary delights the US had to offer, the real proof of whether or not Liverpool could mount a long overdue title challenge would come in the pudding that was to follow.

Chairman Bill McConnell, with his squad and local dignitaries in respectful silence, lay a wreath at the Toronto City hall War Memorial to honour the fallen of two World Wars, the most recent of which many had actively participated in.

Liverpool's 1946 tour of the USA & Canada

12 May – New York All-Stars (Triborough Stadium) 3-1
Team: Sidlow, Harley, Ramsden, Taylor, Hughes, Spicer, Nieuwenhuys, Balmer, Jones, Fagan, Priday.
Scorers: Balmer (2), Fagan.   Attendance: 20,000

16 May – Baltimore All-Stars (Municipal Stadium) 9-0
Team: Sidlow, Harley, Ramsden, Taylor, Hughes, Spicer, Eastham, Balmer, Done, Fagan, Priday.
Scorers: Balmer (4), Fagan (3), Done, Priday.   Attendance: 5,801

20 May – American League Select (Triborough Stadium) 5-0
Team: Sidlow, Harley, Ramsden, Taylor, Hughes, Spicer, Nieuwenhuys, Balmer, Done, Fagan, Priday.
Scorers: Done (3), Balmer, Priday.   Attendance: 16,000

22 May – New England XI (Fall River) 3-2
Team: Sidlow, Harley, Ramsden, Taylor, Hughes, Spicer, Eastham, Balmer, Done, Fagan, Priday.
Scorers: Priday (2), Balmer.   Attendance: 6,387

26 May – Philadelphia Select (Yellow Jacket Stadium) 12-0
Team: Sidlow, Harley, Ramsden, Taylor, Hughes, Spicer, Eastham, Balmer, Done, Fagan, Priday.
Scorers: Done (4), Balmer (3), Fagan (2), Taylor (2), Priday.   Attendance: 7,000

31 May – St Louis All-Stars (Walsh Stadium) 5-1
Team: Sidlow, Ramsden, Harley, Spicer, Hughes, Taylor, Priday, Fagan, Done, Balmer, Eastham.
Scorers: Fagan (2), Priday, Balmer, Done.   Attendance: 12,493

2 June – Chicago Maroons (Soldier Field Stadium) 9-3
Team: Sidlow, Harley, Ramsden, Taylor, Hughes, Spicer, Eastham, Balmer, Done, Fagan, Priday.
Scorers: Balmer (4), Fagan (3), Priday, Taylor.   Attendance: 7,000

5 June – Ulster United (Maple Leaf Stadium) 11-1
Team: Sidlow, Harley, Jones, Taylor, Hughes, Paisley, Nieuwenhuys, Balmer, Done, Fagan, Priday.
Scorers: Fagan (3), Priday (3), Balmer (2), Nieuwenhuys, Taylor, Done.   Attendance: 13,759

9 June – Kearney Celtic (High School stadium) 3-1
Team: Sidlow, Harley, Ramsden, Paisley, Hughes, Spicer, Nieuwenhuys, Jones, Done, Fagan, Priday.
Scorers: Done (2), Fagan.   Attendance: 11,000

11 June – American League Select (Ebbets Field Stadium) 10-1
Team: Sidlow, Jones, Ramsden, Taylor, Hughes, Spicer, Eastham, Balmer, Done, Fagan, Priday.
Scorers: Done (4), Fagan (2), Priday, Fagan, Balmer, Ramsden, Eastham.   Attendance: 8,000

Most Appearances: Sidlow 10, Hughes 10, Fagan 10, Priday 10, Harley 9, Ramsden 9, Taylor 9, Spicer 9, Balmer 9, Done 9, Eastham 6, Nieuwenhuys 4, Jones 4, Paisley 2.

Leading Scorers: Balmer 19, Fagan 17, Done 16, Priday 11, Taylor 4, Nieuwenhuys 1, Ramsden 1, Taylor 1.

Chapter Two
The long awaited big Kick-Off

Sheffield United v Liverpool
Saturday 31 August 1946

"Dear Bee,- Our team will be an arrant failure this coming season. They have signed no-one; although the old familiar names will be reaped up again for our benefit and there is no benefit to be derived from this oft-recurring familiarity of old players who have never been good enough to represent our loyal gang of followers. No club has a better following, no club is served up with such fruitless result. The directors must act at once."

Fans letter to the Liverpool Echo prior to the start of the season.

"Anfield still has its disciples of gloom who can see no future for the wearers' of red; yet it is surely to early to think of them as failures."

Ranger, Liverpool Echo

Seven years with no competitive football ensured that excitement and interest in the new season was higher than ever before. Nowhere more so than Liverpool, where players and fans alike had been counting down the days until the opening game at Sheffield United. The long wait for 'proper' football had whetted the appetite of a war-ravaged city and, as the new season loomed, it was reported that demand for season tickets at Anfield had broken all previous records.

While it was boom time at the box office however, Liverpool's title prospects were being written off before a ball had even been kicked. The absence of league football for so long meant that there was no real form guide by which to gauge the title aspirations of the 22 competing teams but the Reds were certainly not considered to be among the fancied front-runners. Arsenal, Wolverhampton Wanderers, Manchester United, Blackpool, Stoke City and Everton - as reigning champions - and perhaps Portsmouth, were the teams most commentators thought would be challenging for honours come the season's end.

Commenting in the Liverpool Echo a week before the season opener, *Contact* noted:

"General opinion on Liverpool's chances this season is that they will do nothing out of the ordinary. On paper the sameness of the names from which they will choose their teams may make this an obvious thought, yet the American success should have given them confidence and 'paper' form can be proved and disproved in remarkable ways."

Manager George Kay's pre-season message to Liverpudlians would hardly have filled them with confidence either:

"We are not going to be candid. We are not satisfied. Only Income Tax Collectors can say that. But we have a good lot of lads and as and when we can improve the team we shall do so. We want you to see a successful team."

Back at Anfield, at a lunch to celebrate their unbeaten tour of North America, Phil Taylor, Bill McConnell and Jackie Balmer prepare to eat a months worth of egg, flour and butter rations.

Invigorated by the break from post-war British austerity and beefed up by the giant steaks they had dined on in the States, the players reported back for pre-season training on August 6 in comparatively good shape. All had put on weight, some by as much as 4 lbs (nearly 2 kilos).

The same could not be said of Anfield however, where issues with the plumbing meant there was no water to welcome the players and, "the place was in a right mess." With just over four weeks until the long-awaited kick-off there was certainly plenty of work to be done for the ground-staff and the players. Whilst workmen laboured to get the stadium ready in time for the new season, trainers Jimmy Seddon and Albert Shelley put the team through their paces for two hours each day - but not at a fancy training ground with gyms, weights, swimming pools and saunas.

With the club's current training ground at Melwood not acquired until the 1950s, the Liverpool team trained where they played - at Anfield. Reserve inside-forward Stan Palk recalled:

"Most of our training was done on the pitch at Anfield, that's why there was never any grass on it by Christmas! While during the winter months when the pitch was covered in snow or the rain was falling heavily, we used to run up and down the steps of the Kop."

Pre-season training 1940s style. From left to right - Fagan, Taylor, Nivvy and Balmer.

With Liddell, Sidlow and Lambert all yet to be released by the Services the squad itself was not yet at full-strength. Nevertheless, competition for places remained intense and the Board of Directors, who selected the team, was faced with a huge selection headache as the big day loomed.

On the day England and Scotland clashed at Maine Road in a game to raise money for the victims of the Burnden Park disaster, and just a week before travelling to Sheffield, Anfield staged its annual public trial match between the first team and reserves, more commonly known as the 'Reds' [probables] v the 'Whites' [possibles]. The performances here however, would ultimately raise more selection questions than answers.

Always a popular attraction, a crowd of 25,000 witnessed the game, the one notable absentee being rising Liverpool star Billy Liddell, who was in action for his country in Manchester. Many commentators expected big things of the young Scotsman, but Liddell was to suffer a thigh strain in this game that would rule him out of

25

Liverpool's opening two fixtures.

The two sides in the trial match, using the 2-3-2-3 formation that was widespread at the time, were;

'Reds/Probables'
Sidlow
Harley   Lambert
Taylor   Hughes   Spicer
Eastham   Balmer
Fagan   Done   Priday

v

Nieuwenhuys   Patterson   Carney
Jones   Hulligan
Kaye   Easdale   Paisley
Seddon   Ramsden
Ashcroft
'Whites/Possibles'

As the team line-ups were usually a strong indicator as to which players were considered to be in the 'first choice' for the season ahead, interest in these types of games was especially intense. Invariably it was a fixture the 'Reds' were expected to win and, more often than not, the game went to form. On this occasion however,

Two 'probables' and a 'possible'. Taylor, Paisley and Spicer pose for the camera in the Anfield sunshine.

the 'Whites' played exceptionally well to earn a throughly deserved 5-3 victory. At one stage the 'Possibles' even had the temerity to lead 5-1, their goals being scored by Patterson (2), Carney, Hulligan and Jones, whilst on the scoresheet for the 'Reds' were Balmer, Done and Priday. The Directors viewed this trial as the final dress rehearsal before the real business got underway the following week and, although changes were rarely made, the result set alarm bells ringing in Anfield's corridors of power.

The solid Bill Jones, young Bob Paisley, the amateur Len Carney, pre-war first choice left back Bernard 'Barney' Ramsden and veteran South African Berry 'Nivvy' Nieuwenhuys all impressed for the Whites to put themselves in contention for a place in the starting line-up at Sheffield United. Only Paisley eventually missed out as the selection committee rung the changes. The unfortunate 'Reds' who made way were; Welsh international Ray Lambert, Henry 'Harry' Eastham, prolific war-time goalscorer Cyril Done and, most controversially of all, club captain Willie Fagan.

The decision to drop Fagan sparked great debate amongst fans and commentators alike. While unconfirmed reports suggested the Scottish international was perhaps carrying an injury, it was still a huge risk to take for a game against a side who finished the previous season as champions of the Football League North - doing the double over Liverpool along the way. Especially when you consider that the man drafted in to take the experienced Fagan's place was Carney, a 32-year old amateur who, despite playing several times for the first team during the war, had yet to taste competitive action.

Alongside Priday, Hughes and Spicer, Carney was one of four league debutants in Liverpool's team for the opening game, while Sidlow, declared fit despite pulling a muscle playing basketball the previous week, had only four previous Football League appearances to his name as a Wolves player, and that was way back in 1937/38.

Kay's earlier promise to try and strengthen the team was not a hollow one. On the eve of the new season he made an audacious bid to sign Everton half-back Joe Mercer after the England international had submitted a shock transfer request. Unsurprisingly, the Goodison board swiftly rejected Liverpool's offer but it was an ominous statement of intent by the Reds who, under the Chairmanship of Bill McConnell, appeared to be more than prepared to spend some of the previous season's record profit if they thought their target was of sufficient calibre. There is no doubt that the capture of Mercer, a player of undoubted ability and a title winner with Everton before the war, would have given everyone at Anfield a massive lift going into the new season. In his final preview of the forthcoming season however, another local reporter, *Ranger*, defended the men that were being thrust into battle for Liverpool. "Anfield still has its disciples of gloom who can see no future for the wearer's of red," he wrote, "yet it is surely too early to think of them as failures."

As the countdown to the big kick-off gathered pace the sports pages were also dominated by another, much less welcome topic - the simmering row between the Players' Union and the Football League. Delegates from 30 clubs had met in Manchester to discuss the pay demands with Union officials, but just two days before the opening Saturday of the season, the League Management Committee rejected the proposal of revised terms and agreements by the Players' Union - an increase in the maximum and minimum wages and the abolition of the retain and transfer system - to ensure the matter would rumble on. It would resurface throughout the season.

Luckily, Liverpool weren't affected much by this furore. The same however, could not be said of their opening day opponents Sheffield United, who had seemingly lost the services of their star attraction, cultured inside-forward Jimmy Hagan, due to issues surrounding his contract. Just 29 and already one of the era's greatest talents, Hagan had announced he was quitting the game and refused to re-sign - as all players had to do before a new season - citing that there wasn't enough money in the game.

A superb passer of the ball with a sublime first touch and an impressive repertoire of tricks, Hagan had only returned from overseas service in January that year, just in time to play a hugely influential role in the Blades' charge to the Football league North title. Although a household name - only five players had featured in more wartime England internationals - Hagan faced the same problems as many demobbed men, remarking at the time that, "problem number one [for me] is to find a house or flat...Problem number two is employment additional to football."

A renowned deep thinker of the game Hagan, who had scored the winner when Liverpool began the aborted 1939/40 season at Bramall Lane and, like many of the older top professionals, was holding out for better terms and conditions. He only returned after it was agreed he could play part-time while training to be a surveyor. Unfortunately for the Blades, this agreement wasn't reached in time for the opening day and, in a dour game that cried out for a bit of magic, they were to desperately miss his creativity.

As a foreboding sign of what lay in store weather wise for the season ahead, Liverpool ran out at Bramall Lane amid a thunderstorm as, "lightening flashed over a badly blitzed ground." Indeed, the wet weather appeared to have persuaded a number of spectators to find other ways to pass a Saturday afternoon and the 30,000 that braved the monsoon conditions was far less a figure than expected for the supposedly much anticipated season opener.

Liverpool emerged a full 10 minutes before their Yorkshire opponents, an action that caused more than a few raised eyebrows in the crowd. Entering the pitch so early was almost unheard of and even more terrace conversation followed when it was seen that Liverpool came onto the field with three balls, similar to the actions of the famous Moscow Dynamo side that had toured Britain so successfully, and to great acclaim, the previous November. Just as the Russians had done, so Liverpool also took this opportunity to - what we would now term - warm-up, a practice that few, if any, teams practised at the time.

To the amazement of even the assembled pressmen, the Liverpool players tested the ground and their boots, took time to jog and stretch, passed the ball to each other and took pot shots at Sidlow in goal. It was an innovation many teams would adopt as the season progressed - although the fact Liverpool had also copied it wasn't lost on their manager. George Kay told a local reporter after the game, "We'll take a leaf out of anyone's book if it is one that reads well."

When the action got underway Liverpool were less entertaining and seemed content to sit back and soak up whatever pressure the home side applied. Without Hagan, United's team was one of the youngest in the League but they attacked Liverpool who, "just couldn't get started," straight from the kick off. Fast and skilful, their youngsters, "the fastest thing in 22 football boots," forced Sidlow into a string of fine early saves but fortunately the Reds' new number one, "displayed huge confidence between the sticks."

Being a native of Sheffield, Ramsden was cheered and jeered in equal measure by the home fans, although it was more of the latter when they felt he wasted time by booting the ball out under no real pressure - few actions riled a post-war crowd as much as this - and even more so when they thought he conceded a penalty on 35 minutes.

Despite the possession afforded them however, the pacey Blades couldn't cut through the Reds' resolute rearguard. Their final pass often let them down and they wasted a number of promising attacks by simply giving the ball back to the white-shirted Liverpool players. With the Anfield men doing likewise however, it was not a game for the purist. Indeed, so poor were both sides that it looked increasingly likely that a draw would be the final result.

Up front Liverpool's attack, "lacked punch," and their chances could be counted on the fingers of one hand - debutant Carney saw a decent header well saved in the first half by keeper Jack Smith and Balmer placed a couple of shots wide. Other than that the visiting forward line gave their few hundred travelling fans little to get excited about. Conversely, it was Liverpool's defence - a positive sign for the season ahead - that were cited as being responsible for the Reds' win. "The men who made the two points possible were Sidlow, Harley, Ramsden and Hughes," *Ranger* noted, before adding that, "Liverpool never looked likely to lose but equally the chances of their winning were remote until Carney saved the day with a gliding header."

As the hosts began to tire towards the end Liverpool gradually began to assert some authority and, after beating the offside trap, Nivvy centred and Carney, who up until then had had an indifferent game at best, headed home. It was almost the last

*Amateur Len Carney,
unlikely scorer of a
last-minute winner
against the Blades.*

action of the game. The Blades barely had time to restart before the referee blew his whistle. It had been a hard-earned two points for Liverpool whose performance seemed to confirm what most football fans and commentators outside of the city believed at the time - that the Reds were not yet ready to be regarded as one of the favourites for the title.

Elsewhere, the much-fancied Wolves lived up to their pre-season billing with a 6-1 hammering of a seriously depleted Arsenal at Molineux, a result that understandably hogged the newspaper headlines, while there was also a rare moment in the First Division spotlight for minnows Brentford who caused the shock of the day when winning 2-0 against reigning champions Everton at Goodison. Little national press attention was paid to Liverpool's win or Carney's late, late goal. Only time would tell just how significant it would be.

Liverpool v Middlesbrough
Wednesday 4 September 1946

"Our grub rations may be on the tight side still and the weather may be giving us all the pip, but nobody can grumble that they haven't had their fill of thrills during this first hectic week of Soccer's grand reopening."

Ranger, Liverpool Echo

Four days later Anfield staged its first post-war League match. If the narrow and arguably lucky win over Sheffield United had exposed the weaknesses in Liverpool's forward line, their first home game of the season against Middlesbrough only seemed to confirm it. "That the side is not 'set' in attack is evident," wrote *Ranger*, "and no-one, least of all the Board, is going to be satisfied until the front line show more punch."

With key personnel still missing Liverpool's Board named an unchanged side at their Tuesday night selector's meeting thus, "giving Liddell's troublesome thigh injury plenty of time to heal." The Anfield Directors also had an additional request to ponder at this meeting as golfing fanatic and Liverpool stalwart Berry Nieuwenhuys informed them that he intended to retire from football at the end of this season and devote himself to professional golf.

Nivvy had been promised a role as assistant to Bobby Locke at the Transvaal Golf Club in South Africa. The likeable Sringbok had even taken part in the previous month's Irish Open as an amateur, where he, "surprised the stars by finishing in the leading 12." A faithful servant to the club since signing over a decade before, the Board agreed to his request and wished him well in his new career.

Whilst Liverpool were taking the points at Bramall Lane the previous Saturday, Middlesbrough, another unheralded and unfancied side, surprisingly won away at Aston Villa. The Teesiders had finished on equal points with Liverpool in Division One North the previous season but their war-time football record was average at best. They had finished in the bottom half of almost every league they had participated in during the conflict and their best performance was arguably a defeat of a highly rated Blackpool side in a fourth round FA Cup replay in February 1946.

Despite having England left-back and captain George Hardwick, "probably the most handsome footballer playing today, and one of the few to sport a moustache," and his gifted fellow international team-mate Wilf Mannion, "the stocky little lad with the twinkling feet," in their team, Middlesbrough were an inconsistent, although attractive side, and most fans and observers expected Liverpool to record their second win from the opening two games.

In the matchday programme notes the Liverpool Board, who entertained their North East counterparts prior to the game in the Anfield Board Room with sandwiches and refreshments - a new innovation under McConnell's Chairmanship - again reiterated its pledge to do all it could to improve the team.

"Now that football is restored to its pre-war basis, the games will prove to be much harder and keener than those played during the war years - with promotion and relegation once more in operation. All clubs will be anxious to place on the field teams good enough to provide attractive football for their loyal supporters. For our part, you can rest assured that every effort will be made to strengthen the team to make it one of the foremost in the land. Many overtures have been made for prominent players, but our efforts to date have not been successful."

With floodlights at grounds still some years away, kick-off for early and late summer games was scheduled for 6.30pm. It had been almost seven years to the day since Anfield last played host to competitive league action but, despite the anticipation and early kick-off, incessant rain kept the crowd down to a disappointing 30,000. Indeed, the whole occasion proved to be something of an anti-climax. The stay-away fans missed Liverpool's much-talked about, "pre kick-off practice spell," being performed at Anfield for the first time but although the same 11 conspired to give a much improved display than the lacklustre one they had shown at Bramall Lane, here they, "had speed but lacked method."

The Reds showed endeavour and passion, starting the match, "in whirlwind fashion, flinging the ball from wing to wing in dazzling and spectacular football," but in almost a mirror image of their first game of the season - only this time with the roles reversed - they lost by a single goal despite having most of the possession. "Never have so many players worked so hard and achieved so little as Liverpool did," said *Ranger*. It had been, "a long time since I saw so much desperate endeavour allied to such paucity of shot."

Middlesbrough played exceptionally well when not in possession, especially in midfield, but it was still a shock when they took the lead on 11 minutes. A cross by right-winger Geoff Walker seemed to be covered by Laurie Hughes but the Liverpool defender misjudged his header and, instead of clearing easily for a corner, the slippery ball skidded off his head and past the helpless Sidlow. "The only blot on an otherwise fine display by the Reds' centre half."

*Middlesbrough's
Wilf Mannion.*

Although Liverpool attempted gallantly to recover from this setback, at times doing, "nine-tenths of the pressing," they could barely muster a shot at the 'Boro goal and ultimately, "let Cummings get away with an easy passage." In the second period especially, Liverpool spent almost all of the time in their opponents half, but had barely any shots on goal. Nivvy saw a good angled drive go just wide, as did Priday. Together with a first half effort by Balmer however, that was it. "Those three are the sum total of the night's shooting. A poor proportion for so much aggression."

It was clear that Liverpool missed Liddell up front. That Fagan, so often the conduit through which most of Liverpool's best attacking play developed, was also missing was a double blow as it was he who was often the, "key man to hold their front line together." Without the talented Scotsman's vision the Reds were aimless. Instead of a team combining well to produce chances, Liverpool, "just had five hard-working forwards keeping up a cracking pace in sheer desperation." Such play meant that, "the Borough's [sic] rearguard was sorely harassed and almost run of its feet," but due to the haphazard nature of Liverpool's attacking play Cummings and his defence, "always retained command of the situation."

Ramsden, Harley and Hughes, despite his own-goal, were again impressive in defence, "cast-iron", as *Ranger* later remarked. Ramsden especially was singled out for particular praise. Phil Taylor also played well but it was noted that Middlesborough's inside-right was by far the best player on the pitch, gliding everywhere almost effortlessly, rarely conceding possession and giving Liverpool's left-back a torrid time. The balance and ball control Mannion displayed here would make him a legend of the English game in the late 1940s and early 1950s whilst captain Hardwick proved he was still a force in the game. He would skipper the Great Britain side that would defeat the Rest of the World later in the season.

ON WEDNESDAY WE WERE ENTERTAINED BY THE LIVERPOOL DIRECTORS.

THEN WE WERE ENTERTAINED BY THE MIDDLESBROUGH FORWARDS.

MANNION'S BALL CONTROL WAS DELIGHTFUL TO WATCH.

DO AS YOU'RE TOLD

THE LIVERPOOL FORWARDS ALWAYS SEEMED TO BE GOING PLACES BUT THEY NEVER GOT THERE.

HUGHES HEADED THE ONLY GOAL BUT DON'T START CHEERING – HE PUT IT INTO THE WRONG NET.

THERE WERE SEVERAL REASONS WHY LIVERPOOL FAILED TO SCORE AND HARDWICK WAS ONE OF THEM.

GEORGE GREEN

Middlesbrough's win maintained their one hundred per cent start and they, along with Manchester United, Sunderland and Blackpool topped the table after just two games. At the opposite end Leeds, Arsenal, Huddersfield and Aston Villa still awaited their first points of the season.

Despite their defeat, the commitment and intensity Liverpool showed was grounds for optimism. The fans who gathered outside the club offices near the Main Stand after the game however, "apparently with the object of calling upon the directors to make quick team changes," no doubt disagreed. It was left to *Ranger* to point out the obvious - that the Anfield outfit, "will win many a game with half the endeavour they put into this one."

In an unusual move, even by the footballing standards of the time, the Liverpool team given the task of bringing, "method into harness with their speed," in the next game at home to Chelsea was chosen immediately after this defeat - despite the game being three days away. Those Liverpool supporters who had demanded changes appeared to have convinced the Directors and, with a significantly different line-up, their wishes were granted. Would change lead to goals though? The answer was a joy to behold.

Liverpool v Chelsea
Saturday 7 September 1946

"Members of the Players' Union have up to Wednesday to decide their attitude regarding the League's refusal to discuss their request for higher wages and better conditions. They have been asked whether they are prepared to wholeheartedly support whatever move the union executive recommends, including possible strike action."

Ranger's Notes, Liverpool Echo

If the Middlesbrough match had proved to be an anti-climax for the Anfield faithful then the visit of Chelsea to Anfield just three days later more than made up for it. The contrast between the two games couldn't have been starker. One was a decent though laboured performance resulting in a 1-0 defeat, the other a match that had everything, and more; one of the greatest Liverpool games of all-time, the afternoon when, in the eyes of all Liverpudlians, the 1946/47 season finally got underway for real.

Bowing to the demands of those fans who protested after their midweek defeat, sweeping changes were made to the Liverpool team. To everyone's great relief, Liddell finally returned from injury to partner Jones, Nivvy and Balmer in attack. Captain Willie Fagan, whose clever touches and subtle passing had been greatly missed, also returned to make his first start of the campaign. In goal, the injured Sidlow was replaced by Chorley-born Charlie Ashcroft - another Liverpool debutant, whilst in defence Spicer was replaced by a 28-year-old Geordie who had, "spent four years in the desert," during the war, before ending up, "riding on a tank through liberated Rome." Tough in the tackle and with the added attacking threat of a prodigious throw-in, this was also to be Robert Paisley's first competitive game for the Reds.

Despite such drastic changes, much of the pre-match hype surrounded the impending return to Merseyside of former Everton favourite Tommy Lawton, a player rated one of the finest in Europe at the time. Lawton had not longed moved to the capital from Goodison and was viewed as the star attraction in a Chelsea team that had bought big in an effort to stamp its mark on the inaugural post-war League season. An outlay of £29,000 on five players may seem like chicken feed compared to the millions Roman Abramovich would splash out over half a century later, but back in 1946 it still set Chelsea some distance apart from the rest of the Division when it came to spending power.

In addition to Lawton, Chelsea had also added the likes of Len Goulden, Danny Winter and John Harris - all proven internationals - to the Stamford Bridge ranks. Few commentators however, were persuaded that the Londoner's infamous inconsistency would be replaced with something more dependable. In the 1938/39 season they had escaped relegation from the top division by just a single point and although they had won the League South Cup in 1945 after being runners-up in the same competition the year before, they were expected to struggle again this season.

Already the Stamford Bridge outfit had had a lucky escape against Bolton at Burnden Park on the opening day, winning 4-3, and been beaten at home - although this was no disgrace given their start to their league campaign - by Manchester United. Like Liverpool, the Londoners had also failed to score as often as they would have wished so, after what had been such an indifferent start to the campaign for both teams, no-one could have foreseen the drama that was to unfold at Anfield on this sunny autumnal afternoon. No-one perhaps, apart from the management of the Trocadero Cinema in Camden Street, who had decided to show Alfred Hitchcock's 'Spellbound' the evening before. This was exactly what the heaving Anfield crowd were as Liverpool bounced back from the disappointment of defeat to Middlesbrough in the most sensational way possible.

With record post-war crowds already seen at almost every ground in the country, despite Government restrictions on ground capacity due to the Bolton disaster the previous season, it was to be expected that the Liverpool v Chelsea attendance would be a big one. Sure enough, the first League appearance of Liddell coupled with the draw of Lawton, meant that just under 50,000 spectators crammed into Anfield for an 11-goal thriller that would live long in the memory of all those fortunate enough to witness it.

Queues had begun to form at Anfield as early as noon, with the gates to the Main Stand shut at 2.30pm. Fans here simply moved to another entrance but just 10 minutes prior to kick-off an estimated 5,000 saw themselves 'locked out' despite the official attendance showing Anfield was not full to capacity. This though, did not stop a number of youths 'bunking in' by scaling the outside wall of the Anfield Road end!

Liddell's appearance, together with excellent play by both Paisley and Jones, and the much missed guile of Fagan, seemed to transform Liverpool. Whereas they had lacked penetration and confidence in their first two league games, here they were passing with panache and building from the back in the style that the fans of future Liverpool sides have come to expect. With Fagan pulling the strings Liverpool raced into an unbelievable three-goal lead inside the first half-hour.

A minute had not even elapsed when Liddell exchanged passes with Fagan and, "sent a tremendous shot wide of the post to plough a furrow among the heads on [the] Spion Kop." Less than 60 seconds later, Paisley worked his way forward with an uncompromising run and forced a corner. Liddell swung it in so well that Bill Robertson, the Chelsea keeper, could only divert the ball into his own net off the far post. With a goal direct from a corner Liddell had opened his account for the season and netted his first official League goal for the club. It was also the cue for the floodgates to open.

Full of confidence, Liverpool were now rampant. Nivvy saw a shot cleared off the line and Jones saw a header go just wide from another excellent Liddell corner - won by a clever throw from the wide-man, direct off the back of Winter. Chelsea had just one clear chance - a mix-up by Ashcroft that saw Machin's shot creep towards the goal only for Taylor to clear, but on 24 minutes a brief shower came and with it two quick goals in succession.

Collecting a pass from Fagan just six yards from goal, Jones pivoted quickly and struck a sweet shot into the corner of the net to make it 2-0. Six minutes later another swerving Liddell cross was nodded on by Nivvy, and Jones saw his follow-up header nestle in the back of the net. The Kop were ecstatic. This is exactly what they had missed during the long hiatus from 'proper' football that the war had denied them.

Chelsea threatened sporadically, with Lawton seeing two headers easily saved by the debutant Ashcroft, but Robertson was by far the busier of the two keepers. Not long before the break he made two fine saves within 60 seconds of each other, but after some defensive misunderstanding Fagan nipped in to fire a loose ball past him to put the Reds into a seemingly unassailable four-goal lead at half-time.

As the home fans basked delightfully in the early autumn sunshine, so hot and humid were the conditions that many were forced to seek refuge from the packed terraces and onto the dirt track that surrounded the pitch. During the interval the crowd then bore witness to a novel part of the match-day experience of the time when hundreds of boys from the Kop and elsewhere were allowed to leave their positions to take up others behind the Chelsea goal. It was announced that this was not due to overcrowding but merely to prevent any of the young men from fainting due to the heat - the white hot football displayed by Liverpool on the pitch was mirrored off it with temperatures topping 70 degrees.

Liverpool could have been forgiven for taking their foot of the gas in the second-half but within two minutes they'd gone nap. It looked like Balmer's speculative shot from distance would be comfortably saved but, much to his embarrassment, Robertson fumbled and the ball trickled over the line. The home fans, especially those youngsters who had moved to behind the Chelsea goal at half-time, were in dreamland and they celebrated with a minor, good-natured, pitch invasion. Three minutes later it was to get even better. Great skill and determination by Liddell saw him evade a number of sliding, scything tackles to, "weave his way through," the Chelsea defence and courageously score a sixth. The points were Liverpool's, surely?

Tommy lawton (no. 10 extreme left) looks on as Machin scores Chelsea's third.

"Just to let...[people] know there was another team at Anfield," however, Chelsea responded with a consolation goal by Goulden in the 55th minute, while Ashcroft had to save well from Lawton moments later. Unperturbed, Liverpool continued to attack. Jones nearly had his hat-trick, before Paisley and then Balmer saw other great chances go begging.

"This astonishing game continued its thrilling way, and at 64 minutes Lawton was unceremoniously brought down on the edge of the penalty box." Jimmy Argue, Chelsea's red-haired inside-forward came up and, despite Liverpool's defensive wall being well positioned, hit a fine swerving shot past Ashcroft to reduce the deficit further. Six minutes later, "after Balmer had missed a sitter," Alec Machin scored a third for Chelsea, from a corner that many felt was, "definitely a goal-kick." To everyone's amazement he then added a fourth just two minutes later. 6-4. What a game!

The Anfield crowd, "having looked on Chelsea's efforts with benign disinterest," were now stunned. Thoughts began to turn from the improbable to the impossible - 6-5 or even 6-6! Machin went close with a header from a corner not long after. Chelsea just wouldn't give up. Ashcroft spared Liverpool's blushes with a fine save from the Londoners' man-of-the-match Machin in the 80th minute, but with three minutes remaining both home players and the crowd were relieved to see Fagan bundle an uncleared Nivvy corner over the line to make the scoreline an astonishing 7-4!

A GOAL FEAST AT ANFIELD—BY GEORGE GREEN

There was still time for Balmer to hit the post and Jones to fire the rebound over from just four yards before the referee finally blew his whistle to end a pulsating game amid gasps of amazement from all round the ground. The mesmerized crowd could scarcely believe their eyes. One of the truly great Anfield games had ended, with new kid on the block Liddell well and truly upstaging the much-vaunted Lawton. Players and fans alike celebrated as if they had won a cup final and, "for once the police were powerless to keep the youngsters from invading the pitch and mobbing the players as they left the field."

Not since February 1933 - when Everton were beaten by the same score - had Kopites witnessed such a high-scoring game in a competitive fixture and on only six other occasions have eleven goals been scored in the same match involving Liverpool at Anfield. When put into context there can be no doubt that this game is fully deserving of a place in any top ten list of truly great Liverpool games, the nearest modern day equivalent being either of the 4-3 epics against Newcastle in the 1990s.

More importantly though it sent out a message to the rest of the country that, on their day, this Liverpool team was a force to be reckoned with. It was still early days but, as the first league table of the season was published, it showed the Reds were handily placed in fifth position. Four points from three matches wasn't a bad return, especially considering they had only really played well in one of those games, but if aspirations to move further up the ladder were to be maintained then they had to make sure the performance against Chelsea was not an exception.

At this premature stage of the season it was all about staying in realistic touch of the leaders. With three wins from three games Manchester United, playing at Maine Road due to bomb damage at Old Trafford, topped the Division and were already two points clear of Liverpool. Next up for the Anfield men? An intriguing trip to Manchester - to meet up with an old friend.

Chapter Three
The 'Burning Stub'

Manchester United v Liverpool
Wednesday 11 September 1946

"Boxing enthusiasts from all parts of the country have come to Liverpool today to see the all-Northern lightweight contest between Stan Hawthorne of North Shields, and Billy Thompson of Hickleton Main, which takes place at Anfield Football Ground this evening...It is anticipated that the contest will attract a record crowd for an Anfield fight, and advance bookings indicate more than 40,000."

Liverpool Evening Express

Liverpool versus Manchester United hasn't always been the hate-filled fixture we have all now grown accustomed to. Back in 1946 the fans of both clubs even shared a common bond, one that extended beyond their tough working-class Lancashire roots and the colour of the shirts their heroes wore - it was their mutual admiration for the legendary Matt Busby.

At this point in the story it's fair to say he was more of an icon on Merseyside than Manchester. Having only joined United as manager the previous October Busby had not yet had sufficient time to weave his managerial magic at the Old Trafford club but the memories of his inspirational pre-war performances in a Liverpool shirt were, for many Liverpudlians, still very much fresh in the memory.

Widely regarded by Kopites of the time as the 'King of Anfield', Busby had joined the Reds from Manchester City in 1936 and went on to play over 100 league games for the club before the outbreak of hostilities. A classy wing-half he, together with fellow Scots Jimmy McDougall and 'Tiny' Bradshaw, formed one of the most formidable half-back lines in Liverpool history and, such was the respect he commanded among his team-mates, it came as no surprise that he succeeded Tom Cooper as captain in 1939.

An ever-present in the last full-season before the war, Busby led the club with distinction through what was a difficult period on the pitch in terms of success and established himself as a hugely influential figure at Anfield. It was he who is credited with tipping George Kay off about the talents of Billy Liddell, while he also took a young Bob Paisley under his wing and acted as a mentor to the ever-improving

One time 'King of Anfield' Matt Busby during his Liverpool days - now the manager of Manchester United.

Phil Taylor. As his career drew to a close a long association with the club seemingly beckoned but, despite Liverpool offering him a job on the coaching staff, Busby instead opted to try his luck just down the road with Manchester United - where the vacant managerial position was seen as an opportunity too good to turn down for someone with his ambitions.

Only when he penned his autobiography years later did the full story behind Busby's leaving of Liverpool finally emerge;

"Liverpool's coaching offer with a five-year contract and the probability of promotion seemed to provide my main requirement...security. I agreed verbally to accept but, while I was stressing to the directors that my football hopes centred on a managerial job despite being keen on coaching, I was informed quite unexpectedly that the Manchester United chairman Jimmy Gibson would like to see me.

"The sequel was that he offered me the manager's position at United, thus providing me with the opening I had been seeking. Liverpool directors did not take my decision well. In fact, although I was as happy as a player could be with Liverpool, the one black spot on my career there concerned the unfortunate events surrounding my departure.

"Liverpool seemed to think I was going to United in the capacity of player-manager and there were suggestions about demanding a transfer fee from United. But I had no intention of trying to combine the two jobs. I knew it would be quite impossible to achieve all I wished as a manager if I were involved in the full-time playing duties and no transfer fee was paid.

"Having agreed terms with United and finally severed what had been a very happy association with Liverpool, I was asked by manager George Kay to play in a farewell exhibition match for them. But then I got a telephone call from George who told me: 'There's been a change of mind here. The directors don't want you to play.'

"I discovered later that the board were upset because I was joining Manchester United and they had taken the decision to cancel my sentimental journey. It hurt me to think that after nine of the happiest years of my life - yes, even the war years - the club directors should turn against me simply because I preferred to be manager of Manchester United instead of coach of Liverpool."

While the directors were annoyed at Busby's defection to the wrong end of the East Lancashire Road however, the fans took a surprisingly different view. Crossing the great Liverpool-Manchester divide in this day and age would be viewed by many as the highest act of treason, but in 1946 Liverpudlians continued to hold Busby in the highest esteem. Indeed, they did so for many years afterwards, for in 1966 he was voted captain in a poll to determine the all-time greatest LFC XI. Had they known then the extent of the monster he was to create at Old Trafford maybe some would have taken a very different view!

Back in the early days of September 1946 however, Busby's managerial career was still very much in its infancy. After a run of three successive wins had taken United to joint top-spot in the table he was seemingly already heading in the right direction. Despite having no ground to call their own - Old Trafford had been on the receiving end of the Luftwaffe's angst in 1941 and would not be fully rebuilt until 1949 - United, who could boast a team that included seven internationals, were living up to their pre-season billing as one of the title favourites.

After the goal-fest against Chelsea Liverpool were themselves not short on confidence. The Busby-factor also made this a fixture that provoked widespread interest. It was undoubtedly Liverpool's sternest test of the season to date, but their prospects were hampered yet again by the fact that they were unable to field a full-strength 11.

After his explosive league debut at the weekend, Liddell was missing due to service commitments with the RAF and Sidlow, although recovered from his injury, was also, "unable to get release from his Army duties." Such a situation would astound fans today, but it was commonplace in the first few seasons after the War. Until all their players were demobbed Liverpool, like many clubs, were at the mercy of Service officials in granting their players leave to play.

Following a scouting mission, "somewhere down South," chairman Bill McConnell was delayed on his way to Maine Road due to a train crash in London. Until now the name of the Liverpool Chairman's target has been lost in time, but the player he was making enquiries about turns out to have been Chelsea's Tommy Lawton. No doubt McConnell had discussed the superstar's availability in his, now regular, meeting with his opposite numbers in the Anfield Boardroom both before and after the mesmerizing game with Chelsea just a few days previously. Chelsea had spent heavily and perhaps needed the money such a transfer coup would bring.

Without a definitive 'No' reply to his enquiry for Lawton's signature coming from the Chelsea Board, McConnell's attempt to buy him was a long-shot, but the Chairman was keen to add a star to Liverpool's attacking line-up as soon as he could. Unfortunately for Liverpool, news of McConnell's visit was leaked and the Londoners refused to sell their star asset. "Supporters would burn down the stand if he went," was their anguished response!

McConnell's fellow directors did make it to Old Trafford but, as *Ranger* ruefully noted afterwards, most must have wished they hadn't as, "they had to sit through 90 minutes of agony." As rampant as Liverpool had been against a poor Chelsea side a few days earlier, so too were United on top form here. So dominant were the hosts that it wasn't until the quarter hour-mark that their keeper, Jack Compton, got his first touch of the ball. By then Liverpool were already a goal down.

The loss of Sidlow and Liddell hit the Reds particularly hard. Ashcroft made good saves from Charlie Mitten and Stan Pearson early on, but on 12 minutes the latter scored with ease following a defensive mix-up on the right wing that left Aschcroft exposed. Three minutes later Compton received a back pass and touched the ball for the first time. When you consider this was an era when such passes to the keeper were a standard part of the game you get a much clearer indication of United's superiority.

Things went from bad to worse for Liverpool. Harley, "was soon limping," and eventually sent to outside-right, while five minutes after his opener Pearson added another. "The perfection of United," continued, with Jack Rowley adding a third on 37 minutes. With Liverpool's forwards, "being held quite comfortably," by a United defence whose, "work was done at a seemingly lazy pace," it was left to Paisley to have, "the only worthwhile shot," Liverpool could muster during an embarrassingly one-sided first half. Indeed, so good were United, and so underwhelming were Liverpool, that this effort turned out to be the only shot of note Liverpool had in the entire game.

Four minutes after the interval Mitten scored United's fourth to compound the Anfielder's agony. Whereas, "Liverpool moved in fits and starts and soon sputtered out, United were an eleven man team that had no departments." Damage limitation was the order of the evening for Liverpool's beleaguered and shell-shocked players. They, "had to put in extra effort to do so," but although they held out for just over half an hour Pearson grabbed his hat-trick five minutes from the end.

The final whistle at Maine Road was the most welcome sound of the evening for visiting players and fans alike. Liverpool had finally been put out of their misery. To go, in such a short space of time, from the heights of ecstasy that accompanied victory over Chelsea to the depths of despair that followed this annihilation left many Liverpool fans scratching their heads in bewilderment. Such inconsistency was to earn the team the nickname of the 'Crazy Gang'. "Give them a trifling match and they make a race of it," said the club's own magazine. "At other times...they will reveal form that one thought hardly possible."

Four wins out of four kept United at the top of the league, "and with reasonable luck and lack of injuries I don't see how they are going to fail to keep their place," noted *Ranger*. There were a number of reasons for, "last night's debacle," the reporter explained the following day, "not least of which was the perfection of United." Despite the journalists typically honest assessment, Liverpool's poor performance was also a result of absence and injury. The Reds were forced to field a side that was clearly not their strongest and, as Charlie Ashcroft later recalled, injuries to key men during the game ensured that they were always going to be second best.

> *"Jim Harley on the right wing was injured early on and Nivvy was also limping badly too. The pair of them could hardly walk let alone run. It was like playing with nine men. Willie Fagan was just returning from injury and he wasn't fully fit. In the end we hardly got a kick of the ball. No wonder we were over-run."*

— BOXING —

Liverpool Football Ground

Thursday, Sept. 12th 1946

7-30 p.m.   Main Event approx. 8-45 p.m.

Under the direction of Johnny Best

STAN HAWTHORNE

(NORTH SHIELDS)

v

BILLY THOMPSON

(HICKLETON MAIN)

★ STRONG SUPPORTING CONTESTS ★

The above programme will take place WET or FINE.
Covered accommodation for 40,000.

Prices of admission (inc. Tax)

TICKETS—

Ringside on Ground...£3 3 0   £2 2 0   £1 5 6

Covered Stands (Reserved)   21/-   15/-   7/6

PAY AT DOOR—

Stands & Paddock 6/-   Rest of Ground 2/6

Please send Stamped Addressed Envelope when applying for
tickets by post.
Stadium Box Office (Telephone CENtral 6316, 6317, 7297.)

The evening after Liverpool's humiliation against Manchester United, North Shields' Stan Hawthorne outpointed Billy Thompson over 12 rounds at Anfield in front of nearly 30,000 spectators, to win the Northern Area lightweight title. A big boxing fan, Cyril Done (right) is pictured with boxing personalities in the days leading up to the bout.

The feel-good factor of just four days previous had evaporated in emphatic fashion. Although some Reds' fans and some of the players were due to relax the following night; to watch the British lightweight eliminator boxing match at Anfield, not even the most loyal and optimistic Liverpudlian could have come up with a positive that would soften the hammer blow of negativity that had just hit the Reds. Liverpool had seen up close what a team capable of winning the league title should play like. "Matt Busby has whipped them into the best football team I have seen this season," wrote *Ranger*.

Former Red Busby had won this particular battle however, but the war that was the title race of 1946/47 was far from over. While it may not have seemed so at the time, this 5-0 mauling was to prove a defining moment in Liverpool's season. If they were to reach the heights shown by Busby's team it was clear additional personnel were required and a major reinforcement in attack was quickly pinpointed as the number one priority. The club had enquired after a number of centre-forwards in recent weeks, but so far their search had been fruitless.

Chairman and manager discussed the matter once again in the immediate aftermath of the Maine Road shambles. Another target was identified and together they set off through the night in a bid to get their man. All roads led to Newcastle, but Kay and McConnell were not alone.

**Liverpool v Everton
The Race for Stubbins' signature
Newcastle, September 1946**

"If many more clubs are added to the list of those said to be making a bid for the transfer of Albert Stubbins from Newcastle, it will be easier to set out those who are not interested. It will be smaller.."

Ranger's Notes, Liverpool Echo

A young Albert Stubbins in action for Newcastle during the war.

It was a scene that wouldn't have been out of place in the children's cartoon 'The Wacky Races'. Liverpool chairman Bill McConnell and manager George Kay speeding up the A1 to Tyneside with a delegation from Everton in hot pursuit. The object of their desire was Albert Stubbins, a flame-haired Geordie whose formidable war-time goalscoring record had attracted the attention of every top team in Britain. Both clubs were in desperate need of him and, although it would mean breaking the bank to sign him, this was a derby with a difference - and one neither could afford to lose.

Born in Wallsend, Northumberland, Stubbins spent much of the early part of his childhood in America. His family returned home in the aftermath of the Wall Street crash of 1928 and once back in England his talent as a footballer emerged. He originally signed amateur forms with Sunderland but it wasn't long before his beloved Magpies came calling and he signed as a professional at St James Park in 1937. The following year he made his first team debut in the famous black and white striped shirt and soon established himself as an automatic choice, only for war to then be declared to interrupt his blossoming career.

During each of the first six seasons of the 1940s, while also working as a shipyard draughtsman, Albert was Newcastle's top-scorer. Indeed, throughout the hostilities only two other players in the whole of the country – Jock Dodds and Tommy Lawton – netted more goals. Stubbins' phenomenal strike-rate of 231 goals in 187 war-time appearances included 29 hat-tricks; a nap-hand of goals in a match on five occasions; and a sensational scoring sequence of 15 goals in one blistering five-match spell. It was no wonder he was so highly regarded.

Such form was enough to earn him a call-up for England's Victory International against Wales at The Hawthorns in October the previous year and, although he kicked-off the inaugural post-war league season plying his trade in Division Two, his stock was rising with every passing week and he quickly became the most sought-after player in England. *Ranger* noted that, "if many more clubs are added to the list of those said to be making a bid for the transfer of Albert Stubbins from Newcastle, it will be easier to set out those who are not interested. It will be shorter."

In the eyes of Stan Seymour, his boss at Newcastle, Stubbins was the complete centre-forward, comparable with anyone in the game at the time including Tommy Lawton. "The only advantage Lawton may have over Albert," Seymour said, "is with his heading but Stubbins is cleverer on the ball."

The Geordies were pinning their promotion hopes on, "the dashing, bashing, crashing Stubbins," but at 27 years of age his size 11 feet were getting itchy for the top-flight and just three games into the campaign, and amid a frenzy of speculative stories about his future, he handed in a transfer request. The Newcastle Directors were loath to lose their star-man but, late on the night before Liverpool's crushing defeat to Manchester United, they finally relented and granted him his wish.

McConnell and his Goodison counterpart, Theo Kelly, got wind of the request and the race was on. Other managers had coveted his signature but the Mersey rivals had stolen a march on them all by moving quickest and, although the bids came flying in once it became common knowledge, they were now in pole position to complete the deal. The only question was who would he choose?

Upon arriving at St James' Park both parties were surprised to discover the other there but, having quickly agreed a fee with Newcastle, they sportingly agreed to let the final decision rest with the man himself. The only problem now was tracking him down. The man at the centre of what was to be one of the biggest transfer stories of the time was nowhere to be found and Newcastle officials sent out search parties in a frantic attempt to find him.

Unaware that he was the centre of such attention, the 'story' of Stubbins' signing is regularly told; how he and his wife were enjoying a relaxing afternoon at Newcastle's Northumberland Street News Theatre and were only alerted to the fact that something was afoot when a message urging him to 'please report to St James Park immediately,' was flashed across the cinema screen. He met officials from both clubs and, unable to choose between them, tossed a coin to see who would win the race for his signature! The truth however, is much more mundane and, in a world with no mobile phones by which to discover one's whereabouts instantly, far less dramatic.

Contrary to popular opinion Stubbins was completely unaware the club had tried to contact him until he returned to his home that evening after a night out with his wife Anne. In his first column for the Liverpool Echo some days after he signed, he explained in full.

"On the afternoon of the day I signed for Liverpool...my wife and I were having tea in a Newcastle restaurant. Glancing at the evening paper I saw the huge black headline '£13,000 offered for Stubbins.' Reading further I learned that Liverpool and Everton representatives were at Newcastle Football ground, and I thought then that the trend of events was leading up to my transfer to one of the two famous Merseyside clubs.

My wife and I returned home that evening to hear that the Newcastle trainer, Norman Smith, had called at our house during the afternoon. I immediately travelled back to Newcastle, not knowing at the time that another Newcastle official was on his way to my home in Wallsend and passed me enroute."

To greet Stubbins on his arrival at the ground were officials from both clubs. Being the gentleman he was, the target man didn't want to upset one party by speaking to the other first so he decided to let fate run its course - although, again, not in the way many are led to believe. Contrary to Merseyside football folklore Stubbins did not let his final decision rest on a toss of a coin - although it did have a part to play. Speaking in an interview many years later, he recalled that;

"I was 27, Newcastle were in the Second Division, I wanted to play in the top-flight and, suddenly, I had a choice of two big First Division clubs. It was a very difficult decision to make so I tossed a coin to decide which of the two clubs I'd speak to first. It came down heads for Liverpool and I met George Kay and Bill McConnell. I was so impressed by their offer that I made my mind up without speaking to Theo Kelly. I explained to him that I'd decided to go to Anfield and I never regretted it."

So, late that night, after discussions lasting over an hour, Albert Stubbins finally shook hands on a move to Anfield. It required a club record fee (either £12,500 or £13,000 depending on which source is used) to seal the signing – a deal bettered at the time only by the transfer of Bryn Jones from Wolves to Arsenal in 1938 – but it was piece of business that silenced the critics who had suggested Liverpool's inactivity in the transfer market during the summer reflected a lack of ambition.

Given the fact that the Blues had been champions before the war and were considered to be the bigger and wealthier club on Merseyside at the time, it surprised many that he chose Liverpool over Everton. As Stubbins later admitted however, there were a number of important factors that swung the deal in Liverpool's favour;

"I already knew several of the Liverpool players from having played alongside them during war and the fact that Liverpool were planning another tour to America was also a big attraction to me. As a boy I'd lived in America for a while and loved the place. The prospect of returning...with Liverpool was very appealing.

"It had also always been my intention to pursue a career in journalism once my playing days ended and while at Newcastle I wrote a regular column for the local newspaper. When negotiating with Liverpool I explained this to the chairman Bill McConnell and he arranged a similar set up for me with the Liverpool Echo. The arrangement was that for as long as I played for Liverpool I would continue to write in the Echo."

The following night, shortly before 10pm, Stubbins arrived in Liverpool by train from Newcastle. Despite being the biggest signing in the club's history however, Stubbins managed to pass through the barriers of Lime Street Station completely unnoticed, much to the chagrin of George Kay. The boss had been waiting on the platform to greet him, along with club captain Willie Fagan, several journalists and a few cameramen. Fearing that Stubbins must have had a last minute change of heart, Kay was in a panic and had porters frantically searching the carriages for Liverpool's new prized asset. Unbeknown to them however, Stubbins had simply made his way to the Hanover Hotel where the club had made a reservation for him. He was settling down to an early night when a relieved Kay eventually tracked him down!

In an age far removed from the glitz and glamour enjoyed by today's Premier League stars his low-key arrival in the city mirrored the modest life he lived. As down-to-earth as they come, Stubbins may have been the most expensive player in Liverpool's history but it wasn't something that worried or changed him.

"The fact that I'd scored goals for Newcastle gave me the confidence to think I could do it for Liverpool. In contrast to some players who later moved for bigger fees, I never felt any sense of strain over the price Liverpool had paid. It was never a worry to me. In fact, it was an incentive for me."

Described by *Ranger* as, "a sizeable boy, with a boxer's features and a raking stride," Liverpool's new signing cut an imposing figure. Despite his stature (almost 6' tall) Albert was known as 'the genial Geordie' and widely regarded as one of sport's true gentlemen. Given his size, aerial prowess was surprisingly not one of the strongest parts of his game. His greatest attributes were pace, strength and skill, and he was at his most dangerous when running at defences with the ball at his feet - exactly the sort of player Liverpool's style, when at their best, needed.

The capture of a player of Stubbins' obvious quality was rightly viewed by Liverpool fans as a major coup. As the Reds had also beaten their city neighbours to the signing it was also a source of much local pride among the supporters. Whether he was the final piece in the jigsaw that the manager and the Board had been searching for remained to be seen, but just days after the humiliating capitulation against United his arrival instilled a renewed air of optimism around the club and Liverpudlians could not wait to see the new signing in action. The 'Burning Stub' – so called because of his distinctive mop of red hair – was ready to blaze a trail across the First Division.

New signing Albert Stubbins cleans his own boots outside his modest terraced home in Newcastle just after completing his record-breaking move to Anfield.

Bolton Wanderers v Liverpool
Saturday 14 September 1946

"When I arrived at Anfield I also renewed acquaintanceship with Cyril Sidlow, who played against me several times when he was a 'guest' at Darlington, and met the rest of the team which includes two dry humourists in the debonair 'Nivvy' and cheery Barney Ramsden. The atmosphere in the Anfield dressing room is the kind which makes for harmony on the field and I am looking forward to a successful season with the Reds; I know the enthusiastic Liverpool fans will give us every encouragement."

Albert Stubbins - My First Impressions, Liverpool Echo

Stubbins-mania quickly swept through the red half of the city. By midday on the morning after his arrival thousands of Liverpudlians were setting off to cheer him on in his debut at Bolton. The close proximity of Burnden Park meant Liverpool's away following that day was always going to be a healthy one, but the signing of

Stubbins boosted the numbers considerably and meant the scale of the travelling support was more akin to that which would attend a cup-tie.

It was reported that, "the East Lancashire Road was crowded with traffic from Liverpool to Bolton," prior to the game. "After all, it is not every day one has the chance of seeing £13,000 of footballer in one packet, and loyalist Liverpudlians just could not wait for his first appearance at Anfield." The vast army of fans who travelled helped swell the gate to over 35,000 and, with away teams getting a cut of the gate receipts (which they had done from the League's creation in 1888 until the formation of the Premier League in 1992), it was reported somewhat cheekily that, by virtue of the attendance, "Bolton...[had] helped to pay part of...[Stubbins'] fee," already.

As for the man himself, Stubbins only met up with his new team-mates for the first time on the morning of the game. As was widely expected he immediately found himself thrust into the side to take on the Trotters. With four games for Newcastle already under his belt that season, match fitness was never an issue, so the questions Liverpool fans were asking themselves were, just how would the big money capture fit into Liverpool's style of play? Who would he replace? And, perhaps most importantly of all, would his goal-scoring skills transfer from the Second to the First Division as easily as they hoped?

Ranger mirrored the uncertainty surrounding the final line-up. "Right up to the last moment there was doubt as to whether Jones or Balmer would be at inside right." With Fagan ruled out with an Achilles tendon injury, both players were selected, while in another change to the shot-shy forward line that played against United, the now demobbed Liddell returned in place of Priday. After conceding nine goals in two there were also changes at the back, where Ashcroft and Ramsden stood down to make way for Sidlow and Lambert.

Like Liverpool, Bolton had also been a club that showed full commitment to the nation's cause during the war. All but three members of their playing staff signed up for the Armed Forces just days after war was declared. Led by captain Harry Goslin the majority joined the 53rd (Bolton) Field Regiment and together they took part in some of the fiercest fighting of the conflict - the evacuation at Dunkirk, Egypt and the invasion of Italy. Tragically, Goslin was killed in action near the River Sangro in December 1943. Stan Hanson, Don Howe and Ernie Forrest were among others who also came close to death. Thankfully they survived and all three lined up against Liverpool in this match.

Alongside these heroes was a young Nat Lofthouse. Arguably the most famous figure in Bolton's history today, back in 1946 he was just a rookie 21-year old with a meagre four Football League appearances to his name. A former Bevin Boy miner, Lofthouse first appeared for Wanderers as a 15 year old in 1941 and, like Billy Liddell at Liverpool, established himself as a player of huge potential during the intervening years. When the 1946/47 season finally got underway Lofthouse was considered Bolton's brightest star and he had more than played his part in their fine start to the season.

While Liverpool were tumbling to defeat at Maine Road in midweek, Bolton were running out winners by the odd goal in five at home to Stoke. Since their opening day defeat at Chelsea, they had managed to string together an impressive run of three successive victories that had taken them to fourth place. At the start of play the Reds lay two points and eight places behind but an away win would see them leap-frog their opponents and move into the top half of the table for the first time.

On a damp and overcast afternoon in Lancashire it was Bolton who had the best of the early exchanges. Indeed, but for a fine save by Sidlow from Lofthouse and a sliding tackle by Lambert on Willie Moir soon after, Wanderers could have been two up within the first 10 minutes. Stubbins linked up well with Nivvy but nothing was seen from Liddell until well into the first half. Receiving a pass from the new signing Billy sent in a fine return ball but, from 15 yards out, Stubbins failed to connect properly and the shot was easily saved by Hanson the Bootle-born Bolton keeper. A former Anfield amateur, Stan was also the younger brother of pre-war Liverpool winger Alf Hanson.

The wet surface was offering no aid to flowing football, "and lots of long passes landed in the hands of spectators." Then Stubbins showed why Liverpool had paid so much money for him by creating a great chance from almost nothing. Killing a goal-kick from Sidlow stone dead, he turned sharply and sent a fine pass to Jones

Albert Stubbins beats Jackie Balmer to the ball to power a header towards goal on his Liverpool debut.

on the wing. Racing into the area and shouting for a return pass, Stubbins received what he had asked for and, first time, hit a powerful shot towards the goal only to see Hanson pull off a spectacular save.

Despite these efforts Liverpool were definitely not the better side. Bolton were creating the best chances, with Hughes, Lambert and Ramsden again outstanding in defence. Sidlow made a great one-handed save from a Malcolm Barass cross-shot, and Lofthouse, some six years before he was to be famously re-christened the 'Lion of Vienna', was making his formidable presence felt. Good football was hard to come by in such

conditions however, and with the ball, "as tantalising as a bar of soap...lots of long balls were still skidding far ahead of the man for whom they were intended."

Just five minutes before half-time Liddell collected the ball on the touch line and, looking up for a colleague, sent one of his trademark curling crosses into the area. Racing into the danger zone was old stalwart Nivvy. As talented as they come in the air, the South African rose higher than anyone and met the cross with a textbook downward header that finally broke the deadlock. As the jubilant Liverpool players raced to congratulate him and trotted towards their own half for the Bolton restart, the rain came again, "to make the pitch even more of a mud heap."

For most of the second half Liverpool's lead looked decidedly fragile. A fine through pass put Lofthouse clean through on goal within a few minutes of the resumption of play but conditions underfoot conspired against him. The would-be legendary centre-forward slipped in the act of shooting and his shot went tamely wide of Sidlow's goal. The warning signs were there for Liverpool however, and their Welsh number one, "earned his bonus," by making two fine saves in quick succession and punching a dangerous cross clear.

Liverpool's efforts on goal were few and far between in this period although Balmer showed good skills when he, "juggled the ball from one foot to another to beat his man," before forcing a fine save from Hanson. In the 75th minute Bolton's pressure paid off and Liverpool's defence was finally breached. Sidlow saved well from George Hunt's long-range effort only to punch the resultant corner out to Tom Woodward who, despite the almost impossibly tight angle the Bolton winger found himself in, sent a spectacular bullet header past everyone and into the net.

Hoping to gain the win that would have sent them into the top three, Bolton maintained their attacks, forcing Sidlow to make a number of key saves but if Liverpool could hold on for the remaining 15 minutes then maybe they could leave

Burnden Park with a point. This was certainly what the large number of travelling away fans were thinking. Fortunately for Liverpool their new signing had other ideas.

With just eight minutes remaining, Stubbins found himself with the ball at his feet just inside the centre circle in the Bolton half. Moving forward with menace, the debutant found space opening up in front of him and, when he was just outside the area he unleashed a shot that Hanson could only push onto the base of the post and into the net. It was only Stubbins' second real chance of the game but the ecstatic visiting fans had been given a tantalising glimpse into just what he had to offer and why the Board had deemed him worthy of a club record-breaking fee.

Bolton had worked tirelessly in the second half to draw level. They had created more chances and, for want of better finishing, could conceivably have been a few goals to the good. With just a few minutes remaining however, they now found themselves 2-1 down thanks to the magical intervention of Stubbins, and their own profligacy. Coupled with the poor state of the pitch - even at this early stage of the season - they were almost out on their feet.

Liverpool were not about to let Bolton into the game again. Indeed, the Reds were at their most dangerous during this period and could have had a number of goals themselves - a fine Stubbins-Liddell move looked to have set up Nivvy for a simple tap in but the Scotsman's cross was too hard - before Jackie Balmer scored a spectacular third goal to wrap up the points with almost the last kick of the game. "It was an extraordinarily hard match," *Ranger* later reported, "and [with] the going being heavy, hardly anyone could raise a gallop at the finish." After the massacre in Manchester, it was a welcome return to winning ways for the Reds and a dream debut for new signing Stubbins. Predictably, it was he whose name dominated the post-match headlines, something football fans throughout the country would soon get used to. Recalling his debut many years later, Stubbins remembered,

> "...*seeing how the Liverpool defence coped so well with their attack. This gave me so much confidence because I knew the players around me were all capable.*
>
> "*The support of the fans also helped me settle. I always felt I had their support and I'll be eternally grateful to them for that. Later, even if I had a bad game, the crowd would never crucify me like they would some players. As a player it is so important that the fans take to you. Fortunately I had no such problems at Liverpool and everything went so well.*"

Stubbins' arrival had given Liverpool's season fresh impetus. Ahead of the first post-war Merseyside league derby Reds' fans were now walking through the city streets with an added air of confidence and the opportunity to show their Blue neighbours exactly what they had missed couldn't come soon enough. With Everton in poor form most Reds' fans expected to win comfortably but even in 1946 however, form books were routinely thrown out of windows.

Liverpool v Everton
Saturday 21 September 1946

"Never have I known a 'Derby' game which has tickled the public fancy so much as this one – the first home appearance of Albert Stubbins, Liverpool's £13,000 forward, and the hopes that Everton would 'pull one out of the bag' added to the interest."

Ranger, Liverpool Echo

Desperate fans queue for derby tickets in the rain.

Local derby matches have always been intense, the Merseyside derby perhaps more than most. That this was the first competitive game between Liverpool and Everton since before the war, a season in which Everton had won the league, only intensified matters even more. Throw in the fact that just over a week earlier the Reds had pipped the Blues to the much publicised capture of Albert Stubbins and excitement was understandably at fever-pitch.

After just one game in a red shirt Stubbins was already being feted as the new darling of the Kop and it was his impending duel with Everton's, "prince of centre halves," TG Jones, that had every football fan in the city talking. With Anfield's 61,000 capacity reduced to 52,000 due to restrictions put in place following the Bolton Disaster, it was also expected that demand for tickets would far outweigh supply.

Three days before the game the first tickets for the long-awaited match were put on sale, not on the internet, or a dedicated, automated phoneline, nor even at Anfield itself, but at the city centre branch of Jack Sharps in Whitechapel - a specialist sports shop. Well accustomed to queuing for war-time goods, eager fans began to arrive at the store as early as 7am. "In heavy rain a huge crowd of people, men, women and children waited in a queue an eighth of a mile long," noted the Liverpool Echo:

"There were scenes at 10am at the shop entrance, where an otherwise orderly queue pressed into the doorway. The plate-glass window was smashed with the weight of bodies, and two

ladders were passed out of the shop to act as a buffer against further pressure.

"People where lined up four or five deep all the way round. Rain failed to damp spirits, even of the women, who had come better prepared for the weather than most of the men."

Even though the queues were only for Main Stand tickets, and the time when they would be queuing in even more numbers outside the ground itself was still some days away, the scenes were testimony to the interest such a long wait for a 'derby' match had generated;

"Hundreds in the queue were drenched by exposure to some hours of driving rain. Despite this they showed no signs of giving up their quest for tickets, which would save them from queuing at Anfield next Saturday...Several soldiers and sailors were in the line...Some of the men held newspapers over their heads."

Given such intense interest, it did not take long for the tickets to sell out;

"Shortly after 10am it was announced that there were no more tickets for sale, and hundreds of people were disappointed. A policeman estimated that there must have been at least 5,000 in the queue at one time during the morning."

All through Thursday and Friday crowds flocked to Anfield in the hope of purchasing tickets but, with cash payment at the turnstiles then an accepted, and usual, part of the matchday experience, the biggest queues were expected on the day of the game itself. As anticipated, crowds began to gather at the Anfield turnstiles in the early hours and around 6,000 fans were eventually locked out, even though the official attendance – 49,838 – showed that the ground was once again not full to its reduced capacity.

Tickets Please—By George Green

AS IF THERE IS NOT ENOUGH TROUBLE IN THE WORLD WE HAD TO HAVE A NEW WORRY THIS WEEK –"TRYING TO GET TICKETS FOR THE LOCAL DERBY."

A FEW MINDS WITH BUT A SINGLE THOUGHT.

SOME SENT THEIR APPLICATIONS FOR TICKETS BY POST.

AND SPENT THE REST OF THE WEEK SITTING BY THE FRONT-DOOR WAITING FOR A REPLY.

THE GENERAL OUTLOOK IS VERY UNSETTLED

I HAVEN'T A TICKET EITHER

SOME WENT TO THE RESERVE MATCH AT ANFIELD ON WEDNESDAY WITH THE INTENTION OF SQUATTING UNTIL SATURDAY.

THE TICKET QUESTION SEEMED TO BE THE ONLY THING THAT MATTERED.

Expectations of a classic had been fuelled by journalists and pundits alike. "A great game full of thrills," was *Ranger's* pre-match assessment. Everton were viewed as the more illustrious of the two clubs by virtue of their greater success on the pitch – one more League title and two FA Cups to Liverpool's none - and greater resources off it. The Blues could also boast a superior 'derby' record but times were changing - proven by Liverpool's signing of Stubbins. In a further indication of the shift of power in Merseyside football, Liverpool were widely viewed as favourites to claim local bragging rights.

The pre-war 'School of Science' Everton side that had swept to the title so majestically in 1938/39 was a fast-fading memory and the longest reigning League champions in history were not the force they once were. Lawton had gone and had not yet been suitably replaced, whilst their other star player - Joe Mercer - a pre-season target for Liverpool themselves, was unsettled.

Going into the game however, there was little to choose between the two sides in terms of league position. Liverpool were joint eighth in the table with Bolton, but only goal average separated them from 10th placed Everton. The Blues were also enjoying the better run of form having won their previous two games compared to the Reds' run of just one. Nevertheless, it was predicted that Liverpool's style of play - passing and moving and utilising the strength and speed of Stubbins and Liddell - would be too much for a more laborious Everton side. *Ranger* noted that Everton were seen to, "favour the more studious type of game, working the ball to advantage, whereas Liverpool…especially with Stubbins…[would] be all for making a bee-line for goal."

With the war interrupting many playing careers, less than half of those who took to the field had 'derby' day experience. Liverpool could boast only three among their 11 who had tasted the peculiar delights and passion of the fixture; Balmer, Nivvy and Taylor. By contrast, Everton had five such experienced players; inside-forward Alec Stevenson, full-back Norman Greenhalgh, centre-half Tommy Jones and wing-halves Joe Mercer and Stan Bentham. It would have been six had Gordon Watson not reported himself unfit on the morning of the game. Everton duly had to reorganise themselves, with Billy Higgins being named as centre-forward. The former Tranmere man had been signed by the Blues just six months previously and had played barely a handful of senior games. For their part, Liverpool were almost at full strength, fielding the same eleven who had defeated Bolton the week before.

With the majority of the big derby crowd roaring Liverpool on from their, now fully appreciated, warm-up routine, the first attack of note came from Everton. Stevenson found Tommy McIlhatton with a straightforward pass through the middle of the pitch only for the Irish winger to screw his shot out for a goal kick. The Blues followed this with a Higgins header from a Jones free-kick but luckily for Liverpool there was no real power behind it and the ball looped softly into the arms of Sidlow. The Welsh keeper then rushed out smartly to collect the ball before McIlhatton or Fielding could make contact with a fine Saunders pass. It was clear that despite their favourites tag, Liverpool would not have things all their own way.

A Liddell cross-cum-shot was then left by Everton goalkeeper George Burnett, eventually going a foot or so over, but it was Stubbins who was centre of attention. "All were on the watch to see what Stubbins would do when he got his first chance." The home debutant had a shot blocked on ten minutes but then showed he had more to his game than simply an eye for goal when he, "opened the way for Balmer by that old trick of allowing the ball to pass through his legs and to his inside right."

The West Derby man managed to hit the target with his shot but it lacked sufficient power and failed to trouble Burnett.

This effort seemed to galvanise the Reds and they began to play with more composure, creating numerous openings but no clear cut chances. Nivvy, "with a sweeping pass," found Liddell in a dangerous position but, "a sterling tackle," by George Saunders thwarted the attack. It was to be the first of many great tackles the Everton right-back would make on Liddell throughout the game.

Another fine pass by Nivvy then found Balmer and this time the Liverpool forward, "slashed in a powerful drive that Burnett could not hold." The ball ricocheted off his hands into his chest and then spun out for a corner. It was to be the best chance of the match for either side. Balmer then showed why many in the home crowd viewed him as inconsistent when, after he beat two men with a mazy dribble before firing a shot wide from 20 yards, he hit a wayward pass that allowed Jones to build a rare Everton attack.

Everton's T G Jones

Despite this error, "Balmer was Liverpool's marksman-in-chief," and his shooting total for the match must have numbered a dozen at least. That this was the case was down in no small measure to the fact that Stubbins and Liddell were kept relatively quiet by Jones and Saunders respectively. Indeed, *Ranger* singled out both Everton defenders for particular praise, saying later that, "perhaps one day he [Jones] will have a bad game and give me a rest from paying tribute to his brilliant artistry and consistency." Likewise, it was, "a long time since I saw Liddell so securely held – a great tribute to Saunders." It was also noted that Laurie Hughes for Liverpool, although he had a less cultured style to Jones, "was just as effective," at preventing opposition attacks.

The first half ended with Everton under pressure, but with few real goal-scoring opportunities for Liverpool. Despite Stubbins finding himself crowded out in the middle of the park he managed to find Balmer on the wing but he also found himself outnumbered and the move came to nothing. "Stubbins and Balmer [then] collaborated once more, but Jones stood defiant." 60 seconds later, "Liddell also fell against this solid barrier."

Just a minute before the whistle Bentham broke through the Liverpool rearguard and found McIlhatton but the subsequent shot, although on target, was palmed over the bar by Sidlow. From the resultant corner Liverpool broke clear themselves, the ball finally finding Stubbins, but with Jones closing him down his snap shot went just wide. It was the last action of the half.

Jackie Balmer (hidden) fires towards the Kop goal in the first Merseyside derby of the season.
Albert Stubbins and 'Prince of centre-halves' T G Jones (player nearest ball) looks on in front of a packed Kemlyn Road Stand.

The frantic action that had brought the first period to an end was evident again within 30 seconds of the second. Burnett ran clear of his goal line to clear a ball downfield but with the Everton keeper taking his time returning to his goal Stubbins raced to meet the clearance and, "without hesitation he let fly for goal," with a first time shot. "That he did not succeed was due to Everton's covering tactics." It was man-of-the-match Jones who cleared from inside the six-yard box and prevented a wonder goal by the new man.

With, "the respective defences...so much in command that scoring chances were few," most shots at goal were long-range efforts. Balmer shot over the bar from distance to the derision of the Evertonians in the non-segregated crowd who had long ago christened the Liverpool forward 'over the Balmer'.

Stevenson then shot from 25 yards after a good move by Everton, but although Sidlow could only parry the ball to Higgins, he too was guilty of squandering a decent half chance by putting the ball wide when, with more composure, he could perhaps have scored. Taylor also got in on the act when he, "cracked in a fast drive from long-range which Burnett could only turn aside," and Stevenson cleared the rebound.

Everton had created little in the second half so far, but on the hour mark Jones saw his header from a corner well saved and soon after Lambert got in the way of a long-range Eglington shot. With the Everton defence, "supreme against anything the Liverpool forwards could produce," Liverpool became, "uncommonly quiet," at this stage of the game. Indeed, so lacklustre and seemingly downhearted had they become that *Ranger* was forced to note that he, "was astonished at the lack of Liverpool spirit at this point, for it is at moments like this that they usually blaze up." Although the game ended with Everton, "going strongest at the time when it counts most," no goals were forthcoming and the first post-war Merseyside derby had ended goalless. After all the hype the 77th meeting of these two great rivals had been a disappointing anti-climax. While Merseypride remained intact on both sides of Stanley Park however, the Reds did at least manage to get closer to the leaders as Manchester United lost their first game of the season at Stoke. Despite much-fancied Blackpool's victory over Aston Villa, United still topped the table with 11 points, four clear of the Reds who had a game in hand.

As was the new custom, the Liverpool directors entertained their Everton counterparts in the Anfield Board Room after the game. As well as enjoying their neighbours hospitality, the Blues' Board took the opportunity to enquire after Cyril Done, the Reds' centre-forward who, although a prolific scorer in war-time football, had yet to start a game this season. "Tentative feelers were put out by Everton officials at the Liverton derby on Saturday," noted *Ranger*.

Such news today would of course make headlines on both front and back pages for days on end, but as befitted the style and nature of the game in 1946, the Liverpool directors simply stated that they would discuss the matter further at their next meeting scheduled for Tuesday evening. Until they had made their decision - one that centred around whether they could afford to let the player, who was still viewed as excellent back-up for Stubbins, leave at all - press statements, sensationalist or otherwise, were firmly off the agenda.

Liverpool v Leeds United
Saturday 28 September 1946

"I have a feeling that Liverpool's re-organised forward line will do its stuff in the matter of shooting this weekend. To get the best out of Stubbins the ball must be given to him in a proper manner - along the ground. he had few such passes against Everton...Furthermore Stubbins will not have a 'T G' to contend with tomorrow."

Ranger's Notes, Liverpool Echo

What had already been a hectic month for English football was not yet over. Modern managers may wince at the prospect of playing so many league games in such a short space of time, but it was commonplace back in the era of flat caps and baggy shorts. Liverpool had already played four times in 11 days before they welcomed Leeds United to Anfield, aiming to end an eventful few weeks on a high with a return to winning ways.

An ageing side - a dozen of their squad had been with the club since the 1930s - Leeds were not expected to present much of a challenge for a Liverpool team that, after an indifferent start, was beginning to look not only a solid unit at the back, but also a potent force in attack. Indeed, after struggling throughout war-time football, the Yorkshiremen had finished bottom of the previous season's regional table, with just nine wins from 42 games. They had scored just 26 and conceded a staggering 118 goals during that campaign and were among most people's best bet to be relegated in 1946/47.

While the Reds were being held by Everton, Leeds had finally got their season up and running in impressive fashion with a 4-0 drubbing of Bolton at Elland Road. The victory was their first win of the season and one that lifted them off the bottom of the table. Leeds' efforts to build on their morale-boosting victory were not helped by the call up of right-winger Davey Cochrane to the Ireland team that was set to take on England in Belfast on the same afternoon. The Reds had no such interruptions and could call on a full squad for the first time that season. To assist Stubbins and bolster the attacking options, fit again captain Fagan who, "knows the requirements of a centre-forward," made an immediate return, meaning Jones moved from inside-forward to wing-half, with Paisley the unlucky player to drop out.

Jackie Balmer scorer of Liverpool's first goal against Leeds.

On what was another blisteringly hot afternoon the Anfield crowd was again a healthy one, with queues four and five deep reported outside the Kop an hour before kick-off. The official attendance of 51,042 was Liverpool's biggest crowd of the season to date and they witnessed a lively game with Liverpool winning comfortably, although they should have won by more with John Hodgson, the Leeds' keeper, a deserved man of the match.

Liverpool dominated proceedings from start to finish, with shot after shot raining in on Hodgson's goal. In the first five minutes, following a fine pass by Stubbins, the Leeds' keeper turned a fierce shot by Fagan around the post for a corner, "in as good a save as we shall probably see." From the resultant corner the ball was worked to Fagan again but he could only hit the ball over the bar. A similar result from a Balmer shot occurred just a few moments later. It was clear Hodgson was in for a busy afternoon.

Stubbins' lethal combination of speed, skill and strength was causing Leeds centre-back Tom Holley all sorts of problems, but it was from the other wing that Liverpool opened the scoring. A run and cross by Jones - playing in his third different position of the season - was met by Nivvy who, "with characteristic springiness," nodded the ball into the path of Balmer. The old warhorse controlled the ball and shot in almost one movement leaving Hodgson with nothing to do except pick the ball out of the net.

"Made to look like whirlwinds," Liverpool began to play almost as they liked and it was disappointing that they reached half-time with no further goals to add to Balmer's first-half effort. Ramsden hit the woodwork, a Liddell cross almost crept under the bar, and Balmer had two great chances cleared off the line by Jim Millburn. In contrast, Leeds could muster only a few hopeful crosses into an empty box and a long-range Tom Hindle shot that forced Sidlow into the only save of note he had to make in the first 45 minutes. Balmer found himself almost clean through on goal late on but the referee blew for half-time just as the move looked promising and most of the crowd, some of whom were being attended to by ambulance-men in the stifling heat, "cheered the Reds down the tunnel."

The second half started much as the first had ended, with Liverpool doing most of the attacking and Leeds defending gallantly. Stubbins claimed a penalty in the first five minutes after he was fouled in the area but the referee, Prestwich's WB Nixon, incurred the wrath of the Anfield faithful by ignoring Liverpool's appeals. A few minutes later he turned down a blatant free-kick just outside the box when Fagan was clearly pushed off the ball whilst attempting another shot.

Despite many modern-day commentators lamenting the days gone by when players would simply accept the referee's decision and resume the game with a shrug of the shoulders and a rueful smile, a host of Liverpool players showed that such an ideal is a myth, surrounding the man in black at his refusal to give a free-kick for the foul on their captain. The crowd too greeted the refusal with derision, booing the ref loudly. A few oranges were even thrown onto the pitch from the direction of the boys' pen! Rotten ones they must have been though - as to throw good fruit away in a time when they were extremely difficult to come by was foolish in the extreme!

For a time these decisions looked like they may cost Liverpool the points as first Dennis Grainger, then Wales international Aubrey Powell forced good saves from Sidlow and Liverpool's profligacy in front of goal continued. A Nivvy free-kick was floated into the box and an unsighted Liddell, at the back of a bunch of players, was as surprised as everyone when the ball cannoned off his head to go just inches wide.

Halfway through the second half Liverpool finally stepped up a gear and Fagan, who was having a great game, nearly scored when barging his way past everyone in the area only to see Gerry Henry make a last ditch tackle. As the game wore on Liverpool began to create more and more chances. Nivvy was clean through with only the keeper to beat but wasted his chance, then Stubbins forced another great save from Hodgson after cleverly beating a number of men and unleashing a tremendous shot from the edge of the area. On 73 minutes Liverpool finally got their reward when yet another great corner by Liddell evaded everyone except Nivvy on the far post. With the simplest of headers, the South African made it 2-0.

Four minutes later the points looked to be well and truly Liverpool's after the referee gave the Reds a penalty when he judged Milburn to have handled in the area. Perhaps awarding the spot kick was recompense for his earlier decisions as many in the ground thought the Leeds defender was outside the area when the offence occurred. Leeds' players certainly thought so, and it was now their turn to ask the official to reverse his decision.

Any such notions the home crowd had that it was not a penalty - Liverpool's first of the season - were soon overlooked when they saw it was Stubbins who was due to take the spot-kick. With no goals in the Anfield derby a week earlier could this be the star striker's first home goal? Unfortunately, no. Seconds later the Kop could only look on in disbelief, as Hodgson dived splendidly to his right to make yet another great save.

It was a moment that lived long in the memory of Liverpool's new number nine and one he could recall in later years with as much clarity as his many goals:

"Willie Fagan was the regular penalty taker at Liverpool but I was so used to taking penalties at Newcastle that when the ref pointed for a penalty I automatically grabbed the ball and placed it on the spot. I'd never missed one for Newcastle and the Liverpool supporters were all expecting me to score my first home goal but the keeper pulled off a tremendous save.I could not have had a greater chance than with a penalty kick and to make things worse it was in front of the Kop.

"No one should ever miss a penalty when you think about it. You're only twelve yards out with the keeper to beat but these things happen. If someone would have asked me to take another one, two minutes later, I would, although I don't think I took many more for Liverpool. Fortunately we won the game but George Kay was so upset for me that he took me out for tea after the game."

Even here the stark differences between this era and the modern game are pronounced. The force of Stubbins' shot and the heaviness of the ball combined to ensure that although Hodgson saved well, he was nearly knocked-out and broke his wrist in the process. After making the save he immediately, "dropped to the ground in agony," and play was held-up while he received treatment. Remarkably, the brave keeper played on for the remainder of the match and, "fully earned the ovation he received at the end." It was traumatic ending for the Leeds' man however, who, as well as facing an enforced absence from football, would also be away from the pit-face for some time seeing as he was also a miner during the week

- another sign of the times and a scenario that would be unheard of today.

For the record, Stubbins had also fractured the arm of a goalkeeper with a penalty in schoolboy football and was to do it again on a future American tour. During the remainder of his time with the Reds he was to take only one other penalty in a competitive match - in a league encounter at home to Blackpool in March 1948. Not only did he score, but the keeper survived with his arm intact!

Thankfully, the miss against Leeds did not prove too costly and what had been a relatively easy victory lifted Liverpool into the top five on nine points - level with Stoke, Wolves and Sheffield United. There was then a gap of three points to third placed Sunderland.

It was the number of postponed games that makes for interesting reading however. Although most sides had played seven or eight matches, even this early in the season the adverse weather had meant many fixtures had had to be postponed. Middlesbrough, in ninth place, had only played six games, whilst the new league leaders - courtesy of their second victory in four days - were Blackpool on 14 points, who had played, together with Wolves, nine. Manchester United were now second, a point behind.

Despite playing well in arguably only two games - Chelsea and Leeds - Liverpool were still handily placed, especially considering they had games in hand on all the teams around them. Their line-up, particularly up front, appeared to be gelling well, creating chances and, even accounting for the missed penalty by Stubbins, scoring goals. The signs were encouraging and confidence was certainly on the rise.

Grimsby Town v Liverpool
Saturday 5 October 1946

*"Stubbins continues to show lovely touches. Doubtless when he and the
inner men have played together more frequently, we shall see
a better understanding of each other's requirements."*

Stork's Notes, Liverpool Echo

As Liverpool prepared for their cross-country trip to the east coast for the clash with Grimsby Town, the story dominating the pages of the local press centred on the large number of injuries sustained by players so far this season. Questions were being asked as to why such an increasing number of players were suddenly finding themselves laid up on the treatment table. Was the game becoming more violent? Were the players out of control? Or, owing to neglect due to the war, was it down to the poor state of the country's football pitches?

Reds' boss George Kay reckoned he knew the answer and it was none of the above.

"They are trying to play pre-war football on post-war rations," being his simple but intelligent offering on the matter. The Daily Post noted that Everton were without 18 of their 44 registered players because of injury and, while the Reds were not suffering to that extent, they were about to show - as all good teams must at some point in the season - that they had the strength in depth to get through "this injury-ridden part of the season".

Liverpool's preparations for the visit to Blundell Park were hampered by the loss of utility man Bill Jones and the in-form Nivvy, both of whom picked up knocks in the win over Leeds. Into the vacant left-half and outside-right positions came Bob Paisley and Harry Eastham respectively, the pair getting the nod after impressing in a midweek Lancashire Senior Cup first round first leg tie away to Blackpool.

Further proof of Liverpool's quality in reserve came in the form of centre-forward Cyril Done, yet to make a senior post-war league appearance but a man pushing hard for his place. Done was a two-goal marksman at Bloomfield Road as a side which also included the likes of Jim Harley, Tom Bush, Eddie Spicer, Stan Palk and Bob Priday fought back from 2-0 down to secure a share of the spoils. Done, "controlled his forwards expertly," noted the local press, and Liverpool would have ran out deserved winners had Priday not missed two, "gift chances," late in the game. Unfortunately for Done, and as Grimsby were about to discover to their cost, goalscoring was not an area in which Liverpool were to be found wanting. Done's time would come but for now he could only sit back and marvel at an attacking master-class by the Reds.

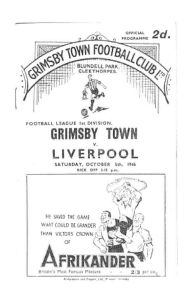

To modern day observers Grimsby Town is a club that immediately seems out of place in the top division, but they had been regular top-flight participants during the 1930s and had even managed to finish as high as fifth in the 1934/35 season. A mid-table team at best just prior to the war however, the 'Fishermen' were a side in decline. On home soil they were regarded as anything but formidable and although victorious away to Bolton the previous week, a Liverpool victory was again expected.

Despite dull conditions, Blundell Park, the smallest ground in Division One, was packed to its 22,000 capacity for the visit of Liverpool and, unlike the previous week when their dominance resulted in just two goals, the pressure the Reds forward line exerted on another of the teams expected to be battling for relegation come the end of the season was to pay off handsomely with, as one imaginative post-match headline put it, a, "Shoal of Goals at Grimsby."

Aided by a strong wind in the first half, Liverpool created numerous chances in the early stages. After just three minutes Stubbins found Liddell on the wing with a fine headed pass and the Scotsman's cross was met by Eastham whose header hit the side netting. Stubbins hit the post with a fierce shot a few minutes later then Balmer, Stubbins, then Balmer again, all saw great opportunities go begging, prompting, "the Grimsby crowd...[to give] a special cheer for the defence."

Next it was Liddell's turn to hit the woodwork, then Tweedy, the Grimsby keeper made a fine save from Taylor's shot. It seemed a case of when, not if, Liverpool would open the scoring with Sidlow in the Reds' goal reduced to the role of a spectator. After 22 minutes a goalmouth scramble in the Grimsby area saw Balmer mis-kick but, "the quickness of Stubbins in picking up the ball and putting into the net was phenomenal." It was a lead Liverpool more than deserved and the goal-scorer had turned away to celebrate almost before the ball had crossed the line.

Within 100 seconds of the restart Liverpool's advantage was doubled through Liddell who showed just why the Liverpool fans held him in such high regard. After receiving the ball in his own midfield, the winger raced almost half the length of the pitch, "at lightning speed," to make it 2-0. "Liddell and Stubbins...stars in a fine forward line...[had]proved unmistakably that they merely need half chances."

It appeared Grimsby lacked any sort of attacking threat but Liverpool's second goal seemed to galvanise their players and they at least began to make more of an effort. Soon after Liddell's goal Sidlow saved at the second attempt after Paisley had mis-kicked in his own area. Another uncharacteristic defensive mistake by Ramsden early in the second half almost let in centre-forward Norman Moore but this aside, Liverpool were, "playing good stuff and keeping the ball on the ground."

Just as Liverpool's two first half goals came in quick succession, so too did their third and fourth early in the second half. On 53 minutes a Liddell corner found Balmer in the crowded area. He stabbed the ball goalwards more in hope than anticipation and, again in the right place at the right time, it was Stubbins who had a simple tap in for his second and Liverpool's third.

Four minutes later Balmer scored his third strike in four games. Stubbins and Fagan were linking up well for the visitors and most of Liverpool's good work came from their, "close harmony." A fine move by the pair ended in a great through ball for Balmer who, although he appeared to be offside, and with the Grimsby defence motionless and appealing for the decision, played to the whistle and stroked the ball into the net. Much to the disgust of the Grimsby players no whistle came and they surrounded the referee in protest. The goal stood however, and at 4-0 the Reds were cruising.

On 64 minutes Fagan dispossessed Mariners centre-back Harry Betmead and, after a great one-two with Stubbins, found himself bearing down on goal. Tweedy did well to block him, but the ball broke to Stubbins who was on hand yet again to shoot into an empty net. Liverpool's record signing had scored his first hat-trick for the club. Or had he? With the Liverpool Echo attributing Liverpool's fifth goal to Stubbins it would seem to be case closed. However, Monday's Liverpool Daily Post, whilst giving a sixth and final Liverpool goal to Liddell - that is not disputed, did not record Stubbins' 'hat-trick'. With few papers listing Fagan's penalty on 65 minutes it is clear that there is some confusion as to the goalscorers in this game. Record compiler Eric Doig, grandson of legendary Liverpool goalkeeper Ted Doig and one of the foremost Liverpool statisticians, agrees that the identity of the final two Liverpool goalscorers is hazy at best, but in such situations sides with the Daily Post view of the game as it is a more considered match report. Adding weight to this argument is the fact that a Grimsby Town historian states that their records tally with those of the Daily Post, Eric, lfchistory.net and other record compilers.

There was no disputing the winners however, and with maximum points safely in the bag - not to mention the goal average column receiving a welcome boost - the only uncertainty now was, "where the rush of goals would end...[the game] might have seven, eight or nine or even more." Six goals to the good, the rampant Reds finally took their foot of the pedal and showed their hosts some mercy.

There was to be no further scoring by the visitors and the only blemish on an otherwise perfect afternoon was the late consolation goal that denied Liverpool's seemingly impregnable back-line a deserved clean-sheet. Lambert, Hughes and Ramsden, "gave the defence the merit of never appearing in danger of defeat," but a dubious penalty awarded against Lambert who vainly protested his innocence for some minutes afterwards along with Phil Taylor, allowed left-winger Billy Wardle to reduce the deficit three minutes from time.

Liverpool's fifth win in their first eight games lifted them up to fourth in the table - five points behind leaders Blackpool but with two games in hand. This scintillating six-goal show had sent out an ominous warning to the rest. After over 20 years in the doldrums, relegation battles and a World War it seemed that, finally, a Liverpool title challenge was under way. Of this, the Daily Post's Leslie Edwards was in no doubt;

> *"Let it be understood, beyond doubt...that this was the best thing Liverpool have done this season. Like the lift attendant, Liverpool FC are going up. They stepped off at Grimsby Town and picked up a nice line in 6-1 victories."*

The strength, standard, style and durability of the Liverpool squad had also been underlined for the first time this season. It would not be the last. The two men drafted in because of the injury situation had done themselves and the club proud. Eastham, "did what he had to do with the ball then promptly passed it elsewhere," while Paisley's, "100 per cent effort," seemingly made him, "undroppable." It was the performance of rising star Liddell however, that was most pleasing and with him, "gradually becoming fitter...this was the brightest news Liverpool have this weekend."

A fascinating footnote to this most emphatic and impressive of victories, and another example of just how times have changed since the immediate post-war era is a story concerning one of the Liverpool heroes at Grimsby that day. Following the match Ray Lambert who, along with a number of his team mates had yet to be demobbed - Sidlow and Liddell among them - had to return to his RAF base at Catterick. In common with a large number of his contemporaries, Lambert could not afford to own a car and so, immediately after getting washed and changed, the Welsh international set off with his kitbag over his shoulder to reach his destination by train.

It wasn't until the early hours of Sunday morning that he arrived at York however, and here the Reds full-back found that a connection to Catterick was still some hours away. Sensing his plight, a friendly railway official tried to get him on an overnight Darlington-bound goods train but he was unsuccessful and so Ray, just hours after playing a starring role in what was undoubtedly the First Division's match of the day, was forced to sleep rough in a freezing station until dawn - his kitbag as a pillow and rail staff as his alarm. For a maximum of £10 a week how many of today's footballer's would contemplate such a trip now?

Middlesbrough v Liverpool
Saturday 5 October 1946

"They played like champions at Grimsby, and many of their followers already have visions of them proving themselves the title-holders at the end of the season... Personally, I would not wish them to take the lead at this stage of the competition for pacemaking is a testing affair. It is much better to be in a handy position near the end of the season and then make your challenge."

Stork's Notes, Liverpool Echo

It was a row that had been simmering in the background since pre-season but, as Liverpool basked in the glory of their resounding win over Grimsby and prepared for their next challenge - a midweek visit to Middlesbrough, the possibility of it bringing the inaugural post-war league campaign to a shuddering halt suddenly reared its ugly head once again. After long and protracted negotiations, the Players' Union and League Management Committee (LMC) remained at loggerheads over a pay dispute that had been ongoing since the summer and which threatened the very fabric of the game.

Players were desperate to cash in on the great post-war boom football was enjoying. With a logic that seems incontrovertible today, but which the game's governing body could not comprehend at the time, Jim Fay of the Players Union said;

"The lads who are playing now and have been doing so for the past two or three years have

66

made the money for the club. They feel they are entitled to get the benefit, as quite a number are approaching the end of their careers."

With the LMC refusing to budge a, "mexican style stand-off," ensued. Wilf Cuff, President of the Football League, was quick to hit back. "The Players Union are endeavouring to force the issue but if they think they can intimidate the League Management Committee they are greatly mistaken."

While supporters may have been revelling in the return to 'normal' league football, the players had had enough and with their cry for a greater share of the rewards continuing to fall on deaf ears the threat of unprecedented strike action being taken escalated alarmingly.

Until now the players at Anfield, while no doubt discussing the situation privately in the sanctuary of the dressing room, had remained tight-lipped on the subject, but while the rights and wrongs of the debate were being dissected at large in the press an unnamed Liverpool player added his voice to the growing sense of unrest among the majority of the country's 2,000 professional footballers when he warned that, "unless our demands for higher wages are met we will strike." In response a Liverpool director promised that, "even if there is a strike, football will continue," suggesting that if such action was taken amateurs would be drafted in to keep the game going. Such an approach may appear altruistic - to ensure fans would be able to watch their beloved game. However, the main reason given as to why such an approach was mooted? Because, "pools betting amounts to millions of pounds."

While everyone waited with baited breath for the matter to be resolved, for Reds fans it was, fortunately, not a disagreement that would be allowed to disrupt the harmony of a team that was enjoying its best form of the season so far. Their emphatic weekend victory may have been lost somewhere deep in the column inches of newspapers more concerned with off-field issues but it was to the north-east they travelled next, riding high on confidence and determined to avenge the defeat suffered against Boro in front of Kop in only their second game of the season. The task they faced was difficult one. Middlesbrough had already yielded maximum points from their three previous home games, scoring ten and conceding just four before Liverpool - with nine goals for and just two against in their last two away games - turned up on Teeside.

In what was the last early season midweek match due to the shortening hours of daylight, a huge crowd was in attendance at Ayresome Park. Government restrictions on early midweek games due to the concomitant loss to industrial output that inevitably followed were still in place and it was easy to see why here. "There was considerable absenteeism in local industry as queues started at midday and the stands were full an hour later." For a midweek working afternoon, such numbers at a 'Boro home game were unprecedented and the vast majority were hoping to see David Jack's side complete a first league double of the season. At half-time however, it appeared the 'Boro fans would be disappointed and another,

"'Grimsby-style rout," seemed to be on the cards. In what was an outstanding opening 45 minutes Liverpool simply picked up where they had left off four days previously at Blundell Park and the same eleven, "six-shooters," quickly silenced the partisan home crowd.

It was Liddell who opened the scoring in the 24th minute, "breasting down an Eastham centre and cutting in to put the ball in the net via the underside of the bar." The same player doubled the advantage 12 minutes later, giving chase to a seemingly lost cause as the ball ran loose towards the last 'Boro defender. After managing to get a touch however, Liddell's mere presence unsettled keeper Dave Cumming and full-back Dickie Robinson to such an extent that they made a complete hash of an attempted clearance and the ball trickled over the line.

Boro were, "undoubtedly a good team," but Liddell's two, "opportunist goals," had made them, "look ordinary". The flying-Scotsman's quick-fire double seemed more than enough to warrant Liverpool a full two points on the road for the third successive away match and, "the 40,000 present certainly sounded as though they were in no doubt that Liverpool had the match pocketed."

The visitors, "general supremacy," in the first half was arguably the stuff champions are made of and the game should have been put beyond Boro's reach during the opening exchanges of the second period. On several occasions immediately after the break Liverpool had opportunities to kill the game off for good. That they failed to punish their lack-lustre hosts however, was to come back and haunt them. Suddenly the game, "took an unexpected turn," and 'Boro, "finished up world beaters!" With, "one of the best inside forwards playing in flaxen-haired Mannion," the home side rallied so well that their fans, who were, "almost in despair," when Liverpool led 2-0 were, "later roused into a frenzy by a Middlesbrough transformation."

The comeback began when pre-war England centre-forward Micky Fenton, a reputed transfer target of Everton at the time, pulled a goal back in the 67th minute. Then, with just ten minutes remaining, inside-forward George Dews levelled matters. At this point Liverpool had to work extremely hard to keep the home side's goals tally to just two and, according to one enthralled reporter, it, "was one of the most stirring and surprising finishes," he had ever witnessed. "The nature of their revival after being so outplayed was one of football's rarer happenings. The mystery was how Liverpool lost their grip on this game."

A thigh injury picked up by Stubbins didn't help matters and as a result he moved across to outside-left where he was not his usual, "penetrative" self. With Liverpool on the ropes and looking more likely to end up losers they staged one last late rally that almost saw them snatch the points at the death, but a Fagan shot from no more than five-yards out came agonisingly back off the woodwork.

"All told," in this classic game of two halves, "a draw was fair." Liverpool had as much of the first half as Middlesbrough had of the second and on reflection the point gained was a commendable one. They'd become the first team to prise a point out of Middlesbrough on their home ground and it stretched their unbeaten run to five games, moving them up one place in the table to third in the process.

"To criticise Liverpool when they played so well for so long would hardly be fair," argued Leslie Edwards in the Daily Post, adding;

> "*At their best the defence was brilliant. Liddell again had a fine game and Eastham was far from being outclassed by Hardwick; indeed he generally got the better of this England international.*"

Whether the players were going to strike or not, the 22 on show here could not be faulted for their commitment. They were bringing some respite to a public that had endured many years of suffering during the war. So long as they continued to serve up entertainment such as this then, in the eyes of the spectators, their demand for a pay rise would be entirely justified.

Phil Taylor, Cyril Done, Jackie Balmer and Bob Priday share a joke at Anfield.

Chapter Four
Done's done deal

Liverpool v Charlton Athletic
Saturday 12 October 1946

"Will tomorrow be the last of professional football for a time? It the players carry out their threat we may have to be satisfied with amateur football for a few weeks. The zero date is the 15th - but I have a hunch that there will be some sort of intervention to prevent what would be a catastrophe."

Stork's Notes, Liverpool Echo

Liverpool's improved run of form meant they were rapidly becoming one of the biggest box-office draws in the country and three days after the trip to Middlesbrough Anfield housed its highest crowd of the season yet. Cup-ties and derby games aside, the visit of Charlton Athletic attracted the first 50,000-plus gate for a league game at Anfield in almost 12 years. While it may have been boom-time at the turnstiles for almost every club in the country, such a statistic contributed to Liverpool being able to boast the largest average attendance in the division come the season's end.

With the ongoing, "football wages dispute rapidly becoming akin to a chess match," such a fact only added further fuel to the players' demands for a pay increase. Given the added income that was being taken at the gate it was becoming easier to sympathise with their plight. While clubs were obviously getting richer the men responsible for attracting fans to the ground - a club's main source of income before TV money created such a massive imbalance - were often struggling to make ends meet.

Despite their celebrity status, the weekly wage packets players in 1946 took home was not much different than the average working man. Indeed, players lived a life far removed from the one those in the same profession enjoy today. Rationing was still in place and affected everybody, regardless of their profession or status. Homes were hard to come by for everyone. Not because they were expensive but because the materials and the fuel needed to build them simply weren't there. The Luftwaffe and six years of war had seen to that.

The weight of expectation and the pressure to succeed was however, very much the same. The days when fame as a footballer was an instant guarantee to a big house, a sports car and a famous WAG on their arm may still have been a good few years off but these players were superstars nonetheless. Ironically, the maximum wage guaranteed that most clubs of the time had their own star name - or names - but at

Liverpool none were bigger in the adulation stakes than record signing Albert Stubbins.

His Anfield career may have still been in its infancy but Stubbins was already on his way to establishing himself as one of the most popular players to ever ply his trade in front of the Kop. The 'burning stub' had yet to be on the losing side in a Liverpool shirt, hence his new moniker - the 'lucky mascot'. In what was a massive blow to their hopes of going a fourth week unbeaten however, Stubbins was ruled out of the clash with Charlton after failing to shake off the thigh injury sustained at Ayresome Park in midweek. Fortunately, a ready-made replacement was waiting in the wings and, even without the pull of Stubbins, 51,127 crammed into Anfield to roar the Reds on. Liverpool's popularity ensured that thousands more were locked out prior to kick-off.

After two away games the Liverpool fans were delighted to welcome their heroes home and esteemed local reporter *Bee* set the scene;

> *"The new Liverpool, who keep the ball on the floor and have men capable of getting of getting goals in all forward positions, will draw a customary 50,000 to say 'well done for the win at Grimsby and draw at Middlesbrough."*

With reserve centre-forward Cyril Done, "fast recovering his best form," the Liverpool selectors had no hesitation in handing him the number nine shirt made vacant by the absence of Stubbins. It was to be Done's official League debut - seven years after his first senior appearance was expunged from the record books due to the outbreak of the war. On that occasion the Bootle boy had netted the winner and, having continued to score prolifically throughout the hostilities, he was eager to make up for lost time.

Like Done, Charlton, who finished as high as third in the last pre-war season of 1938/39 season, had enjoyed a relatively successful wartime period finishing runners up and winners in a couple of Division South Cup competitions. Indeed, they had won the 1944 Division South Cup at Wembley, being handed the trophy by none other than future US President Dwight D Eisenhower, who was in England finalising preparations for D-Day in his role as head of the US Armed Forces just two months later.

Renowned as a good footballing side, Charlton were beaten FA Cup Finalists just five months previous and had finished above the likes of Wolves, Tottenham, Chelsea and Arsenal in that season's Football League South. With players such as Sam Bartram, generally viewed as one of England's greatest-ever uncapped goalkeepers, and prolific England goalscorer Don Welsh - a future Liverpool manager - in their line-up, a home win was by no means a certainty over, "a side with which no club can take any liberties."

On an overcast and windy Saturday afternoon in Liverpool, the band of the Royal

Artillery regaled spectators with a selection of tunes before the game and a collection for the RA Memorial Fund was made before proceedings began. Both Bartram, who had made almost 60 guest appearances for the Reds during the War, and Welsh, who scored 26 in just 21 games during a guest spell at Anfield in the 1944-45 season when he served with the Liverpool Yeomanry, "were not forgotten by Anfield hands," and both were given a rousing reception when the teams were announced.

Keen to prove to the Liverpool directors that he was worth his place in the team Done quickly set about making an immediate impact and he opened the scoring after just nine minutes. From a Taylor free kick, Balmer crossed into the area. Done rose highest to meet it but although he, "got no particular power on his header," and the, "ball had barely sufficient strength to cross the line," it slipped through the hands of Bartram, who "had began in a dithering manner," and into the net. In the eyes of *Bee*;

"Done deserved a goal, if not this one, because he forsook massive efforts and marathon chasing. He was a delight to watch, his ankle flick, his head back a la Westcott was first class and his shooting power was tremendous."

Indeed, so impressive was his all-round display that, "Anfield began to wonder if it were necessary to go to Newcastle to pay £12,500 for Stubbins." While the watching Stubbins must have been no doubt impressed with the form of his replacement he must have been kicking his heels in frustration as Liverpool struggled to build on their early breakthrough. Prior to the game Stubbins told Leslie Edwards that, "the trouble with sitting in the stands is that after watching the game for ten minutes you feel like stripping off and doing it so much better than the other fellow."

Although Done and Eastham went close in the next few minutes it was Charlton who should have scored next - a Welsh header beating Sidlow but bouncing back off the bar to be swiftly cleared by the Liverpool defence, where Paisley in particular, "was having a great game with many characteristically good tackles to his credit." Liverpool's approach work was good but their

Liverpool's 'forgotten' centre-forward, prolific war-time goalscorer Cyril Done.

shooting wayward to say the least, with Done, Paisley, Balmer and Liddell all going close. The Reds were not having the game all their own way however, and it was Charlton who should have scored again when Robinson was clean through only to see his shot deflected wide off Sidlow's legs. After a bright opening, during which, "they battled like giants for half an hour," Liverpool's standards visibly slipped and, "afterwards [they] became commoners."

As the second half began, "Charlton took up the running and Liverpool wilted." Despite good approach play Liverpool's finishing too often let them down. A clever back heel by Balmer found Done, whose quick feet gave Fagan a clear shot on goal but the crowd groaned loudly as his shot could only find the Kop. "Where the Liverpool forwards became fickle and finicky near goal in the second half Charlton went to work with a placidity that was bound to wrench some part of the home defence."

Charlton captain Don Welsh (left) - a future Liverpool manager - and keeper Sam Bartram.
Both had made numerous appearances for the Reds as guest players during the war.

In Robinson, Charlton had, "the most dangerous forward of the day," and it was he who started the move which led to Addicks' equaliser. A one-two found him inside the area where his sliding tackle forced Sidlow to spill the ball and Lambert to hurriedly clear for a corner. From this Welsh took advantage of Sidlow's indecision to beat everyone with a fine header. The performance of war-time Anfield favourite Welsh, "delving, dribbling...and heading better than anyone save Hughes," drew plenty of praise and, like Done before him, he fully deserved to get his name on the scoresheet at a ground where he was no stranger to bagging goals.

In a desperate attempt to force a winner Liverpool made a number of tactical switches. With substitutions not allowed for another 21 years however, any changes could only be positional and were restricted to the starting 11 only. After discussing the situation in the centre circle with his captain Fagan, Liddell swapped places with Done, but still this produced no great change in the tempo of the game.

Indeed, Liverpool's play became even more frenzied the closer the final whistle came. Fagan sent a shot over from long range, then Bartram beat out a strong Balmer shot after the Liverpool forward had beaten three defenders with a mazy dribble before, "Liddell went almost half the length of the field to get a corner from Bartram."

In the last five minutes, "Charlton's goal had a charmed existence." A Balmer shot was cleared off the line by a defender's thigh, then Liddell, "just could not get his foot properly to the ball when not more than three yards from the line." Done and Liddell, "were like human battering rams," during this period.

One Liddell attack in particular exemplified the nature of the game in this era, and the style of the player in particular. The Kop favourite, "spread-eagled three Charlton defenders on their backs, [and] with Liddell also flat...[he]... helped to make the goal area look like a casualty clearing station." The final whistle went soon after to, "complete a day of full throttle excitement and much good football," but, despite the disappointment of another home draw, the Anfield crowd cheered Bartram and Welsh, who'd both had a great game, from the field.

Despite only collecting a solitary point, Liverpool's position in the table was not adversely affected. The Reds were still well placed in fifth, just three points behind leaders Blackpool, with one game in hand. Sunderland's convincing 4-1 win over Everton - Eglington's strike was the Goodison side's first goal in 298 minutes - saw them leapfrog Liverpool into third, but it was Wolves who made the most of other teams' misfortune this weekend. Their 6-1 win over Huddersfield, Liverpool's next opponents, had sent them fourth whilst, after their fantastic start to the campaign Manchester United dropped points again with a draw at Bramall Lane. With Stoke level on points with Liverpool in sixth, all the sides with aspirations to win the title were well placed to mount their challenge.

Aside from the obvious frustration of having to settle for a draw it had been a day to savour for Liverpool marksman Done. Having become the almost the forgotten man of Anfield he'd taken his long-awaited chance to stake a claim for a regular place in the team. That Done, "may not have the polish and finesse of Stubbins," was arguably true noted *Ranger*, but many still viewed big Cyril as a more than capable centre forward. "With good men alongside him he's worth his place in any First Division side." Just a few weeks previous the Liverpool directors had seriously contemplated Done's transfer to city rivals Everton but, if his goal and all-round play against Charlton made them rethink their position, then his performance in the very next game surely made their minds up for them.

Huddersfield Town v Liverpool
Saturday 19 October 1946

"Meeting in Manchester this afternoon, the management committee of the Players' Union had decided to declare a strike of players to become effective as from Wednesday October 23, but while their committee was still in conference Mr. James Fay, the Union secretary, received a telephone call from Mr. Stillwell of the Ministry of Labour in London. Mr. Fay was informed that the question of players' wages would go before a National Arbitration Tribunal, and that the Ministry of Labour was to call a conference between the players, the employers, and the Ministry to discuss matters."

Liverpool Echo

Had Liverpool's mini-revival ran out of steam? After two successive draws the harbingers of doom were predicting just this and many expected what they had predicted before the season began - a rapid descent to mid-table mediocrity. Without Stubbins against Charlton Liverpool had been made to look pretty ordinary, but this was no one-man team and that was soon to be proven in dramatic fashion.

For the trip to Huddersfield, Stubbins was back from injury but a return to winning ways would not be down to him. Having made his mark with a goal on his post-war debut the previous week Cyril Done had the scoring bit between his teeth and it was he who took centre-stage once again as the Reds bounced back in emphatic style.

Had it not been for Fagan being forced to rest a nagging ankle injury that was to sideline him until the New Year, Done might not have even played. With the fit-again Stubbins resuming at centre-forward it could so easily have been a case of him being sent back to the reserves. Fortunately for Liverpool it wasn't and Done filled in at inside-left as the Reds were forced into a number of changes due to the Wales v Scotland home international match taking place at Wrexham on the same afternoon - a match that was to deprive them of Welsh stalwarts Sidlow and Lambert, and rising star Liddell. It was a situation that would in no way be tolerated by a top-flight club in the modern game - with international breaks and weekends now a standard part of any season - but in 1946 it was different. The players themselves did not see anything wrong in this either. For them, to be selected for one's country - even when the renumeration was not great - was an honour. For the three Liverpool players involved in the game it brought additional pride as it was to be their first official peace-time appearance for their respective countries.

Anfield dirctor Ronnie Williams congratulates Cyril Sidlow and Ray Lambert on their appearances for Wales against Scotland.

Familiar faces Priday and Harley returned to take the place of Liddell and Lambert respectively, but there was to be a new face in goal as an injury to reserve keeper Ashcroft meant a call-up for A-team number one Ray Minshull - a player the Reds had signed barely two months previous. In light of Fagan's long-term absence manager George Kay let the players decide who should take the armband while the Scotsman was out injured. A ballot was held and Jack Balmer came out as the unanimous choice to be vice-captain, a role he'd carried out earlier in the season. The selection of Balmer was proof that while he may not have been the most popular of players among those on the terraces he commanded the utmost respect of his team-mates.

It was also a week in which the ongoing pay dispute took another significant twist. At a meeting in Manchester, just two days after Liverpool's draw with Charlton, it was confirmed that the players would be going ahead with their threat of strike action as of Wednesday October 23. For ten minutes it looked as though the season was about to descend into a farce but there was to be a dramatic outcome when the Government intervened to bring the two parties together for discussions.

With the seemingly impending players' strike put on hold for the time being at least, Liverpudlians were as relieved as any that the trip to Leeds Road wasn't going to be their last for the foreseeable future but, as they confidently made their way across the Pennines, the whole issue, together with Liverpool's emerging title challenge, remained the main topics of conversation.

Despite the team changes that had been forced on them, Huddersfield away was not the most daunting of propositions for a Reds side that, even accounting for the recent dropping of points against Middlesbrough and Charlton, was, "settling down to an understanding and gaining renewed confidence." Liverpool had scored eleven goals in three away games since that humiliating defeat to Manchester United in September, so a Huddersfield side that had taken such a heavy beating at the hands of an emerging Wolves the week before, their seventh loss in ten games, and were rooted at the bottom of the table, certainly held no fears for the Anfield outfit.

The halcyon days of the 1920s, when Herbert Chapman laid the foundations for three consecutive First Division titles, were now just a distant memory on the Leeds Road terraces and there was no doubting that the one-time Yorkshire giants were now a fading force. The Terriers had enjoyed a fairly successful war-time period, winning the North-East divisional league in 1939-40 by 10 points, losing just one game out of 20, as they finished above their more illustrious rivals Newcastle, Middlesbrough and Leeds. Similarly, in 1944-45 they had won the first Northern league of the season (August - December 1944) and in Billy Price they had one of the most prolific war-time forwards in the league. Price had struck an amazing 185 goals in just six seasons between 1940-41 and 1945-46, yet even he wasn't able to arrest the steady fall in Huddersfield's on-field performances.

Perhaps with the poor form of their team in mind, Huddersfield fans bucked the post-war trend of large crowds for the visit of Liverpool, and less than 18,000 witnessed the game through the misty rain that lay across most of West Yorkshire that afternoon. Those who made the effort however, were rewarded with an excellent game that was packed full of incident. Despite their league position and the expectation by most observers that Liverpool where overwhelming favourites to win the game, Huddersfield were by no means overawed, and took the game to the Reds straight from the kick-off.

With the wind behind them in the first half, the Terriers attacked the Liverpool goal with intent in the early stages. Finding the greasy conditions difficult to adapt to, and perhaps nervous in his first senior start for the Reds, Minshull, "took time to settle," but both full-backs covered for him, "gallantly and as well as they could," during the opening exchanges. On 20 minutes he mishandled a cross from the right but, despite a goalmouth scramble that resulted in him receiving treatment for a hand injury, he managed to retrieve the ball at the second attempt. Unknown to the rookie stopper this turned out to be a broken bone in his hand but he continued in goal for the remainder of the game - all 70 minutes of it - despite the obvious discomfort he must have felt. Done had a fine effort saved by keeper Bob Hesford but almost immediately the ball was played to the Huddersfield front line and, with centre-forward Lewis Brook ready to fire a shot from within the six-yard area, Hughes slid in expertly to prevent a certain goal and force a corner.

It was clear that despite their lowly league position Huddersfield were not going to let Liverpool have things all their own way. This was demonstrated in the most unlucky of circumstances in the 28th minute when a Huddersfield shot from the edge of the area - that was going well wide of goal - was deflected into the path of Brook by referee Mr J. Williams of Bolton. With the Liverpool defence wrong footed completely Brook scored an easy goal. Despite appeals by the Liverpool defenders the referee had no option but to award the goal and the Reds found themselves behind for the first time since the Maine Road debacle.

Liverpool showed excellent composure however, and refused to let any injustice they felt at the manner of the opening goal affect them. Indeed, within sixty seconds of the restart they were level. After a Huddersfield attack was thwarted by the Liverpool back-line, the ball was brought out of defence with ease and, "a deluxe Paisley pass," found the unmarked Done in acres of space in the home side's midfield. Done turned and, veering to his left, ran a few yards before hitting a fantastic shot into the back of the net from near 25 yards out, "in a way which only allowed Hesford a quick glimpse of it as it passed."

Although, "Huddersfield had played well enough to have the match won," the equaliser galvanised Liverpool and it seemed only a matter of time before their increasing pressure told and they scored another. Stubbins did well to beat a number of Huddersfield defenders but couldn't find the space to have a shot, then Eastham, following a mazy dribble, crossed for Balmer to head an awkward chance over.

Huddersfield continued to use the wind to their advantage, sending a number of speculative long balls into the Liverpool box, but the Red's defence was as solid as they had been for most of the season with, "big Lol," Hughes consistently heading the ball away with, "the persistence of a mechanical ramrod." Taylor too was having another fine game whilst Minshull appeared to have overcome his early nerves, gaining in confidence with every high ball he caught and anticipating the, "speed of the ball off the wet turf with a judgement as mature as Sidlow. For him it was [to be] a very happy debut."

Taylor's good work did not just limit itself to defending and just two minutes before the break he took advantage of slack closing-down by the Huddersfield players to pick out Done wide on the left with another great pass. The forward still had a lot of work to do but, "the first touch of a prolonged dribble tactically took him to the dead ball line from which angle he somehow found the few degrees of opening left to him with yet another fine shot." Liverpool were 2-1 up and the half-time whistle came soon after.

With a lead and the wind behind them Liverpool had most of the play and most of the chances in the second half. "It was good, thrilling football and Liverpool were now serving up delectable stuff", wrote *Ranger*. It was noted that Paisley's famed long throw and his enthusiasm in the tackle were not to the home crowd's liking, but he was having another excellent game at the back for Liverpool. As in the first half, Taylor continued to find plenty of time and space from which to spray passes through to the forward line.

Hesford, the Huddersfield keeper, did well to keep out a Harley free-kick and forced Balmer into a miss when one-on-one after a great flick on by Stubbins. Done showed he was capable of creating chances no matter the fitting of his boots when, whilst fastening his laces he received a pass, stood up, shot just over, then immediately went back down on one knee to continue his task!

Halfway through the half Liverpool's pressure appeared to be rewarded when Priday found himself in the area only to be fouled by full-back Geoff Barker. Unfortunately for Liverpool, Hesford earned the home fans' praise by making a fantastic save from the resultant penalty - taken by Balmer and not Done despite the latter being on a hat-trick. Done should have had his treble a few minutes later however, when a perfect Priday pass found him almost on the penalty spot but he could only shoot wide. In the build up to this move Stubbins had fell awkwardly whilst making a headed pass to Eastham and he received treatment after lying injured for some time. With no substitutes, and after chatting to his captain Balmer, Stubbins was shifted to outside right - a move which resulted in a change of formation for Liverpool but not a change in the direction of their game.

On 76 minutes a flowing Reds' move - involving a great exchange of passes by Eastham and Priday - resulted in the latter crossing and it, "was a gift for Done to get his triumphant third." Just after this Stubbins, still dazed from his earlier fall and head injury, received further treatment. The tough Geordie left the field for five minutes to try and recover and, with smelling salts taken at the side of the pitch, he returned to play a pivotal role in Liverpool's fourth goal of the afternoon. His centre was inch perfect for Balmer to score the easiest of headers and, with the game won, Stubbins duly left the field for the dressing room and Liverpool played the remainder of the game - a little over two minutes, with ten men. "Only Hesford's magnificent goalkeeping prevented another Grimsby rout," noted Leslie Edwards, "Liverpool had scored another win in their extraordinary away gallop on turf which was anything but easy."

As the Reds were romping to victory at Leeds Road, bragging rights in the international match at Wrexham went to Anfield's Welsh contingent after a 3-1 win for the hosts. "The match could not be termed a good one, but our players did their part well," the director's wrote in Liverpool's matchday programme the following week. "The duels between Lambert and Liddell were interesting, with honours even. Sidlow had several of Liddell's specials to save, but he performed his work in his quiet, confident and effective manner."

With the league's top two - Blackpool and Manchester United - meeting at Bloomfield Road, Liverpool's win over Huddersfield meant they had closed the gap on at least one of the sides above them in the table. Stoke's defeat away at Arsenal and Sunderland's surprise home defeat at home to Grimsby Town, ensured that the

Reds ended the day in fourth place - on 15 points - level with Manchester United and Wolves. Blackpool, courtesy of their 3-1 win over United, were now three points clear at the top but with a quarter of the season gone the title race was wide open. Any one of five or six teams had a real chance of challenging for the championship and, despite what certain pundits may have forecast, Liverpool, for the first time in a long, long while, were one of those teams.

Liverpool v Brentford
Saturday 26 October 1946

"The Empire Wharfe arrived at Garston this afternoon with a cargo of 100,000 bunches of Jamaican bananas, unloading of which will start tomorrow morning. The bananas are for the following districts; Liverpool, East Lancashire, Preston and District, Blackburn, Workington and Barrow, Isle of Man, and Newcastle and Northumberland."

Liverpool Echo

Despite an unbeaten run of seven games, Liverpool fans weren't happy. Their team may have rediscovered its winning touch and be enjoying their best league season for many a year, but stories were circulating that threatened to disrupt the feel-good factor of a potential title challenge.

In the aftermath of the impressive victory over Huddersfield it was widely reported that two key players were attracting the interest of other clubs and, more worryingly, it was suggested Liverpool may be seriously considering any offers that were put on the table. The players in question were Willie Fagan and Barney Ramsden, two hugely popular and loyal Anfield servants. The news brought dismay to Liverpool's huge fan-base. The very thought of either of them being allowed to leave had supporters up in arms.

Thankfully for concerned Kopites, no bids had yet been received for either player. Both were believed to be happy at Liverpool but such talk was nevertheless unsettling. Those fans of a more paranoid nature believed it was all part of a sinister plot to upset the equilibrium of a club that was at long last seemingly heading in the right direction. Others vented their anger towards the Anfield Board and argued it was a sign that their perceived pre-war lack of ambition had not yet been fully shed. Such a scenario nowadays would see the radio airwaves turned blue with irate supporters bombarding the phone-ins. Back in 1946 however, it was to the letters page of the local newspapers that they addressed and expressed their hostility to any such moves.

The previous month it had been Cyril Done's future that was under scrutiny, now it was the turn of Fagan and Ramsden to take their place in the speculation spotlight. A swift denial of these rumours could have quelled the unrest immediately but with no official announcement forthcoming, the supporter's patience and faith in the club hierarchy was being sorely tested. "Fagan is the only player Liverpool have to hold the line together," wrote Mr R Davies in one letter to the Echo, "yet now, just as soon as they are getting a good team together, they apparently want to part with the cleverest forward they've had since Harry Chambers." Another pointed out that the directors had only recently stated their desire to sign players not to sell them. "Liverpool were said to be building up, not parting," wrote Mr H W Fairhurst. "If they let Ramsden and Fagan go it will be sheer folly and grossly unfair to the most loyal band of supporters in the country," he continued. Another put the issue even more succinctly, "If Liverpool sell Ramsden they don't deserve success."

Lamber, Fagan and Hughes training on a muddy Anfield pitch.
Any idea the club had of even contemplating Fagan's sale was met with incredulity by many supporters.

Such disquiet on the part of many supporters at the news that three of the club's stalwarts could be sold, was understandable. Despite a number of early setbacks this season, Liverpool had emerged as one of the front runners in the title race. Such success was built on prowess in front of goal - 26 in just 11 games to date - but also a resolute defence. Many felt that Done, Ramsden and Fagan, had more than contributed to this success and, with their combined time at the club amounting to over 28 years, many also felt that, as they had shown loyalty to the Reds during the war years, the club owed them a degree of loyalty also.

In an attempt to assuage supporter's feelings on the issue, *Ranger* reported that it seemed highly unlikely the club would sell any of the players in question. He pointed out that Liverpool could not stop other clubs from enquiring after their players, and that there was, "a big gap between 'approach' and actual transfer." Indeed, the enquiry for Fagan from Bradford Park Avenue had been kept secret even from the player himself, and *Ranger* felt that this was, "indicative of their [(the club's) positive] reaction."

Fagan himself had informed the reporter that he, "had neither the intention or desire to leave Liverpool," whilst Done, "hitting his brightest shooting form at the right time," would almost certainly not be sold either. As for Ramsden, Arsenal boss George Allison had watched him in the game at Huddersfield and although 'Barney', "had not considered the matter fully," it was reported that he too would be kept at the club if possible, especially considering that Arsenal had yet to actually make their interest known.

With the transfer market being, "almost a closed body owing to the unwillingness of sides to lose players they may find it impossible to replace," Leslie Edwards also played down the possibility of any player being allowed to leave the club;

> "*It is the Anfield reserve strength what is helping them to maintain their high league position. The club feel that by having three first class full-backs and resting them judiciously from time to time it must hold the advantage over others. This is a new thought and one very necessary in days when the game is played with greater speed and toughness than for years.*"

It was against this backdrop of turbulent transfer talk that Liverpool prepared for the visit of Brentford. One of the capital's smaller clubs, Brentford is another team whose mere presence in the top-flight may be hard for modern day fans to comprehend but their head-to-head record against Liverpool in the three seasons before the war - their only previous league meetings - was commendable, with little to choose between the two sides.

During the conflict the 'Bees' had enjoyed moderate success, taking part in regional London and Southern leagues and winning the London Cup in 1941-42. They also reached the last eight of the first post-war FA Cup competition, only to lose to eventual beaten finalists Charlton Athletic. In the first proper season after the war they were not expected to finish anything other than mid-table. Indeed, at the start of the season, their manager Harry Curtis had informed reporters he would be happy to do just that.

After four wins from their first five games of the season however, including that surprise opening day defeat of reigning champions Everton at Goodison Park, even he must have raised these expectations slightly. For a brief week in mid-September Brentford had been as high as second, but since that heady start they had managed just a solitary point from their last five games.

A Liverpool team on a fine run of form and with title aspirations for the first time in over 20 years, were expected to win comfortably but Leslie Edwards aired that, despite this, a note of caution should be adopted. "Liverpool are not in a winning groove on their home ground," he wrote, and for that he argued, the supporters should shoulder some of the blame;

"Today at Anfield an elasticated ground would be taxed to hold all who want to see the team which puts 50,000 home fellows into good humour by winning or drawing away and then comes home to Anfield often to play ordinary stuff. Why should this be so? One explanation is that some members of the team prefer any ground rather than their own, not because the pitch falls short in any respect, but because they have a natural aversion to being unfairly barracked. Let the fact be faced - Anfield has its carping critics, most of whom would probably be seen and not heard of they were not cloaked in the comforting anonymity of the big attendance."

Despite the atrocious weather - it rained non-stop in Liverpool on the day of the game - almost 44,000 spectators turned up to see if the Reds could not only maintain their good form of late but also, after three games at Anfield, hopefully witness Albert Stubbins' first 'home' goal. Sidlow, Lambert and Liddell returned to the team after their international break, whilst Done, after his excellent hat-trick in the previous game, deservedly started his third successive match. Despite a Liverpool side at almost full-strength however, the football they offered, especially in the first half, was far removed from the fluid, penetrative style they had shown in recent weeks. Far too often Liverpool gave the ball away cheaply, passed when they should have kept hold of the ball and rushing what few chances they did manage to make.

As predicted by Edwards, the crowd soon grew restless and voiced their displeasure at a number of players as moves broke down and well-intentioned passes went astray. More criticism came their way from the pen of *Bee* who, in his post-match report, commented that;

"spectators at Anfield are the frenzied type who expect everything in red to be a speed merchant and all opponents to be veritable caterpillars. It is not for the games good that footballers sacrifice craft at the altar of speed. We are inclined to be greedy now the club is being hailed as 'League Champions'. It is a long long trail but they can get there by measured football no by frenzied stuff."

As the half wore on Liverpool's approach play improved but they, "were not playing brilliantly in attack." Their lack of sharpness up front was not helped by the excellent Brentford defence, in particular full-back Bill Gorman, who seemed to win every header and tackle he committed himself to. Stubbins was well marshalled by George Smith, the Brentford centre-half whilst Liddell was similarly kept quiet by Cyril Toulouse - a Brentford debutant who amazingly had been playing non-league football in the London Combination League just over a month previously. Chances for the Liverpool forwards were few and far between and even, "this early, it was evident that this was not Liverpool's day." Brentford had a few shots at Sidlow's goal but none amounted to anything more than a half-chance. Just before half-time Liverpool's best move of the game so far fell to Done, but the in-form forward was crowded out and he fell under pressure, with subsequent claims for a penalty ignored by the referee.

Seemingly invigorated by a stern half-time team-talk Liverpool came out for the second half with much more intent and purpose. Stubbins and Balmer had two good chances in quick succession. Done was then crowded out in the area once more and just after Stubbins, with more time than he realised, snapped at a shot that went wide of the Brentford goal. On 49 minutes another fine flowing move started at the back - this time by Paisley, who was having another great game - saw Liverpool finally break the deadlock.

Bringing the ball out of defence with his customary composure, Paisley, "all energy and eagle eye," had nearly reached the half-way line when he sent a 40-yard pass into the corner for Liddell to chase. His first time cross was blocked by Brentford inside-forward and war-hero, George Wilkins, who up until then had played magnificently. Inexplicably however, war-hero Wilkins, father of future England captain Ray, and who would have won a Victoria Cross during the war, "if there had been enough surviving witnesses," waited for his goalkeeper to come and pick up the loose ball instead of clearing it himself. The keeper never came and in the defensive confusion Stubbins swooped in to score.

Liverpool's star signing had his first Anfield goal at last and, according to *Bee*, "it was a delight." Those who had braved the gloomy and goalless first half had been rewarded for their patience.

"The big man [Stubbins] is a great endeavourer with what others would consider unconsidered trifles and plainly wants football not head ball. His delayed success had got on Kop nerves. All is over now. Tension ended."

In Liverpool's next attack Stubbins crashed a shot against the post and, just after, Paisley found Balmer but he, like the forwards before him, rushed his shot and sent it wide even though it seemed easier to score. The Reds were in control at last but although they were, "slinging in shots right and left...few of them were on the target." Apart from one header that went wide, Brentford attacks were rare, with Sidlow a mere spectator for much of the second half. He, "had little to do," said *Ranger* but, "did his difficult work in a business-like manner."

A defence splitting pass from Stubbins just after the hour mark put Liddell clean through but the usually reliable winger sent a weak shot well wide. "Liverpool were outplaying Brentford in every way except by getting goals." On 70 minutes a Stubbins cross appeared to be handled in the area but again the referee dismissed Liverpool's appeals for a penalty. "After being near to their most ordinary form in the first half Liverpool were close to their best," in the second, although they still had just the one goal to show for their efforts.

Late on Balmer showed great vision in attempting to lob Crozier from outside the box but, with the keeper beaten, his fine effort fell just over the bar. It was the last meaningful incident of the game, which ended with both Lambert and Balmer injured and a policeman positioned behind the Brentford goal to seemingly prevent home supporters barracking the keeper or throwing fruit in his direction!

Despite the, "workmanlike but deserved," manner of Liverpool's victory, the win pushed them further up the table. Leaders Blackpool were held to a draw at Bolton, whilst Manchester United's poor run of form continued with a surprise 3-0 loss at Maine Road against Sunderland - the Rokerites leapfrogging Matt Busby's side in the process. The Reds were now third, on 17 points, just two behind the men from Bloomfield Road and still with a game in hand. A title challenge was most certainly on and, slowly but surely, it was gaining momentum.

Blackburn Rovers v Liverpool
Saturday 2 November 1946

"The present minimum wage is shockingly low for these days. And players' contracts are to one-sided. The Union will remain level-headed, aim primarily at remedying obvious injustices to the lesser-known men, and leave the maximum wage to fair compromise - with a proviso for improvement if balance sheets permit...I think we will have heard the last of the dispute."

Ranger, Liverpool Echo

Unbeaten in eight games, with the First Division summit in their sights and 5,000 travelling fans roaring them on to what it was hoped would be a continuation of the impressive away form that had seen them lose just once on the road all season, the Liverpool bandwagon next rolled into Ewood Park to face Blackburn Rovers - a team very much seen as one that would struggle this season. Another Liverpool away win was widely expected.

Although losing finalists in the 1939/40 League War Cup, Rovers were an average side in the league during the war. Few could have predicted their return to post-war football however, when they conceded 111 goals and came second to bottom of the North Division in 1945/46. Despite being able to boast a trio of highly talented players in Bob Pryde, Verdie Godwin and Bobby Langton, this was the start of a steady decline in their fortunes. After a slow start to this campaign Rovers' form had improved and they went into this game on the back of two successive victories - similar to Liverpool - although ten places and seven points separated the two sides.

A week in which local headlines were dominated by Everton finally ending their long search for a centre-forward by splashing out to sign Jock Dodds from

Blackpool, and the Conservatives retaining overall control of the city council in the municipal elections, Liverpool's preparations for the trip to Lancashire were hampered by a number of injury doubts. It was reported that as many as five players were struggling to prove their fitness so, unusually, team selection was deferred at the weekly board meeting. Despite the upcoming game against Blackburn, the club's focus was on a midweek Lancashire Senior Cup return leg at home to Blackpool.

The competition did not figure too highly on Liverpool's list of priorities, arguably similar to the current League Cup, and the early rounds were looked upon as a distraction, especially when sandwiched in between important League games. It was however, a competition that represented another route to success and, while it was unusual for top clubs to field full-strength sides, the Liverpool team selected contained eight players with previous League experience that season. A crowd of just 6,000 were in attendance and although goals from Watkinson and Eastham secured a 2-1 win for the Reds (4-3 on aggregate) and a place in the next round, it was a victory that meant Liverpool, "have to play further home and away ties in the competition when they would rather be free of the risk of injuries."

Blackburn's classy Bob Pryde..

Fortunately, the injury concerns that prevented the board from naming their team for Blackburn earlier in the week had all cleared up by the Saturday and it was an unchanged first eleven that ran out to a great ovation from the thousands of Reds' supporters who had made the short journey north. Such a large number of away supporters would normally have swelled the gate considerably but a local bus strike kept many Rovers' fans away. Among the travelling fans were 40 young boys from the Anfield Boys' Pen, winners of a competition held by Liverpool Echo reporter *Ranger*. The journalist travelled with the boys to Ewood Park, where they were given stand seats, "a red letter day in their young lives," and looked after by Reg Taylor, Rovers' secretary. His Anfield counterpart, Jack Rouse, even arranged for star forward Billy Liddell, to visit the boys after the game.

Both Liddell and Lambert had been expected to be demobbed a few days before the game but a mix-up over records meant that only the Scotsman resumed his

Anfield career as a civilian. On a poor day for most Liverpool players however, Liddell, together with Sidlow and Hughes, were the only ones to have anything like a good game as the Reds turned in a performance that was way below their best. Their recent profligacy in front of goal was all too evident once again and even without a host of regular first choice players, Blackburn were unlucky not to take all two points in a game that proved to be, "a hard unrelenting struggle."

In front of their best home crowd since 1939, "Blackburn were playing good stuff," but the Reds' defence, "as ever, was solid." Hughes displayed his usual calmness under pressure when he cleared off the line early on and Sidlow made two great saves from Ormskirk-born Langton, Rovers' England international inside right, who most observers felt was the best player on the pitch. At the opposite end, Liverpool's, "direction finding apparatus was hopelessly wrong." Their best chance of the half fell to Stubbins, whose flick on from a long Paisley throw looked a certain goal until George Marks, the Rovers' keeper, caught it near the angle. Not long after this Blackburn had the most clear-cut opportunity of the game so far, a snap Godwin header from Langton's great cross that went just over the bar with Sidlow well beaten.

Albert Stubbins is crowded out against Blackburn.

Minutes later Stubbins was involved in a collision with Rovers' wing-half Arnold Whiteside. Despite lengthy treatment, the Blackburn man was forced to leave the field with a damaged shoulder but, even though he returned five minutes later, his injury was worse than originally thought and he was forced off again on 35 minutes, going straight to the dressing room with the training staff in an attempt to recover. With no substitutes of course, Blackburn played the remainder of the half with just ten men. The half-time break proved not to be long enough for Whiteside to regain his fitness and, amazingly for today's fans and players to contemplate, Blackburn resumed the second half with just ten men. For a depleted side however, Rovers, "were playing confidently and well." So much so that they even managed to get the ball into the Liverpool net not once but twice - both 'goals' ultimately being ruled out for offside.

"Defences were so much on top that ten forwards spent the afternoon searching for a loophole that did not exist," observed *Ranger*. Even against ten-men Liverpool were finding it difficult to break Rovers down. A Balmer chance from a quick Ramsden free-kick should have produced more. Had he showed more composure in front of goal he would surely have hit the target. Instead he fired over. Soon after this rare Liverpool chance Whiteside returned to the action having had a painkilling injection. Despite this he was clearly only half-fit and held his arm tight to his body for the remainder of the game, "as though he might not be able to take a risk with it."

Incredibly, Rovers' injury worries continued. First Billy Guest, the left-winger, was forced off the field then, once the game resumed and with Rovers down to ten men yet again Langton, up till then the game's best player, was stretchered off with a leg injury. He wouldn't return. With Whiteside's injured arm making him a virtual passenger, Blackburn effectively played a few minutes with just eight men. Although Guest returned to the fray soon after, it was, "an extraordinary tale of injuries," especially, "in a game which was fought cleanly."

Rovers' injury list forced them into making a number of tactical and positional changes, most notably in the forward line. These did not affect their confidence however, and amazingly they were unlucky not to score when Pryde sent a fierce free-kick just over on 65 minutes. Soon after, Paisley stopped a certain goal when he blocked a shot by Jack Smith on the six-yard line. Liverpool appeared to be hanging on for a draw but then Taylor worked his way towards goal and found Balmer in the area with just the keeper to beat. But with the Reds' captain was having no luck whatsoever he was brought down just as he was about to shoot. To the amazement of Balmer and the rest of the Liverpool players the referee, Mr H Berry of Huddersfield, waved away their concerted appeals for a penalty.

"One of the best rearguard investments Liverpool have made for years," Sidlow then made two more great saves, the first from Godwin and the second from another Pryde free-kick. So well was Blackburn's depleted team playing that even the injured Whiteside managed to force a fine save from the Welsh international. Indeed, had it not been for the Reds number one, "whose phlegmatic

Sidlow, seen here posing for the cameras and some female fans, had one of his best games for Liverpool against Blackburn.

goalkeeping cannot be estimated too highly, and Hughes, whose precision stopping work was superb, Liverpool would assuredly been beaten."

Despite the pressure they had been under Liverpool could still have snatched a winner in the final few minutes. A corner by Liddell late on resulted in the sort of goalmouth scramble that lasts an age and a number of Liverpool players had goalbound shots blocked in quick succession. Eventually the massed ranks of the Rovers' defence cleared and the whistle went shortly after. It was the first time Liverpool had failed to score for six matches.
"Ordinarily one could have said a good away point," wrote Leslie Edwards;

> *"but Liverpool being an away team, with an anything but ordinary reputation, the occasion must be written down as the least effective performance since Manchester United showed the way by 5-0. Such is the penalty of success. The more the side wins, the more they are expected to win."*

Despite a performance that, "did not look anything like a prospective championship side," Liverpool, "did an escalator act at Blackburn, they stood still and still moved upwards." Even though they drew, the Reds found themselves higher in the league table than they had been at three o'clock. Second placed Wolves who, after a poor start to the campaign, had recovered well to win six games on the bounce, surprisingly lost at home to Middlesbrough, who entered the title picture for the first time that season by moving up to fourth on 17 points. 'Boro had two games in hand on leaders Blackpool, who returned to winning ways with a 1-0 home defeat of Chelsea, while Manchester United finally halted their run of losses with a goalless draw at Villa Park.

The Reds were now second - their highest position of the season - but if they were to go one better it was imperative they rediscovered their scoring touch. In the First Division goalscoring stakes it was Stoke's Freddie Steele who led the way with 15. Liverpool players in the top six were largely conspicuous by their absence. Collectively the Reds may have been the Division's joint second top scorers with 27 goals, but the time for one of their strikers to step forward and go on the sort of scoring run Reds' fans have grown accustomed too, was long overdue. The irony was that it would be the man the fans loved to hate whose name they would soon be shouting from the rooftops.

Chapter Five
'Over the Balmer' is Over the Moon

Liverpool v Portsmouth
Saturday 9 November 1946

"Jack Balmer has scored some great goals for Liverpool in his time, but none
better than the third of his hat-trick against Portsmouth.
If ever a shot looked like making a hole in the net that did."

Ranger, Liverpool Echo

The Liverpool forwards didn't need telling. Their form in the last two games hadn't been up to standard and they knew it. All had been guilty of wasting good chances and no-one felt the burden of responsibility more than veteran schemer Jack Balmer. In Fagan's absence the new club captain shouldered the blame and was determined to put things right, but not even he could have foreseen the remarkable events that were about to unfold over the next few weeks.

With five goals to his credit so far, Balmer was second only to Liddell in the Liverpool scoring stakes. However, it was a figure that could - and should - have been higher. Jackie knew it and so did the fans. Despite the all too often barracking aimed in his direction when things weren't going too well, they also knew that on his day he was a player of supreme ability. Fortunately for Liverpool and their followers, this was to be one of his days.

Five days prior to the visit of Portsmouth football fans everywhere breathed a huge sigh of relief when, "the Football League and Players' Union composed most of their differences in a five-hour meeting at Preston," thus ending the threat of a players' strike. It was a surprising outcome given that the Football League had, "seemed opposed to weakening," and although not everything was agreed, most notably the £12-a-week maximum wage so coveted by the top players, the Union declared itself, "well satisfied."

It was players at, "the other end of the scale," that benefited most from the agreement, just as *Ranger* had predicted the previous weekend;

"The present minimum wage is shockingly low for these days. And player's contracts are too
one-sided. The Union will remain level-headed, aim primarily at remedying obvious
injustices to the lesser-known men, and leave the maximum wage to fair compromise – with
a proviso for improvement if balance sheets permit – I think we will have heard the last of
the dispute."

With the threat of industrial action by the players out of the way - at least for the time being all thoughts could once again return to on-field matters. For Liverpool that meant the impending visit to Anfield of a Portsmouth side who were surprisingly struggling at the wrong end of the table. With nine losses from 14 league games, and without an away win all season, the Fratton Park side were just two places above the relegation zone. For most observers however, Pompey were in a false position. Six of their losses had been by just the one goal and more than one pundit commented that Liverpool would have to improve markedly on their recent performances if they were to take the points.

Although the weather was dull and overcast, and there was a potential counter attraction in the November horseracing meeting at Aintree, 43,000 spectators saw Liverpool take on a brave Portsmouth side that, if they had had a full compliment of players come the end of the 90 minutes, would surely have taken a share of the points at least. Liverpool were unchanged for the third successive match although a troublesome knee injury would force Lambert out of the England v Wales home international at Maine Road in four days time.

With the wind bringing in a few spots of rain, Liverpool were lucky to not concede inside the first ten minutes, with first Jack Frogatt and then Jimmy McAlinden clean through only for Ramsden, on both occasions, to come to the home side's rescue with a pair of great tackles. The lively Frogatt then curled a great cross into the area from the left wing that evaded everybody, even Sidlow, and it went no more than six inches wide of the far post. It was a lucky escape for Liverpool who were once again not playing anything like they had done earlier in the season. *Bee* was in no doubt where the blame lay. "Frankly, the Liverpool attack is big and rousing enough, but lack wisdom in combined movement. They are not a chorus, they are soloists."

The first goal threat Liverpool posed was symptomatic of their forward play in their last two games, excellent play at the back and midfield but let down by the forwards who were taking too much time on the ball or opting for sensational strikes at goal rather than placement. In the 20th minute such over-elaboration cost them dear when, in space in the area, Balmer received a great ball from Stubbins only to try and beat one defender too many and Portsmouth cleared easily as he was crowded out. In their next attack however, initiated by Ramsden bringing the ball out of defence with cool assurance, Balmer was unlucky to see a shot go just wide after he had cleverly beaten Reg Flewin the Pompey centre-back.

Minutes later the Portsmouth full-back Billy Hindmarsh, who had been off the field injured for almost 10 minutes returned to the action but he had yet to touch the ball when Liverpool took the lead. Done, who up until now had had a quiet game, found himself with the ball not more than 10 yards from goal and, in the process of shooting, was clearly brought down by Duggie Reid. It was no more a Liverpool penalty than at least two other similar situations in recent games but this time the referee had no hesitation in pointing to the spot. No doubt disappointed at his earlier misses and perhaps also the abuse he had taken from the crowd in preceding games Balmer, who had missed his last spot-kick at Huddersfield three weeks earlier, appeared to take his frustrations out on the ball and he blasted the penalty straight down the middle of the goal, giving stand-in keeper Ernie Butler no chance.

Immediately after the opening goal Hindmarsh received yet more treatment. Unlike earlier however, the defender wouldn't return, and was stretchered off. Only half an hour into the game and Portsmouth found themselves a goal down and a man down, away to a Liverpool side that was second in the table and challenging for the league title. To their immense credit though, the South Coast side did not let this daunting predicament overwhelm them and they continued to cause the Reds a number of problems at the back. At the same time they were also proving themselves to be just as resilient as Liverpool in defence.

As had been the case against a similarly depleted Brentford side just two games previously, Liverpool failed to capitalise on their numerical advantage and, "took more than an hour to nail the victory flag to the mast." Butler saved well from a well-struck Liddell shot five minutes after Balmer's opening goal, but besides the penalty this was the only effort of note the Reds had made up to this point. "Portsmouth were using off-side ideas with good effect," whilst Liverpool were again guilty of too much over-play in the final third of the pitch.

Eventually Liverpool's composure improved and, with the extra man, they began to create more chances. On the right Phil Taylor's cultured wing play began to have more of an influence, dribbling past his marker with ease on more than one occasion and linking well with Eastham. A number of their crosses began to find their way into the Portsmouth area, where Balmer's headed attempts at goal were only thwarted by the fine work of Pompey's defence. It was a centre by Liddell however, that provided Balmer with his best chance, but his first time right-footed shot was palmed away for a corner. The half-time whistle came with Liverpool looking more effective in attack.

The wind had increased gradually over the course of the first half and the ever-darkening sky now brought with it a number of showers that eventually became a persistent downpour. Within minutes of the restart the Anfield playing surface became a muddy mess, especially the central parts of the field, and good football became difficult for both sets of players. With many unable to keep their footing, a number of promising moves broke down by players falling to the turf. "The only man who had not slipped up was the referee," but he managed to do just that on 50 minutes, "much to the crowd's joy."

Liverpool initially struggled to regain the momentum that had seen them end the first-half on top and, soon after the referee fell over, the comedy of errors continued when Done, with a great chance of a shot on goal in the area, trod on the ball. Then Sidlow, normally so assured under pressure, dealt with a Bert

Barlow shot from a Portsmouth corner just as clumsily. Eastham was then sent free down the right wing courtesy of a great overhead pass by Stubbins but a corner was Liverpool's only reward.

Balmer went close, firing a shot across an empty goal, but it was clear Liverpool's recent problems in attack were continuing - even against 10 men. Although Portsmouth were a man short, "they still had lots of pluck and ability, and did not deserve to be a goal down." By contrast Liverpool, "were inclined to make more mistakes than usual," but should have added to their solitary goal when Liddell, followed soon after by Done, beat Portsmouth's offside trap only to be thwarted once more by diligent Pompey defending and their own lack of confidence in front of goal.

Jacki Balmer - scored a hat-trick in this game and was about to embark on a record-breaking goalscoring run.

Liverpool's best move of the half saw Done head on another long Paisley throw to Stubbins in the area. Liverpool's record signing could only head the ball straight towards Butler however, and the goalkeeper collected easily under the cross-bar. Just after the hour mark, Liverpool had three major scares. Barlow saw a shot well saved by Sidlow, then the Liverpool goalkeeper pulled off another fine save to deny Jimmy Dickinson, but the best was yet to come. The Welsh international saved splendidly from Peter Harris in the six-yard box just as the crowd was expecting the winger to score. "Liverpool were extraordinarily lucky to escape in this phase of play," noted *Ranger*.

Although Stubbins had a 'goal' ruled out for off-side – a correct decision by Luton referee H. Pearce, "on the play at the moment, one might reasonably have thought that Liverpool were short [of players] and not Portsmouth." Liverpool had so far failed to live up to their high league placing. This changed in an instant on 70 minutes. Hughes, who was again having a great game in defence, broke up a Portsmouth attack and the ball eventually found its way to Eastham on the right wing. Before anyone knew it; his pinpoint cross to Balmer on the right hand edge of the area had been smashed home on the half-volley. Butler got a hand to the ball but could do nothing to prevent it from spinning into the net. It was a stunning goal – and completely at odds with anything Liverpool had served up so far.

Until this moment the visitors had been, "equally as good, if not better," than Liverpool but, "rejuvenated by this turn of events," it was the home side that were now, "at their best." Eastham in particular caught the eye, playing like a man possessed, winning tackle after tackle, dribbling past players as if they weren't there and sending cross after cross into the Portsmouth area.

Pompey were refusing to buckle however, and the Anfield crowd had another scare when Sidlow uncharacteristically dropped the ball under a challenge from the indefatigable Frogatt but, with the forward lying prostrate on the ground with the ball no more than a yard from him, the Reds' keeper redeemed himself by diving over his opponent's body to retrieve it at the second attempt.

Eleven minutes from time Balmer received a long overdue ovation from the crowd when he scored his third to make the game safe. In almost the same position he found himself in when he struck his second goal, he fired an even more powerful shot into the net. Butler, rooted to the spot, could only watch the ball as it whistled past him. The points were Liverpools' but there was still time for Portsmouth to show they really were in a false position and Reid's shot from 35 yards was well saved by Sidlow in the last minute.

Three-nil scorelines rarely suggest the victors were lucky, but in this case Portsmouth could count themselves extremely unfortunate to have lost by such a margin. "But for losing Hindmarsh for three-quarters of the game, they might have caused Liverpool a pack of trouble," admitted the ever honest *Ranger*.

With Blackpool losing away at Sheffield United, Liverpool closed the gap on the leaders to just a point, and they still had a game in hand. Wolves, Manchester United and Sunderland, who defeated their North-East rivals Middlesbrough and leap-frogged them in the process, all won. The top five sides were now separated by just three points. The title race was hotting up and "so long as the defence does not break," *Bee* thought Liverpool capable of staying, "around the top rung of the League," for some time yet.

There could be no denying that Liverpool's win owed as much to the fact that the visitors played three quarters of the game with ten men as it did to Balmer's hat-trick but, equally, there could be no-one who begrudged the veteran inside-right this rare moment of personal glory. Although he, "did nothing else...he got three when his side looked like languishing," and for that feat alone he was fully deserving of the match ball. Yet still, dissenting voices could be heard amid the back-slapping and congratulatory handshakes, "three should be suffice [sic] for anyone," wrote Leslie Edwards, "but no, the record of two missed are levelled against him."

It was proof that Balmer still had much to do if he was to silence his doubters for good. But try he would. Whilst it would have been too far-fetched to suggest he could repeat his hat-trick heroics in the next game - let alone surpass it - this was the inaugural post-war League season. And anything was possible.

Derby County v Liverpool
Saturday 16 November 1946

"Three employees of Tate & lyle Ltd, Liverpool, with a total of 76 years service with the firm, were each sentenced to three years' penal servitude at Liverpool Assizes today for their part in the theft of nearly ten tons of sugar. A Blackpool engineer - described as 'the co-ordinating mind' in the transaction, whereby the stolen sugar was conveyed to ice-cram manufacturers, was sentenced to four years' penal servitude for receiving and selling the sugar. Two other men received sentences of fifteen and twelve months' imprisonment for receiving."

Liverpool Echo

Buoyed by the first hat-trick of his Liverpool career Jackie Balmer, the Reds' form striker of the moment, geared up for the next match at Derby County by proving his talents were not just confined to the football pitch. At the team hotel prior to the game he took on his team-mates in a game of billiards and, in keeping with the treble theme, won three times in a row! Balmer, it seemed, could do no wrong. But would he be able to top his hat-trick heroics of the previous week as second-placed Liverpool aimed to put more pressure on the leaders? A trip to fifth from bottom Derby, a side who'd taken just ten points from 13 games – may not have seemed the most daunting of prospects but the Rams, one of the enigmas of Second World War football, were not to be so easily discounted.

Although they had not participated in any competitive football at all for the first three years of the conflict, they managed to win the second Division One (North) league of 1944/45 before, in one of the many vagaries of war-time football, finishing fourth in Division One *South* the following season. At the start of the 1946/47 season The Rams were also the current holders of the FA Cup, having scored an impressive 33 goals in 10 games (one replay) on their way to the final just six months previously. In April 1946, before over 98,000 fans at Wembley, they won the first FA Cup since 1939 by beating Charlton 4-1 after extra-time.

Two men who played a crucial part in that success though, Peter Doherty and Raich Carter - two of the biggest stars of the time, had, in the days leading up to the visit of Liverpool, been the subject of transfer interest from Huddersfield Town. The bids were, not surprisingly, flatly refused by the Baseball Ground directors but it would only be a temporary reprieve where one of the duo was concerned.

With no motorways and England's transport infrastructure still recovering from six years of war, even a trip to Derby could take as long as four to five hours back in 1946, so Liverpool stayed in Buxton the night before the game. In so doing they set a precedent they would adopt for all future seasons. At the team hotel Ray Lambert passed a late fitness test on the knee injury that had kept him out of the England v Wales game at Maine Road in midweek – a match in which Sidlow conceded three – and Liverpool were unchanged for the fourth game in a row.

Derby were not so fortunate and were forced to play debutant goalkeeper Alick Grant – signed from Second Division Leicester only nine days previous – as a replacement for the injured Vic Woodley, England's pre-war number one. The late change did not affect them adversely however, and it was the Rams who took the game to Liverpool as the Reds yet again started slowly. Thanks for Sidlow and some sloppy Derby finishing Liverpool could have been three down inside the first ten minutes, "it was luscious stuff with all the trimmings and only lacking the fire of the punishing finish."

Ken Powell beat Lambert for pace down the right inside just 50 seconds but shot wide, then a poor Taylor back-pass was intercepted by Carter only for the usually dependant England centre forward to rush his shot as he rounded Sidlow when it seemed easier to beat the keeper and simply stroke the ball into an empty net. "A flagrant mistake," commented *Ranger*. Frank Broome then rushed onto a fine through ball from only for his first touch, even in the mud, to be too strong and Sidlow did well to race from his goal and collect the ball under pressure.

It was almost all Derby for the first half-hour and, seeing little of the ball themselves, the Anfield men were forced into playing the off-side trap. This did little to reduce the number of Derby chances however, with Powell again showing good skill to control a high ball with his chest, knees then feet before turning and shooting in one movement. Sidlow did well to hold onto it. The Welsh international then saved well from a long Carter shot and a Frank Broome free-kick from just outside the area.

Liverpool's only chance of note in this period was a Liddell effort which the winger, the first to his feet following a scramble in the Derby area, uncharacteristically fired over the bar from all of seven yards. It did not look like it would be Liverpool's day but, as the half progressed, they began to create the better chances and play with a style and confidence their position in the table warranted.

First Paisley, doing, "yeoman service on the left," passed to Eastham who quickly found Balmer in the box, but the skipper's shot was well saved by the Derby debutant. Then Done wasted Liverpool's best chance after being played onside courtesy of a deflection. Again, the Liverpool forward took too much time however, and fired over the bar when a well placed side-footer would surely have opened the scoring.

Leslie Edwards believed the turning point to be midway through the half when Balmer;

> *"took advantage of a short break in play to give [his] co-forwards a signal – the one the sergeant-major used when he wanted his Infanteers to go to earth. But in this case Balmer showed, unmistakably, that it was the ball he wanted there."*

From, "that moment Liverpool began to prosper," and, "having gradually got into their stride…now did their best work." Liddell smashed a great shot against the bar before Rams' full-back Jack Howe made an even more glaringly bad back-pass than Taylor's earlier one for Liverpool. His pass from a tight angle back to his keeper was wayward, and it evaded everyone to trickle across an empty goal for a corner. Balmer's shot from almost the same position just a few moments later was just wide and only just missed by Done's desperate lunge. Any touch and he would surely have scored. After being under extreme pressure, the game had turned Liverpool's way and it was Derby who were now the team fortunate not to be behind.

Two minutes from half-time Liverpool's belated pressure told and it was the man in form who opened the scoring. Almost nonchalantly the Reds' hat-trick hero of the previous week moved towards Derby's goal and with the defence expecting him to pass they backed off. To their surprise, Balmer, "disregarded calls for the ball," from his team-mates then, "feinted to make his opening," and shot as soon as he entered the area. The ball curled beautifully into the top corner and there was nothing the Derby goalkeeper could have done to prevent it.

The second half started just as the first had ended, with Derby under pressure from a Liverpool attack and Balmer finding the net once more. If his first goal had been, "a good one," then his second was, "one of the best goals he is ever likely to get." The Reds number eight beat four men in an amazing dribble into the box and, even though forced wide right of the goal, he still had the skill to flick a lovely shot over the keeper and into the net. So impressive a strike was it, that even a number of the Derby supporters applauded.

The second goal seemed to send Derby into a state of shock and less than two minutes later they found themselves three down. Liddell did the hard work beating two men with another great barging run from the wing and, as defenders closed in on him in the area, it was the easiest thing in the world for Balmer to stroke the Scotsman's pass into an empty net. Two hat-tricks in two games – and this one in just six minutes of play! It was a rare feat, the first time Derby had conceded more than two goals in a game at home that season and a sure sign of his true class.

The two quick goals thoroughly deflated Derby. They'd gone from, "mediocre to worse and were now a shadow of the team that had started so well." The second half was barely five minutes old and, as a contest, the game was all but over.

Despite scoring a hat-trick, Balmer was hungry for more and after an hour he netted another. Chasing the game, Derby were pressing high up the pitch for what would only have been a consolation goal but they gave the ball away cheaply to Eastham and the outside-right played a lovely pass into space for Balmer to run onto. With the home defenders struggling to get back, Balmer bore down goal and lobbed the advancing Grant superbly to score his fourth. Balmer had now scored 12 goals in just 13 games – not a bad return for a man with only the one England cap – and become the first Liverpool player since Fred Howe in 1935 to score four goals in a match.

Many would have expected the game to simply play itself out after this but Derby still pressed and Sidlow made three decent saves before Done narrowly missed a great chance for Liverpool's fifth and a Liddell header scraped the post but the win wasn't just down to the forwards. "Paisley's stern half-back work and the general comradeship of the side with some fine goalkeeping by Sidlow were notable points in a match that was very uplifting." On 87 minutes Carter netted a consolation for Derby but the day undoubtedly belonged to Balmer and no-one was going to steal his thunder, not even the current England international forward. For Leslie Edwards, it was a performance that;

"stamps Balmer once and for all as one of the most brilliant inside forwards in the game. He has his critics, he will continue to have them, but assuming his only lack to be one of confidence in himself seven goals in two matches is just the thing to eliminate this 'modesty'. He will thrive on success."

While Balmer was helping Liverpool to victory at the Baseball Ground, their city neighbours Everton were holding the league's early pace-setters Manchester United to a 2-2 draw at Goodison Park. Combined with Blackpool's surprise defeat at home to Grimsby, the Seasiders' second defeat in a row, Liverpool now found themselves top of the table for the first time that season on 22 points. Wolves' victory over Sheffield United at Molineux kept the Midlanders in the hunt for honours and they joined Blackpool on 21 points, albeit both having played a game more than the Anfield men.

In his popular 'Sportsfolk' column, *Bee* paid tribute to the new League leaders;

"Let us hear the refrain. This is Liverpool FC; the team no-one 'wanted' last August; the team they decried; 'the same old names trotted out,' said vexed correspondents. They wrote begging me to take up the strain and cane the directors. They had beaten America and that meant nothing at all for League football possibilities. And here we find Liverpool FC at the top of the ladder."

The only downside to a memorable day for Liverpool in Derbyshire was shock news concerning Liverpool full-back Bernard Ramsden - who had interested Arsenal earlier in the season and who had so far played in every game at full-back. In a move that highlighted again the uncertainty of life as a top footballer at the time, both in terms of wages and job security outside of the game, Ramsden dropped a bombshell by informing the club's directors that he would be moving to the United States in a little over three weeks – to open a florists shop.

It was reported that Ramsden, who had served in the Army during war and spent time in Greece, "did a good turn to a Greek who had relatives in New York, and Bernard was given the address in case he was ever in America and had the opportunity to look them up." Whilst on the pre-season tour to the USA Ramsden had spent time with the family in question and had, "also met a girl who he intends to marry." Barney told *Ranger*, "everything was in order and that all being well he hoped to leave early in December."

With the US football authorities belonging to the same International Federation as England however, it was clear that Ramsden would not be allowed to play football there unless Liverpool released his registration – either through granting the player a free transfer or demanding a fee from his new club. There was speculation in the press that Ramsden would be joining a club in Brooklyn but he quickly refuted such suggestions and insisted he had no plans to carry on playing.

Having scaled the First Division summit for the first time since winning back-to-back leagues in the early twenties, and with a long-awaited genuine title-challenge on the horizon, the timing of Ramsden's revelation was not the best. It came as a huge shock to both Liverpool fans and directors alike but, with a full-back of Jim Harley's quality waiting in the wings to regain his place, the situation wasn't as bad as it could have been.

Also, let's not forget, in Jack Balmer, Liverpool possessed the most prolific striker of the moment and, in the, "form of his life," and with a unique goalscoring record in his sights, he wasn't planning on going anywhere.

Liverpool v Arsenal
Saturday 23 November 1946

"Our own Balmer and Done, the worst inside forwards that's known.
We think Stubbins is swell, that guy Liddell, Paisley and Taylor and Shelley the trainer.
As we go on through the years, they have the supporters in tears.
The worst inside forwards the worlds ever known, our own Balmer and Done."

Boys Pen song, 1946/47 – related to the authors by John Naylor – Speke.

Not since Dixie Dean scored his famous 60 League goals for Everton in 1927/28 had the goalscoring exploits of one man caused so much interest. Jackie Balmer was the talk of football, his name on the lips of everyone with even the slightest interest in the game and everyone's eyes and ears were focussed on whether or not his remarkable scoring streak could continue. Goodison God Dixie was in fact the last player to score three hat-tricks in a row, hitting a treble in each of the final two games of his record breaking season and then another on the opening day of the following campaign.

No player had managed the feat in the same season however, and for Liverpool fans who had lived in shadow of their near neighbours for the best part of the last two decades the fact that one of their own could now eclipse the legendary goal machine from across the park was an immense source of pride. But with Liverpool's previously much-maligned moustachioed marksman now standing on the verge of footballing immortality the fickleness of the fans wasn't lost on *Bee*. On the morning of the home game against Arsenal he wrote;

> *"I find Liverpool audiences are apt to be somewhat vindictive against certain players. They will not let him [Balmer] get on with his job. They sentence him to football death. You know the names as well as I know them. The list is a long one. How many have decried Balmer? He has taken years to convert the distrusting."*

Ironically, just as they had done at Goodison on the occasion Dixie scored his momentous 60th goal, Arsenal were the opposition at Anfield as Balmer went in search of that elusive third successive hat-trick in the same season and an equally memorable afternoon was anticipated. Unbeaten in their last 11 games, new league leaders Liverpool were not surprisingly unchanged for the visit of the Gunners, who despite being one of the English game's most respected and decorated sides, had now fallen upon hard times.

Prior to the war, they were the dominant force in League and Cup, winning five titles and three FA Cups in the space of just eight seasons, and there was, arguably, no club more famous in the world at this time. It was little wonder the public looked to them as one of the favourites for the title when 'normal' football was restored in 1946/47. Despite a number of victories in early Second World War regional competitions however, the once mighty Arsenal could finish only mid-table in the 1945/46 Southern Divisional league and had lost 6-1 on aggregate to West Ham in the third round of the same season's FA Cup.

Their great pre-war side had simply disintegrated – most of their better players ending their careers through injury, retirement or unavailability because of war-service. With nine losses from 15 games prior to their visit to Anfield, the North Londoners found themselves in serious trouble - just one point and four places of the bottom of the table - statistics that prompted Henry Rose of the Daily Express to lament, "I found it sad to see Arsenal, once our greatest sports ambassadors, as just another football team. The fabric is not worn, it has gone." While Arsenal had conceded 34 goals in 15 games, Liverpool had scored exactly the same amount from the same number of games and few gave the Gunners much of a chance at Anfield on this dull late-November Saturday afternoon.

For the large home crowd another win was expected but everyone present, including the assembled journalists, were asking themselves the same question - could Balmer create history? Perhaps with the prospect of a record-breaking afternoon ahead of them, playing at home before a densely populated Kop, or simply the confidence that being league leaders brings, Liverpool, unlike in their last few games, started brightly.

As early as the fourth minute an excellent Eastham cross was met by Liddell on the half-volley but his goal-bound shot hit Done and screwed wide for a goal-kick. Barely 60 seconds later yet another well-directed Liddell shot, this time hit even more cleanly than his last, struck another of his team-mates - Eastham being the unfortunate Liverpool player on this occasion. From this shot, the ball broke loose in the area and, in the mad scramble that followed, Eastham tried to get past the great Arsenal centre-half Leslie Compton but, "bounced off the giant...like a pea off a drum." Not long after, Hughes was injured making a great header and had to leave the field to receive attention on a head wound, returning a few minutes later amid, "great joy in the Anfield camp."

Compton found himself in action once more when he headed a Ramsden free-kick clear to thwart Done but the Liverpool number ten was as lively as ever and causing the Gunners back line all sorts of problems. After receiving a throw from Liddell he promptly turned and made a beeline for the visitors goal. As one, the home crowd urged him to shoot, "and Done obeyed it magnificently with a fine cross-shot which swung a few feet wide of the far post."

Jackie Balmer's first goal of the game - a penalty - against Arsenal.
He was just two goals from greatness at this point.

On 12 minutes, Arsenal had their first chance of the game when centre-forward Reg Lewis, scorer of 15 of the Gunners' 23 goals to date and the man who three seasons later would break Liverpudlian hearts at Wembley, did well to force a corner after beating a number of defenders in the area with a mazy dribble. From the resultant kick Sidlow saved well under the bar.

Liverpool then worked the ball forward only to lose it on the halfway line whereupon an Arsenal mis-kick gifted Liddell the ball almost immediately and, with it, a clear run on goal. The dashing winger, "came speeding through," and after a one-two with Done found himself in the area with the goal in his sights. But as he, "was on the point of shooting," Ireland international wing-half

Paddy Sloan tripped him and it was as clear a penalty as you would ever see. The ref had no hesitation in pointing to the spot and the Arsenal man was lucky not to be sent off, as he no doubt would if a similar incident occurred in the modern game.

"There was no hesitation in the penalty award," wrote *Ranger*, "nor was there any doubt about Balmer's low and well-directed shot, which gave Liverpool their lead." The hat-trick hero of the previous two games was on the scoresheet again. One-nil to Liverpool after just 15 minutes and Balmer was closing in on the record. High on confidence already, Liverpool were playing some great football. Arsenal's defence may have been, "shaky and apprehensive," but this was all down to the number of chances the Reds were creating. "Rarely this season have Liverpool started with such confidence and ability."

At no time was their newly found confidence more evident than on the half-hour mark. First a great pass by Lambert found Liddell in space in the midfield. His first time ball was played to Done and, bearing forward, his fierce shot was deflected an inch over by the slightest of touches from full-back Joe Wade. It was a great flowing move and, barely a minute later, another, "enormous shot," - this time from Liddell - was caught at the near post by keeper Ted Platt. "Liverpool were superb," expressed *Ranger*, adding that, "for thrills the game contained more in [this] five minutes than most in forty-five." Another shot towards goal by Done was then turned behind for yet another Liverpool corner. The home side must have had at least a dozen by now and from it, Liddell's customary curling centre was headed away from under the bar when it seemed certain he would score.

On 37 minutes Liverpool were made to pay for their failure to convert these chances as Arsenal scored a well-worked equaliser completely against the run of play. A long-range shot from Lewis was partly stopped by Sidlow but it somehow managed to evade the Welsh international's grasp and squirmed over his body and over the line. If the Anfield crowd were surprised at this goal, they were to be in total shock just two minutes later. Another good move by Arsenal, as they attacked in numbers, led to Jimmy Logie, the smallest player on the pitch, nipping into the six-yard area after another goalmouth scramble to put the ball into the net, "at his leisure."

After dominating for most of the first-half, Liverpool now found themselves 2-1 down. Showing tremendous spirit however, the 'Crazy Gang' didn't panic. Indeed, Liverpool, "were still playing splendidly, but without the necessary luck in finishing to make the big difference." A Stubbins shot and a Taylor centre were well saved by Platt and on another day these may well have earned more reward.

The start of the second half was notable for another great run by Liddell, who knocked the ball past the advancing defender before rounding both him and the linesman to race down the touchline with the pair in hot pursuit, and also a couple of injuries to key Liverpool players. First Paisley was dazed in a heavy collision and forced off for treatment to his jaw, then Hughes reopened a wound just above the eye when heading a ball bravely away. He too had to leave the field for stitches to be applied. For a brief spell Liverpool found themselves reduced to nine men. During this time Lewis spurned a good opportunity to increase the Arsenal lead when hitting a tame shot at Sidlow when a much firmer effort would surely have sealed the points.

A Liverpool reshuffle followed and, "a damaged side was welded into a winning side when all seemed lost at the hour." The main switch saw Taylor move to centre-half, where his vision and experience allowed Hughes, visibly suffering with that earlier injury, to take up a position at outside-right where the prospect of any aerial combat was minimal. As a result, Eastham went inside-left and Done to half-back. It was a sound move and, "although one saw links frayed through injury…the spirit of the eleven came to life."

On 61 minutes Liddell, "who had never been more spectacular," set off on another, "scintillating run." He, "carved his way five yards from goal and then flicked the ball towards the far post with the outside of his foot." Arsenal's defence managed to half-clear only to see it fall at the feet of Balmer 15-yards out. With the crowd frozen in anticipation Jackie made no mistake and fired home into the roof of the net. "Rarely has an Anfield goal given such joy," exclaimed *Ranger*, "the scene…almost reminiscent of that when [Dixie] Dean got his 60 goals at Everton." Liverpool had their equaliser. Balmer had his second. The hat-trick of hat-tricks was on!

A Liverpool reshuffle followed, mainly to place Taylor at centre-half where his vision and experience could ease the burden on Hughes, who was visibly suffering with that earlier injury. It was a sound move and Liverpool's chances increased. Under pressure from Balmer, Platt dropped a back-header by Stubbins, who then

BALMER DOES IT AGAIN — BY GEORGE GREEN

fired wide from close-range. Barely had the Anfield faithful recovered from this near miss when Eastham broke up a promising Arsenal attack and started the move that led to Liverpool's third goal. He brought the ball forward and, with a perfect pass into space ahead of Balmer's angled run, beat Arsenal's off-side trap. Balmer collected the ball with a great first touch, veered to his right, looked up, steadied himself, "and put the ball into the net for the biggest cheer Anfield has ever known."

With the crowd delirious at the history they had just witnessed, the goalscorer, "was [first] mobbed by his delighted comrades," and then a number of spectators ran onto the pitch to congratulate the record-breaker. It was some time before the game restarted. Even a few of the Arsenal players offered their congratulations as he made his way into his own half, Compton in particular making sure he shook Balmer's hand.

In a frenzied effort to hold onto their lead Liverpool's controlled game and disciplined approach deteriorated. It was noted in the stands and on the terraces that they began to not only waste time, much to the disgust of the visiting press core – few things annoyed 1940s fans and commentators alike as time-wasting - but also to foul needlessly and generally break up play whenever possible. "Full of enthusiasm and the lust for another goal [Liverpool] were a bit too hearty in some of their work, and the record of first-half cleanliness was certainly not maintained now."

Keen to add an incredible eleventh goal in three games, Balmer found new energy up front and chased every ball and harried every defender. In the 78th minute he chased what looked like a lost cause near the right hand corner flag but found himself crowded out when he eventually managed to win the ball. From this tight space however, the hero of the hour selflessly managed to retain possession and eventually worked the ball to Stubbins on the angle of the area. It was the big number nine who powered home the fourth from this position to seal the points for the table-toppers and end the hottest individual scoring streak of any Liverpool player.

At the final whistle every player on the pitch, plus the referee and linesmen, made their way to Balmer to offer their heartfelt congratulations. As he headed towards the tunnel, waving at the crowd, a fickle Anfield gallery rose as one to applaud the triple hat-trick hero. For a player who'd suffered their wrath on countless occasions in the past such long overdue appreciation for a fine club servant meant this was a moment for him to savour. As this great sporting feat reverberated around the country, "John [sic] Balmer has ample merit to stand on," wrote *Bee*, "much of his unpopularity was unjust, a little patience would have put it right. Today, however, Balmer has triumphed in historical manner."

At football grounds up and down the country one of the first questions asked by players, supporters and directors was 'how many goals has Balmer scored?' Reds' reserve keeper Charlie Ashcroft, who was away with the second string at Derby County that afternoon, recalls a similar story:

"As we came off the pitch all we were interested in was events at Anfield and how many goals Jackie had scored. As we got to dressing room the director who had travelled with us came rushing in to tell us the news and the place erupted. Everyone was delighted for him and, coupled with our win that day, it was a very happy journey home."

It went almost unnoticed that Liverpool's 4-2 victory had taken them two points clear at the top of the table. With Blackpool suffering a shock loss to Leeds United, Wolves drawing away at Preston and Middlesbrough being held at home by Portsmouth, Manchester United were the only other top five team to win on this Saturday. At last, Liverpudlian title claims were starting to be taken seriously. In what had been one of Anfield's all-time great games the Reds had shown, "true greatness," and belied their reputation. "They have learned to love a battle, to fight back, to be consistent. They are playing like a team inspired."

With tough games looming against Blackpool and Wolves a much sterner test of their credentials was to come. This however, was not a time to be worrying about what lay ahead. History had been made and, fittingly, Anfield's biggest crowd of the season so far – 51, 435 – was there to witness it. It was the cue for a good old Scouse celebration. Balmer was fully deserving of the many post-match plaudits that came his way and it was his name that, quite rightly, dominated the back-page headlines of all the local papers, with the Echo noting the following Monday that;

"surely there has only once been a previous occasion on which a Liverpool crowd has risen to a son of the city with such fervour…the Anfield match…[is]…as memorable as the never forgotten one when Dean scored his 60th against Arsenal at Goodison Park.

The same paper noted that Balmer could have even been transferred earlier in the year, with Arsenal enquiring as to his availability before the start of the season;;

"If that had happened we would have been robbed of a local sportsman and a good-class player. We can ill afford to discard from strength…Balmer lives by his intricate footwork; if he had the poundage of a Dodds he would sweep the football earth in his triumphs. He has to do everything by his talent because [his] physical attributes are not highly developed. He works his way through a defence; barging through wil never get him the opening he desires. So let us appraise the whole side for winning where least expected, for continued collection of points, and for upholding the honour of the city's football strengths."

Jack Balmer's finest hour had indeed become, "one of the red letter days in the history of the club," and it should never be forgotten.

Chapter Six
The 'Crazy Gang' personified

Blackpool v Liverpool
Saturday 30 November 1946

*"Let us hear the refrain. This is Liverpool FC; the team no-one 'wanted' last August; the
team they decried; 'the same old names trotted out,' said vexed correspondents.
They wrote begging me to take up the strain and cane the directors.
They had beaten America and that meant nothing at all for League football
possibilities. And here we find Liverpool FC at the top of the ladder."*

Ranger, Liverpool Echo

With more points and a better goal average than the rest of the teams in Division
One, Liverpool were riding on the crest of a wave and the omens were looking
good. It was now 12 games undefeated for the Redmen and the last time a team
from Anfield had enjoyed such a startling sequence of results the season ended with
the Championship pennant flying high above the Kop.

Even the club's harshest critics had been forced to doff their flat caps in
acknowledgement of a run that, while taking many by surprise, had certainly been
no fluke. Their surge to the top was, "causing many enquiring eyebrow lifts," and
in what was described, tongue-in-cheek, as, "soccer's greatest sensation," a
Liverpool supporter even wrote to, "hero of the hour," Jack Balmer, requesting
from the West Derby man an, "acceptance of apology for his barracking in former
days!"

It was undoubtedly a good time to be a Red. After the euphoria of Balmer's
thrilling hat-trick of hat-tricks it was a trip to the Seaside that was next on the
Liverpudlian agenda and in the days leading up to the game at Blackpool it was
reported that, "the Anfield phone has been almost red-hot from applications for
stand tickets." Liverpool's biggest away following since before the war was expected
at Bloomfield Road and such was the clamour to see the league leaders that special
trains had to be laid on for the huge number of travelling fans, with departure
times brought forward, "to allow of earlier entry into the ground."

In what was an eventful few days in the lead up to the match that pitted first against
fourth, Oldham Athletic were beaten 3-1 at Boundary Park in the second round,
first leg, of the Lancashire Senior Cup. McLeod opened the scoring, "with a good
shot from outside the area," and a goal apiece from the Shepherd brothers, former
Marines Bill and Arthur, sealed victory in the second-half for what was a virtual

second string Reds team. On the same day Billy Liddell played in the Scotland side that drew 0-0 with Ireland and Liverpool's injured club captain Willie Fagan got married, the bride wearing nylons obtained by Fagan during the close-season tour of America and the three-tier wedding cake being a gift from Anfield chairman Bill McConnell.

The big news away from Liverpool was the transfer from Everton to Arsenal of Joe Mercer, a player the Reds had made a cheeky enquiry about just prior to the opening game of the campaign. While a player of Mercer's undoubted ability would have been a welcome addition to the Liverpool squad, having since embarked on this impressive unbeaten run it could be argued that he'd now struggle to get into the Liverpool team and so, on the eve of the trip to Blackpool, his move to Highbury passed with no regrets from the red side of Stanley Park. Twenty-four hours later however, they may have been ruing their

decision not to submit a second bid. The fourth-placed Tangerines may have gone into this game on the back of a worrying run that had seen them lose their last three but it was to be no donkey ride on the beach or walk along the prom for the visitors. Blackpool were not considered one of the country's top sides for nothing and they were bracketed among the fancied frontrunners for the inaugural post-war title.

When war was declared in September 1939 and league football abandoned for the duration of the conflict, three games had been played in the top division. Blackpool, under the guidance of their forthright, cigar-loving manager Joe Smith, a former playing colleague of George Kay at Bolton, had won all three – the only side to do so - and topped the table when the season came to its premature end. The town was also an important training centre for forces personnel during the war and the club found they had the pick of war-time guest players, including the legendary Stanley Matthews, then of Stoke City, but a player they would sign on a permanent basis late in the 1946/47 campaign.

With a host of top players at the club, Blackpool enjoyed unparalleled success in war-time competitions; third in the North West League of 1940-41, winners of the first Northern Division 1941/42, runners-up in the second stage later in the year and back-to-back winners of the first Northern Division in both 1942/43 and 1943/44. With no fewer than six guest players in their team for each leg of the finals Blackpool also won the 1942/43 League War Cup and were runners-up the following season. Although they could finish only ninth in the 1945/46 Football League North, with the prolific and dynamic Stan Mortensen, one of the game's greatest ever centre-forwards in their side, together with Harry Johnston, as composed and determined a centre-half as any in the country, Blackpool were a more than capable side who, had indeed, topped the table for a six-week spell prior to Liverpool's recent ascent.

The leaders knew they would have to play exceptionally well if their proud unbeaten run was to be maintained and they received a welcome boost when, in their white away shirts, they ran out onto the Bloomfield Road pitch as, "the thousands of followers of Anfield…[who had]…made the trip by car, coach and train," greeted them, "to the larger cheer." The official attendance was just over 23,500, with Liverpool fans making up around 5,000 of that figure at least. Along with their roars of their supporters, "rattles and whistles added to the atmosphere," with "a barrage of nine rattles immediately in front of the press box," in particular making the Liverpool Echo match reporter, *Contact*, glad he, "wasn't using the phone."

With Paisley's bruised jawbone still too sore for him to play, Liverpool were forced to make their first change in five games and so Bill Jones, "utility man par exellence," was called up to start in his place. The man who had scored two goals in his last senior game against Chelsea, when he played up front, was at his best going forward again and Blackpool's right-back Eric Sibley did well to block an excellent pass from him that would have given Liverpool a great chance to take the lead after just six minutes. Four minutes later Liddell should have opened the scoring for Liverpool when he intercepted a poor back-pass by centre-half Eric Hayward. Billy's first touch, with the ball bobbling on a heavy pitch, was not a good one however, and keeper Jock Wallace, who's son of the same name later managed Rangers and Leicester, bravely collected the loose ball at the Scotsman's feet.

In the 13th minute Blackpool had their first chance and it was a case unlucky for Liverpool because unlike the visitors the home side took it, "to take the lead with a glorious goal." What seemed like an over-hit cross from the left-wing by Alex Munro soared over everyone only to fall at the feet of Jimmy McIntosh who, "volleyed it with perfect timing to the far side of the net." George Dick should have added to Blackpool's opener just two minutes later but the inside-forward, "blazed away at the ball and the chance," from only 10 yards and fired over. Soon after Mortensen who, "was always alive and had a fair share of the ball," saw a goal-bound shot deflected for a corner. The game was certainly turning out to be the stern test everyone thought it would be.

As they'd done in previous games when behind Liverpool didn't panic. Hayward was now playing exceptionally well for Blackpool at the back and he thwarted another great Liverpool attacking move when he prevented Eastham's clever reverse pass from finding Liddell in the area. Soon after Balmer was extremely unlucky not to add another goal to his rapidly-increasing tally when a strong shot from just inside the area beat Wallace easily. But, to his and the thousands of travelling Liverpool fans' disbelief, the ball came back off the inside of the post and rebounded safely into the arms of an equally disbelieving, but relieved, goalkeeper.

The visitors were playing well, creating opportunities and piling on the pressure in the hope of an equaliser. Twice in the space of two minutes Wallace rushed from his goal to smother decent Liverpool chances, on the second occasion coming out of his area to do so and dragging Jones to the ground. The resultant free-kick by Balmer was passed square to Done but his shot was well saved. The Tangerines' number one was called into action yet again soon after when he saved a first time shot by Stubbins after a clever back-heel pass by Balmer. It was all Liverpool now.

A cross from Eastham was headed back to Done by Liddell but the Scot sent this, "first rate scoring chance," high and wide. Done, Stubbins, Liddell and Balmer were working tirelessly to create chances and their endeavor was finally rewarded on 35 minutes when Balmer scored a fully deserved equaliser. Winning the ball in the tackle at the right hand corner of the penalty area, Balmer showed good composure to step to his right, then step forward, look up and send a low shot towards goal that, although striking the woodwork again, this time, "made up for his previous bad luck," by ending up in the back of the net.

Five minutes later Liverpool should have gone ahead when Wallace, up until then in great form, spilled a Liddell shot into the path of Stubbins. From less than six-yards out and with the goal at his mercy the ball bobbled up again on the poor surface and his side-foot shot went just over. On the stroke of half-time Taylor almost knocked himself out when he headed the heavy ball clear with the crown of his head and he required smelling salts at the side of the pitch from trainer Albert Shelley to help bring him back round. Post-war footballs were large and heavy, especially so if wet, and if you headed one incorrectly it would leave a bruise at best. So heavy where they that reserve keeper Charlie Ashcroft remembered that, "you would be doing well if you could get the ball over the half-way line," from his kicks.

Liverpool resumed the second half full of confidence that they could go on and take the two points. They had played well in the first half, creating numerous opportunities and more than holding their own in defence. Apart from a handful of chances, however, most of the second half belonged to Blackpool with McIntosh, Munro and, "quicksilver," Mortensen, in particular, the danger men for the hosts.

On 50 minutes Ramsden, who would not now be emigrating to the USA as he could not obtain a visa, prevented McIntosh from scoring with a great late tackle in the area just as the forward was preparing to shoot. The Liverpool right-back did the same against Mortensen just five minutes later before a Jimmy Blair flying header was saved splendidly by Sidlow.

With Blackpool now, "right on top," and playing, "as though they knew it," the visitors were very much under the cosh. Ramsden saved Liverpool again when he headed a Johnson lob off the line with Sidlow beaten but it was only a temporary respite because on 65 minutes a George Farrow free-kick was headed on by Mortensen and the ball fell to Blair who's cross-shot flew arrow-like into the top corner. It was a deserved second for Blackpool who seemed to be creating chances at will. Within a minute Mortensen was brought down at the left angle of the area by Jones but the subsequent appeals for a penalty by the Blackpool players were turned down by Southport referee Mr W Prescot. McIntosh then saw three shots blocked in quick succession before Farrow smashed a 30-yard free kick against the bar.

The woodwork, and some profligacy of Blackpool's own in front of goal, came to Liverpool's rescue again on 80 minutes. Sidlow failed to hold onto a well-struck shot by Blair and the ball fell to Munro, "the brightest and best of the home forwards," only five yards from goal but his shot, "flicked the outside of the far post and stayed out."

From having a great game at the back for Liverpool Ramsden was now being beaten by Munro almost every time the Blackpool forward ran at him and he duly, "came in for some barracking when Munro was treated unceremoniously." A former long-time prisoner of war, Munro appeared, "to have the joyous abandon of a man released only the day before." The Blackpool forwards were now revelling in their supremacy and, "had taken such command Liverpool's front line was rarely seen."

Mortensen went on a great run that deserved a goal, beating three Liverpool players in the process, but sent his shot wide, then, on 87 minutes, the man, who would seven years later become the first player to score a hat-trick in the FA Cup Final at Wembley, finally got the reward his performance deserved. Winning a throw-in on Liverpool's left, Farrow shaped up as if to send a long throw into the area but instead fooled everyone bar Munro to whom he sent a short one instead. Munro quickly played it back and from Farrow's centre the ball was flicked on by Blair to Mortensen who had the simple job of tapping it home at the far post to make it 3-1. The points were surely theirs now.

Despite being outplayed for almost the entire second half Liverpool, to their immense credit, managed to make Blackpool hold on for their win by scoring straight from the restart - a five player move resulted in Done scoring to make it 3-2 with just over two minutes to go. "Amidst tremendous excitement," another flowing Liverpool move ended up with Liddell fizzing a shot just wide, but it was to no avail. The full-time whistle blew soon after and Liverpool's long unbeaten run was over. All good things must come to an end and Leslie Edwards' was sympathetic to the Reds' plight;

> *"Liverpool met a team a fraction better than themselves. The losers played well, they fought hard and refused to be panicked by the possibility of defeat. Let it be said without delay that the match could have gone either way. For Liverpool there was no disgrace. The truth is that*

the ball dragged on a heavy surface and ran kindly for no one. Blackpool, knowing the place better, were less likely to find it bothering. They have played less ably and won. Defeat was bound to come. There are plenty of opportunities for a fine side to create another winning sequence."

Despite the loss to one of their main title rivals, Liverpool remained on top of the table on 24 points, together with Wolves who defeated another of the main title challengers, Manchester United, 3-2 at Molineux. Blackpool's victory lifted them to third on 23 points but with Stoke and Middlesbrough also losing it was, perhaps, not all doom and gloom for the Anfield men. With Wolves at home next however, Liverpool could ill- afford to drop anymore points in what was undoubtedly their biggest game for many years.

Liverpool v Wolves
Saturday 7 December 1946

"It is all very well being at the top of the table. It is another matter to stay there. That is going to be Liverpool's worry for the next few months. It means that each and every game from now on is going to be of a cup-tie nature….the testing point will be round about Christmas, when there is a welter of holiday games. How often have we seen the scene change after the Christmas games?"

Liverpool Echo

The Liverpool crowd has long been renowned for being one of the most fair-minded and sporting in the game. In times of trouble they are famed for getting behind their team and providing support when it's needed most. Such a reputation was not forged overnight. It has taken many years to establish and one which every right-minded Liverpudlian is immensely proud of. But every generation of football fans have among their ranks a small pocket of critics who are too quick to condemn any poor result or on-field misdemeanor. The Kopites of 1946/67 were no different. After seeing their side suffer a first defeat in 13 games at Blackpool, a minority of natives became impatiently restless and an immediate scapegoat was sought by the boo-boys. With the usual target of their angst – Jack Balmer – having recently found a new pair of scoring boots, the pack were hunting for new prey and no sooner had the final whistle sounded at Bloomfield Road than they were getting their teeth into another victim of their fickleness, as. Leslie Edwards noted;

"Already the team is being faulted, surely a 2-3 verdict can be recorded without seeking a scapegoat. Or is football memory and sentiment (like other commodities) in short supply? Thus, Stubbins, who missed a great chance because he mistimed a shot with the inside of his boot, and others who found the ground troublesome, may be sacrificed on the basis that blame for defeat must rest on someone."

The fact it was superstar centre-forward Stubbins who was now incurring their wrath was proof that no-one was exempt. It was also proof of the high demands fans placed upon their team. Over two decades may have passed since any silverware of note had been brought back to Anfield but rather than lower expectations this long barren spell had served only to heighten them. The unbeaten run had given Reds' fans a tantalizing taste of the good life - and they were hungry for more.

The previous week's loss also provided ammunition to those who argued that the Reds were in a false position at the First Division summit, "there by virtue of others' failures rather than any credible title challenge of their own," some claimed. And although the barometer of form indicated that Liverpool, were indeed, a decent side, another criticism levelled at them was that against stronger teams they often come up short.

Defeat at Blackpool, albeit an unlucky one, meant Liverpool were now hanging onto their lead at the top of the league by the skin of their teeth. After two weeks of looking proudly down on the rest they were clinging on by the slenderest of margins. With goal average not goal difference the first barometer of success after total points when the 1946/47 league table was calculated, just 0.4 of a goal now separated Liverpool from their nearest challengers Wolves, although they did have the cushion of a game in hand, and, as fate would have it, it was they who were due next at Anfield.

Despite an average war-time record that read; winners of the small 1939-40 Midland Regional League, a 1942 victory in the League War Cup, and semi-finalists in the same competition two seasons later, Wolverhampton Wanderers were a side many expected to be at or near the top of the table once 'normal' football resumed after the war had ended.

Wolves' captain Stan Cullis

Although they could manage only sixth place in the Southern Division in 1945/46, and were dumped out of the FA Cup at the fourth round stage by Charlton Athletic the same season, the Midlander's were nevertheless a side awash with talent.

In his pre-match report *Ranger* noted that Wolves were able to boast, "no fewer than six internationals (war-time included), with Stan Cullis, captain and driving force, the light-haired Billy Wright – successor to Joe Mercer in the England side, and one of the finest wing-halves in football today – and pre-war international Galley making a brilliant half-back line." Other notables included former New Brighton forward Dennis Westcott, "a product of Wallasey junior football," who had netted 14 times from 14 starts this season so far, Jesse Pye, who himself had, "a dozen to his credit," and Willie Forbes, a recent buy from Dunfermline, who had linked well with Jimmy Mullen, another England international, on the left-wing.

Although they'd never won the League, successive second-placed finishes in the two seasons immediately prior to the outbreak of war marked Wolves down as one the teams to fear in 1946/47 and by the time of their visit to Anfield they'd fully recovered from a disastrous start to the campaign which had seen them lose their first three games. Unbeaten now for the past month, they'd taken over Liverpool's mantle as the form team of the division and had showed their mettle by twice coming from behind to defeat fellow title challengers Manchester United the previous week.

To those Liverpudlians whose glass was constantly half-empty the visit of, an in-form, Wolves was viewed as a daunting prospect, one that could extinguish all hopes of the title if lost. To those of a glass half-full nature it was another massive game and one which provided the ideal opportunity for Liverpool to reaffirm their credentials with a win. Either way it was a match that drew what was to be Anfield's biggest crowd of the season and the highest, bar cup-ties and derby games, since January 1935. It also marked the first occasion for Cyril Sidlow to line-up against the club he'd been signed from ten months earlier and saw hot-shot strikers, Balmer and Westcott go head-to-head in a mouth-watering duel.

Even accounting for Wolves' star quality and Liverpool's recent setback *Ranger* could see no reason why, especially with home advantage and the anticipation of a big crowd, the Anfield outfit could not win this game. "If their defence is up to earlier standard and the attack functions with…cohesion and understanding," he wrote, then the points were Liverpool's. Moreover, "in what promises to be a thrill packed encounter," they could extend their lead over their closest rivals in the process. In both respects however, Liverpool came up woefully short and, as they had found against Manchester United earlier in the season, the game would effectively be over before half-time.

With the gates closing on a heaving crowd that totalled 52,512 and included the touring Danish national side, the visitors ran out to a great cheer from the 3,000 vociferous travelling supporters and after winning the toss Wolves skipper Cullis elected to attack the Spion Kop end in the first half. Liverpool's team showed just one change, Paisley returning in place of Jones after recovering from the jaw injury that forced him to miss the defeat at Blackpool.

The appalling and unpredictable weather, including, "snow, thunder, lightning, hail – and bright sunshine," that had affected most of North Western England in recent days meant that, although both sides had early chances to open the scoring, they found it hard to control the ball on the muddy Anfield surface. Inside the first two minutes Westcott was fouled by Hughes just outside the box – the former Everton reject already causing the Liverpool back-line problems - and Lambert did well to clear the resultant free-kick which skidded low across the slippery surface. Balmer then found Stubbins in a good position but he skewed his shot well wide from 20 yards when the ball was caught up in a sodden area of the pitch.

Taylor was having another excellent game and was finding Eastham with ease on the right. But although Eastham's subsequent centres were decent enough, "Cullis and McLean were there to hold up Stubbins and Liddell." Taylor then had the home crowd holding its breath as he hooked a clearance over his shoulder and towards his own goal but thankfully Sidlow managed to scramble across and jump high to catch the loose ball as the Wolves forwards loitered with intent.

Together with Westcott, Tom Galley was also giving the Liverpool defence a hard time and on 16 minutes his run and dribble seemed to have been halted fairly by Paisley some five yards outside the area but the referee, Mr J Briggs of Cheadle, thought otherwise. The home crowd did not agree and they voiced their displeasure loudly. Johnny Hancocks took the free-kick but his shot was blocked by Ramsden. The ball came straight back to the outside-right however, and he sent a first time cross back into the box for the unmarked Westcott to loop a cushioned header over Sidlow's despairing dive and into the top left-hand corner. First blood in the top of the table clash had gone to the men from the Black Country.

Albert Stubbins (right) attempts to score an equaliser v Wolves.
Done and Liddell look on for Liverpool, whilst Stan Cullis is also keeping a close eye on things for Wolves.

With the capacity crowd roaring them on, the Reds attacked in numbers to try and gain an equaliser. A fine three-pass move that took the ball the length of the pitch in seconds was started by Taylor, who found Balmer, who in turn then found Stubbins, but the centre-forward's shot from 18 yards was blocked by Billy Crook. Taylor then tried another over the shoulder shot – only this time at the opposite end – but Bert Williams was alert to the danger and saved well.

"The Wolves' goal bore a charmed life," during this period noted *Ranger*, "when first Liddell, then Done and Balmer came through in menacing fashion only to see their shots strike a defender and cannon away." Liverpool were playing well in attack but Wolves' were not only defending in numbers, once they had possession, they also looked more than dangerous in attack. "It was hard, keen football, notable mainly for the quick tackling of both sides."

Mullen then went on two long, mazy dribbles, both of which were blocked by Lambert. On the half-hour mark another run resulted in a corner being awarded to Wolves' – much to the disgust of the Kop crowd near the Kemlyn Road corner who felt so strongly that a free kick should have been awarded to Liverpool owing to a perceived foul by Westcott on Paisley, that they threw a number of oranges (some full and some half-eaten) towards the corner taker!

Wolves' Dennis Westcott

Four minutes later Hancocks and Pye both had shots beaten away by Sidlow in quick succession. The Welsh international could do little with the second rebound and the loose ball fell to Westcott who buried it in the back of the net from eight yards to double the visitors' advantage. Soon after this goal the police and ambulance-men helped around 30 spectators from the corner of the Kop near the Main Stand as the pressures of a packed home terrace began to tell. Alarmingly, "one or two of the more elderly ones had to be escorted," onto the cinder path that then ran around the pitch and the more serious casualties were, "shepherded down the player's exit."

Any hopes of Liverpool salvaging something from the game were gone within five minutes of Wolves' second goal as the Reds' defence, normally so disciplined and assured, were uncharacteristically caught ball watching. A hopeful Wolves' punt up the middle of the pitch was seized on by Westcott. The former Raker did exceptionally well to control the ball and knock it past Hughes in almost the same movement and then it was between Sidlow and his former teammate as to who could get to the ball first. Unfortunately for Liverpool, the centre-forward won, lobbing the ball over the advancing keeper and into the net. The inevitable collision saw

116

Sidlow upended and almost do a somersault over the hat-trick hero but, unlike it would surely have been today, no foul was awarded.

The home side were visibly shell-shocked and 60 seconds later, Westcott incredibly scored a fourth in almost identical circumstances, this time rounding Sidlow with a feint and dribble to stroke the ball into an empty net after he had again beaten Hughes to a long pass. It was 4-0 to Wolves and Liverpool, having come up short against one of the division's better sides once again, didn't know what had hit them.

"Not for a long time has the Liverpool defence been made to show up so poorly," wrote *Ranger*. "The truth is...[they] could not match the winners for combination in attack and solidity in defence." In contrast, the Liverpool defence had been out-thought and out-fought, with Hughes in particular given a torrid time by Westcott. There was even time for Wolves' star of the day to net a fifth before the first half ended – although Liverpool's blushes were spared when it was ruled out for offside.

With the home crowd utterly deflated, Liverpool started the second half aggressively – searching for a goal that would surely now be little more than a consolation. Their play however, "did not cause the Wolves', with their commanding lead, any undue anxiety." Indeed, so much better than the Reds were their Midland rivals that *Ranger* was moved to say their play, particularly going forward, "was an object lesson," for Liverpool, whose passing paled in comparison. Whereas Westcott, Pye, Forbes and Mullen seemed to weave flowing moves across the pitch, on the one occasion when Done found Stubbins with a similar pass the number nine looked up for options only to see he was the furthest man forward and the move quickly broke down as Cullis, "the king-pin of the team, who had Stubbins in his grasp throughout," dispossessed him.

Liverpool's misery was completed when their defence was caught too far forward and Hughes slipped in the mud, allowing Mullen to, "rub salt into the wounds," by going on to score a fifth. Soon after Mullen, "who was now giving Lambert many anxious moments," was pulled up for offside and he showed his displeasure – and received the barracking of the home crowd – by smashing the ball fully 50-yards from the Liverpool area. Unlike today, no booking followed this obvious sign of dissent. It was an incident that didn't go unnoticed by Daily Express reporter Henry Rose, but rather than condemn Mullen for his act of petulance it was those in the Boys' Pen who he vilified in a scathing, over-the-top, attack two days later.

"Something should be done about the young hooligans in the pen reserved for schoolboys at Anfield. Their concerted booing and cries of 'send him off' in the Liverpool v Wolves match horrified me. I suggest the Liverpool board close the pen for a few weeks and bring them back to their senses – if any."

The Boys' Pen was then situated in the standing enclosure that ran along the front of the old Kemlyn Road stand, between the halfway line and Anfield Road, and the war of words between Rose and its inhabitants would rumble on for many months before he eventually, after much campaigning, played a major role in getting it moved to the top left-hand corner of the Kop.

Once that particular furore died down Liverpool continued to try and claw back some degree of respectability by forcing at least one goal. A Balmer shot was fumbled by Williams who gathered at the second attempt, while a Taylor free-kick was headed against the bar by Stubbins before their determination eventually paid off 13 minutes from time when Balmer (who else?) converted a penalty after being brought down in the box. The Liverpool forward had now scored in five consecutive games, taking his tally for the season to 17, but this latest effort was nothing more than a consolation. Four-goal Westcott had overtaken him at top of the scoring charts and, not content with his already impressive haul, he went close to a fifth in the dying minutes with a fine curling shot from 12 yards out that hit the post.

By then of course many home fans had already left the ground bemoaning yet another humiliation by one of their closest rivals. The final whistle couldn't come soon enough for both home supporters and players alike, while the travelling fans celebrated wildly after witnessing their team go top of the League for the first time that season with one of the most impressive away performances ever seen at Anfield. It had been Liverpool's biggest home defeat in almost a decade and the architects of it were ironically two men – Cullis and Westcott – who had 'guested' for the Reds during the war.

There were some who took the view afterwards that if Wolves hadn't got their first goal from an alleged, "unjustifiable free-kick," then, "the issue might have been different." But the hosts could have no complaints and in his post-match summary Ranger waxed lyrical about Wolves' championship potential. "With their ideal blend of youth and experience, [they] promise to be a menace right to the end [of the season]," he noted, before summing up the game with typical verbosity. Wolves, "fell upon the Anfielder's like the ravenous animals of the same name, full of goal-hunger and just as relentless as their four-footed counterparts. One felt sorry for the home side, whose defence was tossed and tantalised by the visitor's quick moving and accurate forwards, and whose own attack so sadly lacked fluency and cohesion."

It had most definitely been a football lesson to remember. Defeat meant Liverpool dropped to second, two points behind Wolves (albeit still with a game in hand) and a point above Manchester United and Blackpool – who lost 4-1 to Stoke in what was another important clash that weekend. The Potteries outfit climbed to fifth on 22 points. It was certainly not going to be easy for Liverpool to win this league, but Wolves had not seen the back of the Reds and it would be a different story when the two next met later in the season. The fixture list had paired the duo together on April 12 at Molineux. If both sides maintained their form until then, what a game that could potentially turn out to be!

For now though, all Liverpool could do was lick their wounds and get on with it. How they'd respond to this morale-shattering reverse would tell us a lot more about their character and, in turn, their now seemingly faltering title prospects.

52,523 SPECTATORS INCLUDING THE LIVERPOOL TEAM WATCHED THE WOLVES AT ANFIELD ON SATURDAY.

IT WAS NOT FAIR – LIVERPOOL SUPPLIED THE BALL AND CULLIS WOULD NOT LET STUBBINS LOOK AT IT.

BUT WESTCOTT SEEMED TO GET THE BALL WHENEVER HE WANTED IT

WESTCOTT SCORED GOALS QUICKER THAN SIDLOW COULD TAKE THEM OUT OF THE NET

ARF A MO

WE MUST TAKE OUR HATS OFF TO THE WOLVES, PROVIDING THEY ARE NOT DRAWN AGAINST SOUTH LIVERPOOL THEY STAND A GOOD CHANCE OF GOING TO WEMBLEY.

THE MIGHTY WOLVES ATANFIELD—BY GEO. GREEN

"Liverpool made a wise investment when they bought houses for half a dozen of their married players. No-one can give of his best when worried by domestic problems. It has been a source of anxiety for Cyril Done for instance. Now the lads have an easy mind, and are bound more strongly than ever to Anfield, for the firs question a married player asks these days when a transfer is mooted, is, "What about a house?" Getting one isn't weasy and I know at least two big proposed transfers this season which have foundered on this rock.

Sunderland v Liverpool
Saturday 14 December 1946

"The question of extra food for football players has been asked in the House of Commons. There is no doubt that nutritious food is highly important to any athlete, and this is not so much the amount of food consumed but the right type to build up energy. In these days of course, a correct diet is difficult, and it is a matter of opinion whether or not Soccer players are entitled to more than the average citizen. Last season Liverpool toured America and their success over there is well-known to football fans. The Reds players place much credit for that success on the excellent diet they enjoyed in America."

Albert Stubbins

An acute shortage of adequate housing posed major problems as Britain slowly readjusted to life after the war and professional footballers, including those at Liverpool, suffered like the rest. With many skilled tradesmen still to be de-mobbed, large swathes of blitz-scarred inner-cities lay derelict, leaving indelible eyesores on a landscape ravaged by six years of hostility and austerity. The demand for new homes far outweighed supply and the number of homeless cases rapidly increased as troops returned from abroad only to find they had nowhere to live.

It's a scenario that may be hard to now envisage in an era when it's not uncommon for even an average lower league player to be living it up in a ten-bedroom mansion, out in the country, with its own private swimming pool and a garage as big as an aircraft hangar. But in 1946 good quality houses were like gold-dust and when it came to clubs negotiating terms and conditions with their players they became hugely important bargaining tools. For those footballers with families the situation was an even greater cause for concern.

Football clubs also knew that being able to provide players with suitable accommodation was a key component in building a successful team. Stability off the field bred stability on it and, with this clearly in mind, Liverpool's board of directors boldly sanctioned the purchase of six newly-built semi-detached properties in the then leafy suburb of Broadgreen. Despite the struggling economic climate of the time it was a move viewed as, "a wise investment," and the first six inhabitants of these new club houses were family men Willie Fagan, Phil Taylor, Cyril Done, Billy Liddell, Eddie Spicer and Albert Stubbins. The road on which the houses were situated - Westfield Avenue - would soon be dubbed, "the Downing Street of football," and the neighbours would meet up every morning to travel into training together at Anfield. "No-one can give of his best when worried by domestic problems. Now the lads have an easy mind and are bound more strongly than ever to Anfield," said *Bee*, who added;

> "the first question a married player asks these days when a transfer is mooted, is, "What about a house?" Getting one isn't easy and I know at least two big proposed transfers this season which have foundered on this rock."

The promise of a house no doubt played a big part in the capture of Stubbins and to them all it was an early Christmas present, their minds now free to concentrate solely on football matters. While the wives made plans for their new abodes, the men joined up with the rest of their team-mates for the long trek north to Sunderland.

With one or two players carrying slight knocks after the Wolves game the directors delayed selecting their team until late in the week but after two successive defeats changes were inevitable. "Liverpool's utility man," Bill Jones came in at right back with Ray Lambert moving across to replace the dropped Barney Ramsden on the left of defence, whilst Cyril Done was missing through injury. Berry Nieuwenhuys, who like Jones had featured in the first few games for Liverpool only to be replaced when others returned, came into the attack at outside right with Harry Eastham, who showed again the versatility in this Reds' side, moving to the opposite flank behind Liddell.

Although they had not taken part in any regional football during the first season of the Second World War, Sunderland finished a respectable tenth in the 1941/42 first Northern Division and, with Albert Stubbins as a guest player, were runners up in the same season's Football League Cup, losing to a strong Wolves' side, containing

Cyril Sidlow in goal, 6-3 on aggregate in the two-legged final. A fine third place in the 1944/45 North Division was followed by a good run in the 1945/46 FA Cup were they lost at the quarter final stage to Birmingham.

A fine attacking side – with Cliff Whitelum scoring an incredible 134 goals in 163 war-time games - Sunderland had nevertheless sold Raich Carter, one of English football's greatest centre-forwards, to Derby County that summer and he had been sorely missed. Despite a good start to this season, the Rokerites had lost their last four games and, even accounting for Liverpool's last two results, this was seen by many as an ideal opportunity for the Reds to return to winning ways.

Poor weather was again a factor in the weekend's footballing calendar and a number of games were postponed both in the Football League and in the second round of the FA Cup. Indeed, so bad was the fog on Wearside that there looked to be little chance of this game kicking-off on the morning of the match, but by mid-afternoon rain had helped improve visibility and the game went ahead - although the weather had, "made the pitch very heavy and treacherous."

Liverpool's new look formation enjoyed plenty of possession and they created a number of chances in the early stages. On 10 minutes Balmer did well to evade a tackle by centre-half Billy Walsh outside the penalty area but, after he had brought the ball forward, he sliced his shot wide of Birkenhead-born Johnny Mapson's goal. Liddell then embarked on a typical forward run, "in the course of which he beat three men by sheer speed when it looked odds-on their getting to the ball first. A good tackle at the last moment saved the day."

The heavy ground was making good football difficult for both sides, but Liddell was in his element. On the quarter-hour mark he did exceptionally well to cut inside after receiving a great pass by Eastham and his subsequent shot from 20 yards was only inches wide.

Soon after, Liddell turned defender when he prevented a cross by Whitelum from entering the danger area by getting his face in the way of the ball. In the wet conditions however, with the leather ball exceedingly heavy, such an act was akin to taking a punch to the face off a heavyweight boxer and sure enough the brave Scotsman had to receive immediate treatment from Liverpool, "sponge-man," Albert Shelley, after going down with concussion.

On 20 minutes Liddell had recovered sufficiently enough to turn provider when his first touch pass, from another excellent Eastham through ball, found Balmer on the edge of the area. Despite his earlier miss from almost the same spot Balmer took aim again and this time, "lashed the ball into [the] goal." Sunderland hit back though and refused to let Liverpool's early lead affect their play by then creating some good chances of their own. Centre-forward Dickie Davis hit a speculative shot from distance and with Sidlow watching in anguish the ball thankfully, "spun…[just] inches wide of the Liverpool post."

Sunderland were now attacking at every opportunity and but for some sterling work by Jones and Liverpool's well worked offside trap, they would surely have equalised before they did. In the 28th minute a great shot by Jackie Robinson appeared to have beaten Sidlow but the Welsh international managed to get a hand to the ball for a fantastic save that brought gasps from the crowd. In trying to collect the ball again however, Sidlow was beaten by Davis who, "threw his boot at the ball to make it a goal." The Reds' keeper received treatment after this mad scramble but a free-kick in his favour was never going to be given and the goal stood.

After being pegged back Liverpool defended in numbers and, for a time, they looked anything like a team challenging at the top of the table. Sidlow bravely continued to dive at the feet of the Sunderland forwards – mostly Robinson, who was having a fine game, and Liddell was then forced to head another cross clear. Again, he was floored by the impact and the same happened to Paisley who also received the wet sponge from a busy Shelley after heading away another fierce Whitelum shot.

Liverpool were clearly rocking at this stage and it required a motivational intervention from the skipper to get things going again. "Early on it looked as though Sunderland were going to mop us up," said Balmer afterwards, but, "the lads responded with every ounce to my call for an extra effort."

Five minutes before the interval Liverpool forced a corner following good work by Liddell. Taking the kick himself, the Scotsman whipped the ball into the box in his customary fashion. So fast and accurate was the delivery that it created havoc in the Sunderland area – Jack Stelling the right back failing to connect with a header and the ball hitting the keeper's chest and deflecting into the net to make it 2-1 for the visitors. Just three minutes later, Balmer was unlucky when, "with a flick of the boot as Mapson came out," his effort trickled past the post.

"The second half opened with as many thrills in the first ten minutes as many games have in their entirety," observed *Ranger*. Sidlow saved yet again at the feet of Robinson – this time just two yards out – and was again injured in the tackle but continued all the same. Twice in quick succession Stubbins was put through on goal with only the keeper to beat but on each occasion Mapson did extremely well to narrow the angle and force the miss. Balmer then failed to connect properly on the muddy surface with a Stubbins pass when a little over five yards from goal.

With the middle of the pitch, "churning up pretty badly," both teams opted to use long ball tactics and Sidlow saved well from a dangerous Whitelum effort. On 65 minutes Liverpool won a throw on the Sunderland left, not far from the area. Liddell delivered it to Stubbins, whose clever back header found the returning Nivvy. Despite his first time shot at goal having little power it curled away from Mapson to drop into the Sunderland keeper's right-hand corner. Was the Reds' title challenge back on?

It was all Liverpool now. Balmer sent another shot whizzing just past the post, then a terrific shot by Liddell was well held by Mapson. Stubbins proceeded on a great weaving run, beating three players in the process, only for the ball to stick in the mud just as he was about to shoot.

With 13 minutes left Liverpool wrapped up the points with a great goal involving over half a dozen players. After winning the ball in his own half Jones played it to Taylor in the midfield who, in turn, carried it for 15 yards before finding Balmer. The captain then played, "a lovely pass," to Nivvy on the right and the South African floated a cross to the far post. It reached the head of Liddell who nodded it back towards goal and, after a fumble by Mapson, Stubbins, on one of his wartime stomping grounds and at the club he'd started out as a junior, eventually headed the ball into the net. Victory was assured and the 'crazy gang' were back on track.

Even the local Sunderland newspaper agreed that, "Liverpool fully earned their decisive win and were the best balanced side to oppose Sunderland this season." *Contact* too, thought the win fully deserved, highlighting that;

> *"The successes in a 4-1 win were Paisley and Taylor...Liddell's hard work after a heavy knock was worth more than the single goal he obtained....Nivvy, returning after three weeks without a game, did his job well without flourish, scored once and was in the lead up to another."*

On one of the highest scoring weekends in the top division – only two of the 11 games played saw less than five goals – Liverpool's sixth away victory of the season kept them in second place. Wolves smashed five past Bolton without reply at Molineux to retain top spot, with Westcott scoring four once again to emulate Balmer's feat of ten goals in three games. Elsewhere Blackpool lost by the same scoreline – at home – to Middlesbrough in what was the biggest game of the day. Stoke's 4-1 win at Brentford saw them leapfrog Manchester United – who lost yet another away game against lowly opposition, this time at Blackburn - into third.

This win may have gone some way to restoring the faith following the previous week's 5-1 mauling at the hands of Wolves, but Liverpool now had to convince those on the Kop that they were still very much a team with realistic title aspirations.

The imminent increase in the number of games was highlighted when the Reds were paired with Third Division South side Walsall in the third round of the FA Cup. Never having won the trophy - much to the delight of their Blue counterparts in the city - it was hoped Liverpool could make an impression in this competition for the first time in a long time. An away tie at one of the league's minnows was a decent enough start.

Liverpool v Aston Villa
Saturday 21 December 1946

"The next fortnight is going to be a severe testing time for the majority of clubs.
Those most adequately equipped with tip-top reserves are likely to come best out of the
Christmas and New Year glut of games, which place a strain on playing resources at any
time, but more particularly when the grounds are frozen..."

Ranger, Liverpool Echo

As the busy festive period approached Liverpool's board of directors took on the role of Scrooge as struggling local rivals Everton came knocking on the gates of Anfield asking for a helping hand with their last minute Christmas shopping. The object of their desire was once again Cyril Done, a player they'd expressed an interest in earlier in the season. On that occasion, after howls of protest from Reds' supporters, the Blues were eventually given short shrift and Done's immediate future at Anfield seemed secure, especially after his hat-trick at Huddersfield in October.

But, having scored just one goal since and with a number of other unnamed clubs also enquiring about his availability, the rumour mill went into overdrive yet again, forcing the Liverpool board to call an emergency meeting in order to discuss the matter. Everton's revived interest had got the local grapevine buzzing once more but, "with the heavy Christmas programme almost here and the cup-ties just around the corner," *Ranger* did not envisage the club selling their prolific war-time goalscorer. "I fail to see any advantage in letting Done go," he added, citing the need, much in vogue in the modern game and supposedly a rare part of this bygone age, that the big and bruising forward provided excellent cover in case of injuries.

Contact agreed with his colleague, with as good a defence of a large squad as any modern day manager could write;

"With the holiday programme and cup-ties imminent, Liverpool can afford to rest content
that in the case of injury they have the players to fill first team positions with ability, and
with no detriment to the side as a whole. And that is what a side with championship hopes
needs most of all, especially during the testing second-half of the season when a possible run
in the Cup makes the programme heavier still."

With the Toffeemen languishing in the lower reaches of Division One and finding goals hard to come by – they'd netted just 22 compared to Liverpool's 51 and no team in the League had scored fewer, even bottom club Huddersfield – they were in desperate need for a player of Done's quality. But despite it being the season of goodwill to all men no helping hand from the red side of Stanley Park was forthcoming and Everton were sent packing - back to the Goodison drawing board with an empty begging bowl. To the delight of Done's many admirers, Liverpool directors agreed with the what the local newspaper correspondents had wrote and it was announced, "they could not afford, in view of the approaching Cup-ties and their championship bid, to entertain [any approaches for the Liverpool forward]." Done however, was to play no part in the busy Christmas and New Year programme.

The first of five games in a fortnight saw Liverpool entertain Aston Villa on the last Saturday before Christmas and after an impressive 4-1 victory at Sunderland it was same again as far the team selection was concerned. Villa, despite their mid-table position, could boast one of the best defences in the division – indeed they had conceded six fewer goals than Liverpool - but also one of the poorest forward lines, with just 31 goals in 20 games.

Although the Midlands side did not take part in any competitive football for the first three years of the Second World War, they finished well-placed in every league they subsequently took part in after 1941/42, culminating in a fine second place (on goal average) in the 1945/46 Division South. They had also won the League North Cup in 1943/44, beating a strong Blackpool side 4-3 on aggregate in the final, before losing by the odd goal in nine to eventual winners Derby County at the quarter-final stage of the 1945/46 FA Cup.

LIVERPOOL MEET ASTON VILLA ON THE ICE

Prior to the game ex-Everton player Fred Geary, a famous forward from the 1890s, presented the directors of Aston Villa the match ball that was used in the 1897 FA Cup Final that Villa had won 3-2. Unlike today's drawn out ceremonies however, the presentation was conducted in barely 90 seconds – just in time for a photograph to mark the occasion - not because of the bitter cold, but due to the fact that freezing fog had delayed the Aston Villa train and everyone was in a rush to get the game underway. The visitors had arrived at Anfield barely 10 minutes before kick-off with the players scrambling to get changed enroute. Their directors received the award on a pitch that, despite being heavily sanded, remained extremely hard underfoot.

The poor weather, icy conditions and perhaps the close proximity to Christmas, affected both the standard of play and the attendance. A crowd of 35,000 - down a staggering 17,000 on Liverpool's previous home game – witnessed a slow to warm up game in every sense, especially during the early stages. Despite the Villa players' keenness to get changed as quickly as possible, kick-off was delayed for ten minutes. Fog lingered in certain areas of the stadium and the, "ice bound ground…did not allow either side to play normal football." It is certain that in the present era the game would have been postponed due to a frozen pitch – just as Manchester United's 'home' game against Portsmouth had been called off the same afternoon.

With both sets of players justifiably worried about injury on the hard surface, the opening minutes of the game were played at almost walking pace. "Keeping a foothold was one thing," remarked *Ranger*, "playing football something entirely different." Indeed, few moves of note could be made at all, prompting the reporter to add, "there were some nice touches…but nothing [was] concrete except the state of the ground."

Conditions meant that, "there was an almost entire lack of shooting," in the early stages and it wasn't until the twelfth minute that Liverpool created the game's first real chance. Balmer won possession outside the area and slipped the ball to Liddell who, although outnumbered, bore down on goal in his customary manner. A first tackle failed to stop the Liverpool star whilst a second merely resulted in the ball rebounding of his body towards the goal. Although Joe Rutherford, the Villa keeper, came out swiftly, "and fell on the ball as Liddell attempted to shoot," the ball bounced awkwardly away and the Villa number one cleared, "almost from the goal line." As many keepers had already done throughout the season, Rutherford received treatment following his collision with Liddell but was able to continue after a few minutes.

On 18 minutes Stubbins scored Liverpool's opening goal after a great piece of opportunism. Vic Potts was harried by Eastham on the wing and, seeing his opportunity for a pass to a teammate reduced by great work off the ball by the Liverpool forwards, was forced into a rash back-pass to Rutherford. Liverpool's record signing nipped in to intercept and warmed the shivering Anfield faithful by hooking the bouncing ball into the net after rounding the keeper. The home crowd's joy was short-lived however, as just three minutes later Villa equalised after a speculative shot by Dickie Dorsett - who had guested for Liverpool during the war and would later become reserve team trainer at Anfield - took a harsh bounce on the icy surface and was misjudged by Sidlow. Almost immediately afterwards, most of the crowd thought Liverpool had regained the lead when Liddell;

> *"went clean down the centre with the incisiveness of a knife, and the crowd, feeling certain that this must be a goal, were ready to cheer when he pulled a shot from point-blank range wide of the post."*

It was a glaring miss. Even the great Billy Liddell was human after all.

It was during this passage of play that Villa wing-half Bob Iverson was injured. Although he received treatment he never fully recovered. The injury to, "one of their best schemers," seemed to disorganise the visitors and Liverpool began to dominate. On 35 minutes another superb in-swinging corner by Liddell was almost headed in by Balmer but he was just beaten to the ball by Scottish international full-back George Cummings. After the opening timidity due to the treacherous conditions both sides were now creating chances regularly and only a great tackle by Jones on left-winger Les Smith soon after kept the scores level.

Five minutes from half-time yet another great corner by Liddell caused panic in the Villa area but Nivvy, in his customary position at the far post - only this time with his feet planted firmly on the ground, sent a bullet downward header into the back of the net.

Proving that it wasn't just Jackie Balmer who bore the brunt of the home crowd's frustrations when things didn't go their way, Nivvy's goal prompted *Ranger* to make an impassioned defence of the likeable outside-right, "if the few jaundiced 'supporters' who booed Nivvy before the start are capable of regret," he wrote;

> *"they should have felt it later, for the South African brought to the attack speed, ability to provide the right type of centres, and finishing power, all attributes it has lacked on the extreme right for some time."*

In the remaining minutes of the half tempers began to flare on both sides and, "more than a little spirit entered the game." This could be bad for both teams it was noted, "anything over robust [on the icy surface] was sure to cause trouble," or injury.

With the afternoon drawing to a close and the sky darkening over Anfield due to the late kick-off and the inclement weather, "the light suggested that to finish the game would be quite a performance." A goal ahead, solid in defence and with Stubbins having another fine game in the icy conditions, Liverpool started the second half in rapid style and they dominated the second 45 minutes.

In the first minute Rutherford did well to collect a Balmer shot at the second attempt on the hard surface. The keeper then took the full force of a Stubbins shot in the face and needed treatment for slight concussion. He soon recovered and play quickly switched to the opposite end and a Villa free-kick by Cummings proved a refreshing change to the common practice of trying to steal a yard or five from a dead ball situation. The Scotland international took the kick a yard behind the spot where it should have been taken, prompting *Ranger* to note it was, "a little point the stand crowd did not fail to recognise," and the Liverpool fans in that part of the ground took time to applaud the opposition player's integrity.

On the hour mark, "Liddell should have scored after a lovely pass by Stubbins," but hit the side-netting from close range. The Liverpool midfield was having one of its best games of the season. "Paisley was playing brilliantly," while Taylor, Jones and Lambert, "were [all] very much on top of their work." Indeed, following a well-placed Nivvy header from a corner, Paisley, "went very close to a third goal," with a long range effort that went just wide and in an almost identical situation, "Taylor too, made a very good scoring effort," only to see his shot through a crowd of players only caught by Rutherford at the last moment.

On 70 minutes, "the Villa goal had a remarkable escape when Liddell centered and Balmer shot from three yards out." With the keeper beaten, the ball hit Cummings in the chest and was deflected wide. Immediately after this chance Balmer scored his 14th goal in seven games, "by bamboozling the defence," who expected him to square the ball to Stubbins in the area but instead saw him hit a fine, "angled shot which beat Rutherford from start to finish."

Liddell then shot high when well placed before Balmer with, "the full force of his boot with a right-footer," doubled his tally to score Liverpool's fourth just six minutes after his first. It wrapped up the points up nicely and Balmer's 15th goal in just seven matches was, "evidence not only of his good marksmanship, but [also] of the co-operation of Stubbins, whose display…was the best since his arrival here."

With Liverpool, "well on top and Villa…scarcely seen," there was still time for more scoring chances from the home side. Nivvy sent a centre across goal that evaded everyone, then Balmer nearly got his fourth hat-trick in seven games before Nivvy again was unlucky to hit a shot straight against the keeper's legs when clean through. The referee blew for full-time soon after with the ground almost in darkness. Liverpool had won, scoring four for the second game in a row after conceding eight in their previous two – living up to their erratic and inconsistent reputation.

A return to the disciplined defensive displays that had done them proud in the early stages of the season appeared to have returned, and this was cited as another reason for their morale boosting victory;

> *"Bill Jones gave a great show at full back, playing as though he'd never been anywhere else, and with Lambert at the top of his form, and the half-back line never better, the Villa attack rarely got out of their grip."*

Two victories had followed two defeats and their title challenge appeared to be back on track. Second on 28 points with a game in hand on leaders Wolves – 2-1 winners at Stamford Bridge - who had 30, Liverpool, with their, "attractive football and combative spirit," had rediscovered their form just in time for the holiday fixtures. With only four more days until Christmas, another two points was the perfect gift for their supporters but, with the imperious Stanley Matthews and his in-form Stoke City side - who had title aspirations of their own - up next in a crucial 24-hour double-header on Christmas Day and Boxing Day, would the festive cheer continue?

Chapter Seven
No festive cheer

Stoke City v Liverpool
Wednesday 25 December 1946

"Liverpool's holiday games will have a big bearing on their championship bid. They do not need me to tell them that every point is vital, and that any thrown away now will be doubly hard to pull back when the cup-ties add possible complications to the fixture list."

Ranger, Liverpool Echo

The concept of playing football on Christmas Day may be a difficult one for contemporary followers of the game to grasp. The only 'footy' action on this most holy of dates these days is played out via the latest computer consoles but, between 1894 and 1957, for the players and supporters of Liverpool FC it a common occurrence. Tradition dictated it was and no-one batted an eyelid. For the players involved, missing out on time with their families at this special time of year was an inconvenience they could have well done without and especially so for the Liverpool team on this occasion. The fans loved it though, so much so that a loyal contingent from Liverpool forsook Christmas dinner with their loved ones to cheer the Reds on in the Potteries. With no international qualifying tournaments, no meaningless friendlies and no inter-club continental competition the public lapped up whatever football they could, where and whenever it was played.

Fearing a reprimand by the Football League, who viewed the previous week's late kick-offs with disdain – "Fog, frost and train delays are not regarded by them as valid reasons," for the recent, "crop of late starts," the Reds travelled to Stoke on the afternoon of Christmas Eve rather than early on the day of the game. Liverpool's festive double header in 1946 held particular intrigue, for their opponents, Stoke City, were a team bang in form. Second against fourth, with just three points separating the two teams, it was an opportunity for one to pull clear or the other to close the gap and maybe overtake.

For Liverpool, arguably the surprise package of the season so far, it was a stern examination of their credentials and previewing the games in the Christmas Eve edition of the Echo, *Ranger* noted;

"With Wolverhampton Wanderers hanging onto the leadership, Liverpool will be aiming at maximum points from their Christmas away and home engagements with Stoke City. Tomorrow they appear at the Victoria ground, where only two sides this season have beaten the Potters. There will be a big crowd for the return encounter at Anfield on Boxing Day. The constitution of both sides will depend on how the players come through the Christmas

Day fixture, but if Lambert and Matthews are fit there should be a great tussle between them, as well as between Stubbins and Franklin, and Hughes and Steele."

The prospect of Hughes going up against Stoke's veteran England international Freddie Steele, who earlier in the season had netted 14 goals in just 10 games, was one that the fans and pundits had been looking forward to but, unfortunately it failed to materialise as a severe bout of flu forced the Reds' centre-half to miss the clash. Hughes had been one of Liverpool's best performers of the season and deemed a worthy claimant for an England cap in some quarters. Earlier in the season *Ranger* had heaped praise on the Liverpool defender noting that he was, "six feet in height, with a record of withstanding centre-forwards of every trade with remarkable success."

Stanley Matthews

The Potters were the only side Liverpool had yet to face and the big danger was undoubtedly that renowned 'wizard of the dribble' Stanley Matthews. One of English football's all-time greats, he would later become the first European Footballer of the Year and the only player to be knighted while still plying his trade. In 1946 Matthews was 31, an established England international at outside-right, of 'superstar' status and the man upon whose shoulders Stoke were largely pinning their title hopes on. Despite his standing in the game he was yet to win any domestic honours but many observers felt he now had a genuine opportunity to put this right. Together with club captain and fellow England international Neil Franklin, the aforementioned Steele and left-winger Alex Ormston, a Matthews' inspired Stoke were many people's pick to win the Championship.

Not that their war-time record had been anything to shout about. Although topping the Western Division in 1939/40 - finishing above both Merseyside and Manchester clubs - Stoke enjoyed only limited success during the hostilities, mainly due to the absence of Matthews. He played in less than half their games the following season and only 38 times between 1941/42 and 1945/46. It was a situation that Victoria Ground officials often complained about but, with other teams more than happy to have him as a guest – he was a fantastic draw at the box-office - and the Army requiring his services for a host of games and events, their complaints fell on death ears. With their 'star man' now back playing regularly however, the Potters had recovered from a poor start this season – just one point from their opening four games – to steadily climb the table and they went into the game with Liverpool unbeaten in three and without a loss at home since late-October.

As predicted by commentators in recent weeks, the strength in depth of the Reds' squad was now called upon and John Easdale, the replacement for Hughes, became the 21st player used by the club in the first team since the start of the season. Easdale had endured a near ten-year wait for his official debut and he was joined in the team by a fellow rookie, albeit one with slightly more senior experience. Ray Minshull was a late call-up to the side after Cyril Sidlow took ill on the morning of the game.

With reserve keeper Charlie Ashcroft also injured, an urgent telegram was sent to Minshull's Southport home and he duly responded to plug the gap between the sticks. The Daily Post reported that the young keeper, "and his wife were driven from Liverpool to Stoke by a chauffeuse of a city taxi firm, who knew her clutch as well as Minshull knew the goalkeeper's sure clutch." On his one and only previous senior appearance – the 4-1 win at Huddersfield in October – Minshull had earned rave reviews and he impressed again at the Victoria Ground as Liverpool went in search of their first peace-time Christmas Day victory since 1931.

Freddie Steele

In Stoke however, nine of whose team were all local men, Liverpool found a side in top form – Matthews especially so. From early in the game it was easy to see how the Potteries' outfit had emerged as title contenders themselves and their, "all-round skill and splendidly co-ordinated teamwork would have mastered almost any team in the country." Matthews, in particular, was in outstanding form. Both he, and the left-wing pair of Ormston and Frank Baker, gave the Reds' back-line a torrid time and but for Minshull, Liverpool could easily have been on the wrong end of a rout.

Midway through the first half, after good work by Ormston, Matthews received the ball deep in the Liverpool half on the left wing. Running at Lambert with pace and menace he beat the Welsh international with a jinking, stuttering, run before eventually crossing for Steele, nipping in front of Easdale, to score with a well placed volley. Soon after, the same players combined again only for Minshull to push another Steele effort onto the bar and over.

Shortly after the restart Liverpool felt they should have had an equaliser when

Liddell managed to put the ball in the net only for the referee, Mr C Fletcher of Northwich, to disallow it due to an earlier infringement by Balmer. Despite protests by a number of players the decision stood. "The best part of Liverpool's team was their attack, skillfully marshalled by Balmer," so this wasted effort was particularly frustrating especially as, less than 10 minutes later, Steele scored his second. Again Matthews was the architect, sending an angled centre into the area for Stoke's leading scorer to again latch onto.

Ray Minshull

Moments later Minshull saved well from Matthews, Ormston and then Steele in quick succession, earning him the appreciation of his teammates and the sporting crowd. "He was Liverpool's man of the match," penned Leslie Edwards, "and the ovation given him by the crowd for repeated saves [at the end of the game] was well merited." The Echo also gave praise to the inexperienced keeper, adding that;

"Liverpool have found in Ray Minshull, of Southport, a goalkeeper on Elisha Scott lines... [He] played magnificently at Stoke and received an ovation. That was compensation for being on the losing side for the first time this season. He has played about seventeen matches in the first team or reserves or 'A' team, and this was the first time he had failed to draw a bonus of some sort."

Liverpool did their best to rally and but for the, "grand Stoke defence," they may have added more goals than a late headed consolation by Stubbins from a Nivvy cross with eight minutes to go and the game ended 2-1 to the hosts.

The big winners of the day were the team due at Anfield in three days time, Sheffield United, who ran out 6-1 victors at home to Brentford. Table-topping Wolves scraped a 1-0 away win at Sunderland to increase their lead at top but with third-placed Middlesbrough drawing 3-3 with Leeds at Elland Road there were no positional changes in top four. Although they hadn't played badly, this latest 'top of the table clash' defeat handed Liverpool's critics yet more bullets with which they would try to shoot down the Reds' title ambitions. The Daily Post were more supportive in their summary of the match however. In a game that thrilled the large crowd with, "high quality football, incidental features and testing pace on heavy ground," the Anfield outfit had, "suffered no loss of football prestige by reason of their...defeat."

As the beaten Redmen trudged off the muddy field they could have been forgiven for letting their thoughts wander to the festivities that were taking place back home but with the return fixture coming up at Anfield less than 24 hours later the turkey - if they had any - and tinsel would have to wait.

Liverpool v Stoke City
Thursday 26 December 1946

*"It was well worth a Boxing Day trip to Anfield if only to see Matthews.
He has been criticised as not a good club player, but a careful analysis of
everything he did yesterday proved that Stoke were never more dangerous than
the few seconds immediately after he had been given the ball."*

Ranger, Liverpool Echo

Given the fact they had seen more of each other than their own families over this Christmas holiday, the Liverpool and Stoke players could have been forgiven for exchanging gifts and cards rather than handshakes when they renewed acquaintances at Anfield on Boxing Day afternoon. It was a long-held tradition that the Christmas Day fixtures were reversed and so Liverpool were handed an immediate opportunity to exact revenge for the previous day's 2-1 defeat. It was a result that had left the Reds four points adrift of leaders Wolves, so anything less than a home win would cast severe doubts on their ability to last the distance in the title race.

With 21 of 42 league games completed, the half-term report for Liverpool's class of 1946/47 could have read; great improvement shown, effort can't be faulted, outstanding at times but prone to silly mistakes and costly lapses in concentration, consistency must be worked on but plenty to be optimistic about. Grade? Probably a B or B+.

With confidence high in the Potteries, Stoke, who themselves had performed admirably during the first half of the season, were unaltered for their visit to Anfield but Liverpool made one change, handing veteran defender Tom Bush his first start of the campaign at centre-half in place of John Easdale who, in attempting to mark Freddie Steele the day before, had found the step up from reserve team football difficult to say the least. Laurie Hughes remained ill in bed with flu, as did Sidlow so, after his heroics at the Victoria Ground, Ray Minshull kept his place in goal.

Driving rain and a bitterly cold wind did little to dampen the Merseyside public's enthusiasm for this game and they turned out in force to not only see their heroes play but to also witness at close hand the mercurial talents of the great Stanley Matthews. Liverpool's matchday programme notes praised both Matthews and his side;

"One of the most attractive teams playing today is Stoke City, and their visit today will be welcomed, particularly if their famous winger, Stanley Matthews, is playing. His sparkling runs down the right wing and his uncanny ball control are a source of trouble to all

133

defenders and our left flank will have to be in good form to circumvent this brilliant exponent of wing play. Matthews in his best form is a football feast and some of his displays for England have never been equalled by any of his illustrious predecessors."

Maybe the club purposely hyped up the appearance of Matthews in an attempt to justify their decision to increase the price of stand tickets for this fixture, an action that, unsurprisingly, met with an angry response from some supporters and there was even talk of a boycott. But when the tickets in question eventually sold out it indicated, "that whatever their views, the vast majority of supporters don't mind paying extra to be sure of a seat."

Almost 50,000 spectators eventually crammed into Anfield, while the unofficial attendance was undoubtedly higher due to a large number of fans 'bunking in' at the Kop end by simply climbing over the stadium wall to escape the pre-match chaos at the turnstiles. Those who made it were not to be disappointed.

'Bunking in' at the Kop end - Boxing day game v Stoke City, 1946.

There had been little time for rest and recuperation but, to their credit, the players on both teams played their part in what turned out to be a tense but thoroughly enjoyable encounter. The first half was notable for the sterling work each defence did to nullify the opposition's attack. Good play by both sides in bringing the ball forward from midfield was countered by even better defence and there were few real chances for either side early on, although after half an hour Stubbins did attempt to catch Stoke keeper Arthur Jepson off his line with a speculative shot from distance that was eventually saved with ease.

The second half continued in much the same vein – "a game of arts and crafts in midfield with the honours likely to go either way" - until Eastham broke free down the left on 68 minutes and hit a diagonal pass to Nivvy, lurking dangerously as ever at the far post. The South African made no mistake with another pinpoint header and the deadlock was broken. "The new and more thoughtful Liverpool surprised some of the 50,000 who filled Anfield for the Stoke match," wrote *Contact*, "they played lovely, neat but unproductive football for three parts of the game and then a Nivvy goal against the wind and bitter rain put them into a winning mood."

With the large holiday crowd still jubilant the visitors were unlucky not to draw level. As Matthews danced through the home defence, Minshull advanced off his line to narrow the angle but just when it looked as though he'd done enough Matthews, "merely hooked the ball over the goalkeeper and only the bar and Steele's miss from the rebound precluded a goal."

Eastham restored calm to the Liverpool cause with some excellent play in midfield, while Liddell was as committed as ever, causing problems for an increasingly tired looking Stoke defence. By contrast, Liverpool seemed as fit as ever, testimony to their conditioning by trainers Albert Shelley and Jimmy Seddon, moving *Ranger* to note that, "apart possibly from Wolves, if there is a better trained side in the First Division than Liverpool, I've not seen it. They are invariably going as strong at the end as the start."

At the other end superstar winger Matthews, although his side trailed, didn't disappoint. He was, "the footballer complete in this game…practically his every use of the ball was, for Liverpool, excruciatingly effective," and it was easy to see how, with him in this form, Stoke had emerged as serious title challengers themselves. "A careful analysis of everything he did…proved that Stoke were never more dangerous than the few seconds immediately after he had been given the ball," wrote a clearly impressed *Ranger*;

> "*Matthews toys and trifles with the ball and the opposition. The full-back who goes into the tackle, believing Matthews is going to hold the ball, finds it astutely moved elsewhere. Then, when he decides to hold off, Stanley holds on and coaxes and cajoles his way through at walking pace. It all looks very simple. No player moves faster for half a dozen yards and none does more with less effort.*"

Unlike the previous day's game however, Ormston was not at his best following an early knee injury, and Matthews could not carry his team alone, especially with Liverpool picking up where they had left off in the Potteries. Minshull was again a safe understudy in goal, albeit he had less to worry about in this return fixture than he had the day before. That this was so was down to the Red's defence, in particular Jones who, at right-back, was exceptional once again and his performance did not go unnoticed by those in the press box, with one seasoned observer commenting that, "after [only] two or three games there he looks good enough to play for England much less a club side."

The high level of Liverpool's fitness was often referred to in 1946/47.
Pictured above is the team training at Anfield whilst below is the stadium gym - then situated beneath the Main Stand.

The Reds' never-say-die attitude was epitomised by Stubbins just five minutes from the end. After a fine move involving Taylor, Eastham and Balmer, the number nine found himself at the edge of the area surrounded by three defenders. There seemed little chance of a goal in such a tight situation but the crowd favourite, "switched the ball to his left foot and scored a second to complete the joy." A minute later he missed a glorious chance to add a third, getting too far under a chip from Liddell and heading safely into Jepson's hands but the points were safe and, "so all was well."

It had been a well-earned and fully-deserved victory. Stubbins may have been the match-winning two-goal marksman but credit also went to, "the speed and shooting of Balmer; the fast and full blooded winging of Liddell; Eastham's earnest roaming, and Nieuwenhuys' wise 'nodding'." Again there was special praise for the defence who, even accounting for the absence of Hughes, appeared to have returned to their resolute best. "It was the immaculate Taylor, ably supported by some strong heading by Bush and characteristically tough tackling by Paisley which kept Stoke out," noted Leslie Edwards, while Lambert too, was singled out for his battle with Matthews. The Welshman, "did as well as most who have the unenviable task of tackling the ghost in football boots."

The only sour note to the day was the news from the West Midlands that two late goals for Wolves at Molineux saw them come from behind to snatch a 2-1 victory against Sunderland. Along with Arsenal, 2-1 winners at home to Portsmouth, Wolves were one of just two teams to complete a Christmas double and it meant their lead at the top remained the same. Liverpool's win over Stoke kept them very much in contention and, having finally beaten one of their title rivals, many fans started to believe once again and went off to enjoy the remainder of the festivities in a much more positive frame of mind. The Anfield action didn't end there though and while the players headed home for a well earned rest before the next game in two days time, late that night the club offices were burgled and a safe blown open in an attempt to steal the previous afternoon's gate receipts. Fortunately the takings had been banked immediately after the match and, just like Stoke, the would-be thieves went away empty-handed.

Chapter Eight
Who wants to win the league anyway?

Liverpool v Sheffield United
Saturday 28 December 1946

"After the storm – the calm. Today is the welcome period of rest for players and officials after two stern and hectic holiday games, but it is short-lived, and tomorrow vital issues are again at stake."

Ranger's Notes, Liverpool Echo

The country's insatiable appetite for football was never more ravenous than over Christmas and attendances at English league grounds during the festive period topped the three million mark. At Anfield, a crowd in the region of 50,000 squeezed through the turnstiles for the second in time in three days to witness what would be Reds' last game of 1946, further underlining Liverpool's standing as one of football's biggest box office attractions. Sheffield United were the visitors and the gates were once again closed well before kick-off.

While this may not have been an ideal scenario for the fans who had to battle their way in and run the risk of being locked out, in terms of club finances it was a godsend;

"thus warming the treasurer's heart and making a long-worn overdraft fade from the banker's sight. The overdraft had been £28,000, today it is hardly noticeable and shortly it will become a credit balance for the first time in a generation."

On the pitch, Liverpool were hoping to complete their first league double of the campaign, having defeated the Blades away on the opening day, although since then, United had won 10 of 19 games in the top division – losing only five – and had settled nicely in mid-table.

Jimmy Hagan's dispute with the club had not been resolved to his satisfaction but, with no club allowed to sign him so long as the Blades retained his registration – precisely why the players' strike had been proposed in the first place - he was forced to return. Indeed, he had only missed the first three games of the season and his experience and vision complimented United's young side nicely, and he was to play an instrumental role in this game, with one observer noting, "if there is a finer inside-forward playing today, I am the Emperor of China."

The mesmeric form of Hagan must have been a nagging source of embarrassment to Anfield officials for he had been on Liverpool's books for two years as a youngster, starting in 1933, where he was, "set menial tasks on the ground to await the day when he should be 'blooded' into football." An England schoolboy international, Hagan's unique talent was, unfortunately, not fully appreciated by the directors of the time and at the tender age of 18 he was allowed to join Derby County. The scale of Liverpool's loss would soon become apparent and thought of 'what might have been' must have crossed Liverpudlian minds many a time in the years that followed.

Jimmy Hagan

Widely acknowledged as Sheffield United's most notable player of the 1940s and quite rightly considered to be one of the greatest-ever Blades, Hagan was the undoubted star of the side that travelled to Anfield for this final fixture of the calendar year. Having missed out on the opening day clash with the Reds he was eager to show once more just what Liverpool had missed out on when they had failed to spot his potential all those years ago.

Along with bottom club Portsmouth, eighth-placed Sheffield United had been particularly hard hit by the recent adverse weather and, as a result of postponements; they had played fewer games than most in the division. With at least two games in hand on some of the teams around them - a fact that would have a significant impact on the title race later in the season – it could be argued that they were a better team than what their league position suggested.

On their previous visit to Merseyside a fortnight before however, the local press had spotted a weaknesses in their game and *Ranger* fully expected Liverpool to exploit this. "[They] work the ball nicely, have solidity in defence and good combination in attack," he wrote, but against Everton they, "threw good work to the winds by refusing to shoot when the openings were there," and he stressed that, "no side can afford to do that with impunity against Liverpool, whose own prolific goalscoring feats usually give the opposition defence plenty to think about." Their 3-2 victory at Goodison upset many Evertonians and to prove that the recent Done affair had caused no rift between the red and blue boardrooms, the programme notes for this game outlined Liverpool's desire to, "avenge the home defeat sustained by our neighbours at Goodison Park a few weeks ago."

A home win, "to end the old year with a nice double," was most definitely expected, but Liverpool, minus Phil Taylor, who was ruled out with a foot injury, "were not themselves," and with the visitors, "wisely generalled by Hagan," things didn't go according to plan in what was a fiery encounter.

In unseasonally bright sunshine, Liverpool had the better of the early play. A long curling pass by Eastham found Nivvy on the wing but the South African's centre hit the side-netting with Balmer and Liddell both unmarked in the area. It was clear that the veteran Springbok was feeling the effects of four hard games in three days, and as the match went on he was hardly able to, "raise a gallop." Balmer blazed the ball over in uncharacteristic disgust a few minutes later after play was called back for a poor offside decision against Stubbins. The Reds' skipper, the intended recipient of Stubbins' through ball, was clearly onside and the home fans vehemently let their feelings be known on the matter.

On 15 minutes United left-winger Colin Collindridge was stopped in his tracks by a fine tackle from Jones, and, soon after, Minshull turned a good effort round the post from the same player. On both occasions the United centre-forward had been found by Hagan, whose, "generalship was already evident." Hagan was having a fine game, "a link between full-backs, half-backs and forwards," and it was through him that United enjoyed a, "spell of…superiority which had Liverpool distinctly worried," just before the half hour mark. Bush headed a dangerous cross out for a corner and Jones was kept busy by the speed of the United front line, although he, "was playing as well as anyone, coolly and calmly, and with consummate ability."

Soon after, Balmer shot wide when he perhaps should have passed to the better placed Liddell, and then Eastham, from barely five yards out and with a clear shot on goal, unselfishly passed to Stubbins, but, "Furniss came from nowhere to clear," his side footed shot. The latter chance was to prove a pivotal moment and the general consensus afterwards was that, "had Eastham rammed the ball into the net instead of passing to Stubbins it would have changed the whole course of the game."

The action was end to end, "but there were still notable holes in the Liverpool defence." Nightingale shot straight at Minshull after a series of errors saw Liverpool give the ball away at least three times in quick succession. The warnings were there for Liverpool and on 36 minutes they were made to pay for their lack-lustre start. A rare mis-kick by Jones let in Collindridge. His snap-shot was well saved by Minshull but the rebound fell to Hagan who shot towards an empty goal only for Lambert, standing on the line, to handle for a penalty. Unlike today, when a red card would be shown straight away, Lambert was only booked, although Alex Forbes, a tough tackling wing-half who would come back to haunt Liverpool at Wembley four years later, tucked the spot-kick away with ease to give the Blades a 1-0 lead.

Having wasted several good chances themselves Liverpool could have no complaints when, "the defence cracked," and for the watching *Bee*, "it was aggravating to see Liverpool probable winners for forty minutes and then find them peter out." United were full of confidence following the goal and again Hagan was the focus of all their good work. Just two minutes later, "it took an army of defenders to keep out…one of his best dribbles."

Five minutes before the break play switched suddenly to the other end and Liverpool equalised with a splendid goal, albeit against the run of play. Lambert took a quick free-kick in the middle of the pitch. Balmer then found Stubbins just outside the area. The centre-forward ran to his left, beat one man, then turned inside to beat another before finishing with his right foot. It was a stunning goal that showed why Liverpool had spent so much money on the Newcastle striker in September. The half-time whistle came two minutes later with most of the 50,000 strong crowd hoping the Reds could improve in the second half to maintain their title challenge.

Within four minutes of the restart however, Liverpool found themselves behind once again. Hagan beat three Liverpool players, "with a full-speed dribble," before sending a long cross-field pass to Harold Brook who, although beating Lambert for pace, sent his shot just wide. It was one of those days for the Liverpool left-back and just a minute later Nightingale shot from almost the same spot just as a tackle from the Welsh international came in. His tackle looked to have forced the Sheffield striker to fire wide but the ball took a wicked deflection of Lambert's boot and completely wrong-footed Minshull to bounce into the goal.

At this point United were playing the better football, with Liverpool, "far too inclined to work without method." Although the Reds seemed to have more of the ball, their attacks paled in comparison with United's but Jones and Paisley were playing as well as ever and Minshull produced two fine saves to deny Walter Rickett on 65 and 85 minutes respectively. By contrast Liverpool's forward play was poor. Balmer shot well from long-range but it was straight at Jack Smith in the Sheffield goal. Liddell and Eastham then swapped

SHEFFIELD TAKE THE POINTS — BY GEORGE GREEN

positions – Liverpool's "usual plan when things are black and time is short," - but, "the United defence did not appear likely to crack," even for 'King Billy'. Indeed, but for two Liddell shots that were easily saved by Smith near the end, the Blade's keeper had a pretty quiet second half. With United's defence, "steady as a rock throughout Liverpool's endeavour," the Anfield men's attempt to keep pace with the leader's seemed to have stalled.

Paisley may have, "shone," and, "Stubbins had rarely played better," but one had to hold their hands up and admit that Liverpool had been, "well and truly beaten by a better side," and, "it was well that Jones, Lambert and Minshull were so sound otherwise the defeat might have been greater." If they had taken some of their half chances, most notably the one fluffed by Eastham, then, "the boot might have been on the other leg," but there could be no getting away from the fact that former Anfield 'find' Hagan had been the, "star of the day." *Ranger* purred that;

> *"He was invariably the starting point of every Sheffield attack, gave the defence plenty of help in times of stress and was a supreme artist in all he did. It is a long time since we saw so brilliant an all-round display."*

Bee also waxed lyrical about the outstanding performance of Hagan, "he took throws, rearranged corner kicks, went to the wing, called for the ball, cajoled it, tickled it and went just far enough to draw opponents out of normal range." It's no surprise that a player of such influence later entered management and enjoyed great success on the continent, most notably as boss of Portuguese giants Benfica, but from Liverpool's point of view, they were just glad they wouldn't have to face him again that season.

Although dismayed at a third home defeat, the Reds remained in second place but the gap between them and the leaders had now increased to five points, courtesy of Wolves' 1-1 draw at Arsenal. Blackpool's home win over Brentford saw them join the Reds on 30 points while Preston, thanks to a Tom Finney-inspired 3-0 win at Leeds, entered the title frame for the first time.

Four games in eight days had proved a hard slog and Liverpool's record of two wins and two defeats was typical of their recent form - inconsistent and unpredictable. So 1946, a memorable year in which the club had made great strides on and off the pitch, had ended on a low note but it was now time recharge the batteries for what would hopefully be an even better 1947.

Chelsea v Liverpool
Saturday 4 January 1947

> *"The games in the Football League today are likely to be watched anxiously by managers of the leading clubs. Injuries suffered in these games may easily spoil a team's chances in the FA Cup third round matches next week."*

Bee, Liverpool Daily Post

Liverpool welcomed in the New Year with a day out at the park. But while their bodies were at Goodison their minds were elsewhere, switching between Ayresome and Burnden, as they looked anxiously over their shoulder at the chasing pack of fellow title challengers. Two defeats out of three over Christmas had left them vulnerable and their position as second to leaders Wolves was under threat.

With no match of their own on New Year's Day, the Reds took in the Everton game against Aston Villa, the result of which was of no major consequence to them in terms of league placings, but the same could not be said of the matches involving fourth-placed Middlesbrough, at home to Grimsby, and fifth-placed Preston, away to Bolton. Just a point separated Liverpool from them both and, as it turned out, without setting foot on a pitch, Liverpool dropped two places to fourth as both took maximum points. It was a far from ideal introduction to 1947. It was to get worse before it got better.

It was another three days before Liverpool played their first fixture of the year away to Chelsea. Manager George Kay and his players went into the game with a New Year's resolution – to rid themselves once and for all of the inconsistency that was threatening to derail their title challenge. Since going top of the table with a victory at Derby in November the Reds had won five and lost four - anything but Championship form. But ahead of the trip to London there were plenty of reasons to be hopeful. Their away form remained among the best in the division and no side had scored more on their travels. Together with the fact that earlier in the season they had smashed seven past Chelsea in a never to be forgotten 11 goal epic at Anfield and that a trio of key players – Hughes, Taylor and Fagan – were all declared fit and ready to return to action, it was an optimistic Liverpool squad that travelled to the capital.

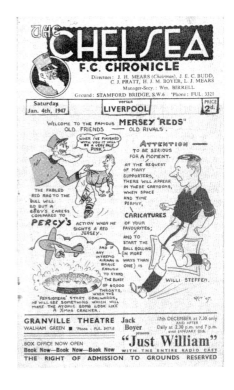

It had been three months since club captain Fagan, the victim of a persistent ankle injury, had last figured in the first team and, after proving his fitness in a reserve outing the previous week, his long-awaited re-appearance was viewed as a major boost, with *Ranger* noting that with him back;

> *"Liverpool will be fielding their strongest attack for some months...[their] forward line needed a man of his stamp and ability to weld it into a real team unit capable of getting the utmost from what has sometimes...been rather haphazard individual behaviour."*

With Taylor and Hughes also welcomed back into the fold the pre-match signs were certainly encouraging, "every vital department should be at its best again, so that the chances of a Liverpool victory are much enhanced."

A glance at Chelsea's recent form also suggested that this game should be marked down as an away banker on the coupon. Given the many expensive players they'd signed and the high pre-season expectations placed on them, the Londoners' campaign thus far had been a massive let-down. Hovering just below mid-table, with only one victory in their last eight - and that was against lowly Huddersfield, - this was, "a measure of the pensioners' success." Such optimism however, can often be ill-founded. This was to be one of those instances.

Just like at Anfield in early September, this game – the only top-flight fixture in the capital that day – began at a fast and furious pace. In front of a capacity crowd of almost 60,000 (it would have been nearer 80,000 had Government restrictions not been in place) both teams went close in a busy opening spell. Chelsea centre forward Johnny Paton flashed a shot just wide inside the first five minutes. Shortly afterwards, "Liverpool's defence twice had desperate moments." Former Everton star and Liverpool target Tommy Lawton went close with a snap shot from the left, then turned provider as he set up Dick Spence only to see the winger thwarted by Laurie Hughes who, "showed speed enough to get back and punch the ball for a corner."

Liddell then fluffed a half-chance but it was Liverpool who were under more pressure. With Chelsea, "bright and breezy and full of promise," Hughes and Paisley had to be at their best. "When Hughes for once misjudged the bounce of the ball," on the hard, dry pitch however, he was relieved to see Lawton hit, "a very hot shot only a fraction wide." On 15 minutes Paton had the ball in the net for the Londoners but it was ruled out for offside. It was a close decision.

Taylor and Liddell combined well to set up Balmer but he was crowded out, then Taylor and Jones, "indulged in some lovely inter-passing to get themselves out of difficulty," as Chelsea retaliated. It was frantic stuff.

On 20 minutes Liverpool had a great chance to take the lead, the first in a sustained spell of pressure. A Jones cross was headed away by Winter but his clearance fell at the feet of the returning Fagan, who hit the ball first time on the half-volley. The captain, "looked a certain scorer," but, "Medhurst's save was one in a thousand." The keeper then saved smartly from Stubbins before Liddell, bearing in from the left, "hit a peach of a shot just wide of the far post." The entire Liverpool team was playing well, not just the forwards, with Taylor, "the artistic genius," whose, "half-back play was superb," in particular, having an inspired game.

Although Liverpool were starting to dominate the game, so much so that, "there were times when only Hughes stood in their half," it was Chelsea who took the lead on 27 minutes with a goal of frustrating simplicity. Spence crossed and Lawton's header, although not powerful, had enough pace to beat Sidlow who, despite getting a hand to the ball, should have done better.

Despite the goal the game continued in the manner of the first half hour, with both sides creating numerous chances. Paisley and Taylor both, "went very near to success," as did Stubbins, "with a dribble half the length of the field," while another marginal offside decision saved Liverpool from going two goals down. Lawton also went close for Chelsea, but it was Balmer, from a threaded Stubbins pass, who got a deserved equaliser on 35 minutes with a fantastic shot on the turn just inside the area. It went in off the underside of the bar and, with their tails up, Liverpool, ended the half well, with Nivvy and Balmer again going close.

"There were times when Liverpool's honest plodding suggested that here, again, they were likely to win away," but any momentum Liverpool had hoped to carry into the second-half was dashed within just two minutes of the restart. Again Spence was the creator, his pinpoint cross finding Len Goulden in the area and it was his cushioned header that set Lawton up for a simple side-foot shot into the back of the net to put Chelsea 2-1 ahead. Spence then headed against the underside of the bar before Paisley, who, "was getting through an enormous amount of work," cleared from the foot of the post.

On the hour mark Liverpool's defence was again caught out by a straight forward Chelsea move. A Paton cross that Sidlow perhaps could have collected, was headed home by Goulden. A second defeat on the run looked inevitable for Liverpool but ten minutes later they were extremely unlucky not to get back into the game when a header from Balmer was cleared by Winter from what appeared, "to be a position feet inside the goal." Despite their protests to both referee and linesman however, all Liverpool got was a corner. A goal was the least their play deserved.

Liverpool defend a corner kick away at Chelsea in January 1946. Ray Lambert is on the near (left-hand) post,
then Paisley, Fagan, Laurie Hughes heading away, Sidlow, Taylor and Jones the no. 2 at the far post.

In manager Harry Hibbs, the former England and Birmingham goalkeeper, the Saddlers also had someone with previous experience of dumping Liverpool out of the cup. Liverpudlians with long memories will have remembered that it was he who put paid to their dreams at Anfield in 1931 when he produced a man-of-the-match display as the Reds drew a third round home tie against the Midlanders, eventually losing the replay 2-0.

Interest in this tie, the first-ever competitive meeting between Walsall and Liverpool, was understandably high and away fans were advised not to apply for seats as the hosts could, "sell the stand ten times over," and that the, " allocation will all go to our own supporters." Nevertheless, as snow storms swept across Britain and power was cut off in many parts of the country, a healthy contingent of Reds journeyed to the Midlands to roar on their heroes as they got their FA Cup campaign underway. Despite both clubs agreeing to wear their home colours a late change of heart by London referee Mr G Clarke, who feared red and claret was too much of a clash, meant Liverpool took to the field in their white away shirts and Walsall in blue.

The pitch, inspected thoroughly by Kay prior to kick-off, had been heavily sanded and it was the home side that adapted quicker to the difficult conditions with Gilbert Alsop, a veteran of the 1933 team, going close in the first minute, before Sidlow was then forced into a early save by Doug Lishman, a player who just three years later would line-up against Liverpool for Arsenal in the Cup Final at Wembley.

Training at Anfield took place no matter the weather. From left to right; Taylor, Ramsden, Fagan, Stubbins and Balmer.

Walsall were revelling in the superiority they had shown during the opening exchanges and only four minutes had passed when their bright start paid dividends. Laurie Hughes conceded a corner and from the resultant set-piece Lishman played it short to Albert Newman. His cross caused a frantic goalmouth scramble from which centre-forward Fred Kelly, "stabbed the ball home," to fire Walsall into a surprise lead.

There was no time for Liverpool to be shell-shocked though because within seconds they had fortuitously levelled when, from an Eastham centre, defender Reg Foulkes, "beat his own goalkeeper with an intended headaway." Goalkeeper Jack Lewis was taken, "completely by surprise," and could only knock it onto the underside of the bar, from where it bounced downwards and over the line, with Done on hand to knock it in if it hadn't already entered the net.

"Away went [Walsall's] hard won advantage," or so we thought. The spirited Saddlers stunned their more illustrious visitors once again in the 22nd minute of what was turning out to be a thrilling cup-tie. The limping inside-forward Dennis Wilshaw, on loan from near neighbours Wolverhampton Wanderers, was the scorer, finding space on the left edge of the Liverpool area and cutting inside to, "score with ease." Phil Taylor led the protests, claiming that Wilshaw was in an offside position but the appeal fell on deaf ears and the goal stood.

Shortly after the half hour mark it was Walsall's turn to appeal for a linesman's flag but play was waved on once again and Done, although a reported two-yards offside, raced through and, "wisely finished," to draw Liverpool level for a second time. A minute later, with the Walsall players still coming to terms with what they believed was a gross injustice, Liddell cut inside and drove a shot past goalkeeper Lewis to put Liverpool ahead for the first time in the match.

Five goals and just over half an hour gone - this was classic. "Blood and thunder cup-tie football," at its best. From here on in though there was only ever going to be one winner and, "once in the lead Liverpool changed the complexion of the match."

Any hopes the hosts, and indeed any neutral observers, may have had of witnessing an upset faded further just after the break when Balmer, showing, "first-rate promptitude and power," struck twice in 15 minutes to seal victory. The first, after 48 minutes, followed neat wing play by Liddell who, "cut in and flicked the ball out to Balmer," leaving the skipper with the task of, "smashing the ball home." Shortly after the hour mark he doubled his tally with a first-time shot from Taylor's centre.

At 5-2 it was game over and Walsall's spirited challenge slowly fizzled out. Lewis pulled off a fine save to deny Liddell his second of the afternoon and Taylor missed an open goal in the closing stages as chances went begging to increase Liverpool's margin of victory. It had been an exciting game, "and only the action of the boy who kicked Bob Paisley as he left the ground marred the aftermath."

According to Leslie Edwards, the Reds, "finally won playing exhibition football," but any more goals would have been harsh on Walsall who, "went on trying to the end when it had become obvious that it was not their day." The Daily Post scribe was quick to note that Liverpool's passage into round four had been secured with the help of, "two or three rubs of the green," but it did little to change his belief that this could be their year and he quickly countered that, "no club reaches Wembley without a measure of good luck." Whether fortune had played its part or not, Liverpool were safely through and for players, officials and supporters alike, that is all what mattered.

Five top-flight sides – Aston Villa, Blackpool, Huddersfield, Leeds and Sunderland – experienced no such 'luck' and suffered the embarrassment of crashing out at the first hurdle against lower division opposition, while on an afternoon of thrills and spills the length and breadth of the country, Chelsea and Arsenal fought out a 1-1 draw in the tie of the round before 70,000 at Stamford Bridge. Third round day had certainly lived up to expectations and fingers were now crossed for another favourable Liverpool draw in the next round.

Liverpool v Bolton Wanderers
Saturday 18 January 1947

"Nothing tickled the crowd's fancy more than Jones' coolness and his dummying of outside-left Wrigglesworth and Lofthouse. Both were cajoled into thinking that he must pass back to Minshull whereas, at the last moment, he turned the ball and went on to make the clearance himself."

Contact, Liverpool Football Echo

Victory over Walsall had come as a timely boost to the morale of a Liverpool squad that was seemingly suffering from a festive hangover and, as they made their return to league action after a two-week absence, hopes were high that it could act as a springboard for them to get their weakening title challenge back on the track. Two successive league defeats had taken the shine off what had been a positive first half to the season but there was plenty of renewed confidence around Anfield as the Reds prepared for the visit of a Bolton Wanderers side that they had already beaten 3-1 at Burnden Park back in September – a result that proved the catalyst for the 12-game unbeaten run that had taken them to the top of the table inthe first place.

The Trotters had gone from bad to worse after that game and were languishing in 16th place, just two points off the relegation places and without a league win since the first week in December – a dismal run of seven games and which included a 5-0 thumping at leaders Wolves – but like Liverpool they had put five past lower division opposition in the cup a week earlier.

The big surprise ahead of the match was the announcement that Cyril Sidlow was to be dropped, with the board of directors citing his poor form of late as the reason. Stepping in to take his place was Minshull, who had proved himself a more than able deputy when Sidlow was out injured earlier in the campaign and who was, ironically, a native of Bolton. Unfortunately, while Sidlow was keeping goal for the second string in a 2-2 draw at Burnden Park, his replacement endured an afternoon to forget against his home-town club. On the same day, 12 people were injured following an explosion in the Mersey Tunnel and Liverpool's championship aspirations also suffered a severe jolt.

The early signs were encouraging enough and Minshull found himself with little to do as Liverpool began stronger in what was a thrilling start to the game. Before a Bolton player had even touched the ball Stubbins glanced a header just inches wide of the far post from a Liddell centre and an opening goal seemed only a matter of time away. An offside decision that went against Balmer soon after was highly questionable, although there could be no question about the paucity of his subsequent left-footed shot, "he only half hit the ball when not more than seven yards out," noted *Contact* and, "even then he was wide."

It was a moment that set the tone for the remainder of the half as Liverpool failed to convert a host of chances during a one-sided first period, the highlight of which was a, "scintillating round of passing...that left Bolton's players chasing shadows." But as the ball was switched swiftly from one end to the other a misunderstanding between Stubbins and Nivvy saw a promising move eventually flounder. Liddell, Stubbins and Balmer were all guilty of squandering good goalscoring opportunities, with the latter incurring the crowd's wrath when, with another close-range effort he, "was as wide as the Atlantic."

It wasn't all one way traffic however, and Bolton looked anything but a side struggling at the wrong end of the table. According to the Football Echo they, "were playing as well as any side at Anfield for some time," and the Liverpool defence had to be on their guard throughout, especially with recent signing from Manchester United Billy Wrigglesworth living up to his surname. Jones and his fellow defenders however, were enjoying another fine game and few Bolton attacks came to fruition at this stage.

But while all was well at the back, up front Liverpool's woeful wastefulness continued. Of the five front men only Eastham, "with the ball delivered in unselfish manner to his comrades," caught the eye with many believing that this was his best game yet in a red shirt. Too often though his fellow attackers, "having beaten defences by subtle art, swift driving force, and fairly good combination," failed to find the target. "It seems as though they were pitying Stan Hanson, saying, 'He's only a Liverpool lad.'" *Bee* also noted that the Bolton keeper should;

"pass a vote of thanks to the forwards for failure to trouble him when five times Liverpool had no-one to hinder them. The easier the chance to mark a goal the more certain the ball

was crashed. They crash shots rather than walk them in. Cause, too, may be found in lack of confidence, fear of outraged onlookers, or the feeling that the chance was too easy to miss."

Whatever the reason; such profligacy was to cost Liverpool. They began the second-half in much the same vein as the first and, with the Kop roaring them on, they remained the better team, but once Bolton managed to do what the Reds couldn't the game changed dramatically. Hughes was penalised for making what many thought, "a successful tackle," on Lofthouse and from the resultant free-kick the visitors took an unexpected lead, "the ball was put into the goalmouth, and [Malcolm] Barass beat Minshull with his head as the goalkeeper came out to make the catch."

That was on 61 minutes and just moments later Liverpool suffered another, more devastating blow, when Hughes was forced out of the action, with what was later revealed to be a broken bone in his ankle. The trailing hosts were left to play the remainder with just ten men. It was an incident that took the wind completely out of Liverpool's sails. After being, "harassed and perplexed for nearly an hour," Bolton were suddenly revived and, "with a live wire like [Nat] Lofthouse to lead them, were always a menace after the opening goal." Within two minutes they had doubled their advantage, "Minshull this time got to a high ball and pushed it away, but before he or any other had time to recover Lofthouse had slammed the ball into the goal from ten yards range."

The points were sealed and Liverpool could do nothing but struggle on in vain until finally being put out of their misery by the final whistle. Before then Bolton found time to increase their lead, "with the best goal of the day...a strong, longish, glorious drive by [Willie] Moir," from 30-yards and the Reds were left to ruefully reflect on a game that should have been sewn up before the break. Liverpool, "could and should have won by a wide margin," wrote *Bee*, but, "in front of goal they were at their worst...they screwed, sliced and pulled like a truly bad golfer."

With Wolves slumping to a surprise 4-1 defeat at Brentford and second-placed Preston being held to goalless draw at Charlton things could have been worse, but Manchester United's 4-2 victory at third-placed Middlesbrough saw them move above the Reds who now occupied fifth position.

Despite seeing their side suffer such a heavy loss thousands of fans hung around Anfield at the end in the hope of getting their hands on tickets for the following weeks FA Cup tie at home to Grimsby – further proof, if needed, of the lure of the competition. Their tempers may have been frayed after the performance against Bolton but not their loyalty and, "the supporter will declare all is forgiven if the players win next Saturday."

Liverpool v Grimsby Town (FA Cup 4th round)
Saturday 25 January 1947

*"Have a care caustic Liverpool supporter, that you don't slip on the slippery street today.
This is to remind you of the dangers the players faced on Saturday."*

Bee, Liverpool Daily Post

The fourth round of the FA Cup came as a welcome relief to Liverpool. After suffering three straight losses in the league, the wheels were in danger of falling off their championship-chasing bandwagon and it was to the cup that the Reds now channelled their energies. The prospect of a day out in the sun at Wembley may have still been a long way off on what was another bitterly cold wintry afternoon at Anfield, but the widely held belief among most supporters and pundits alike was that it was the FA Cup rather than the First Division where Liverpool's best chance of success lay.

Despite suffering with a temperature of 102 degrees earlier in the week, chairman Bill McConnell was determined that, "nothing will keep me from this game," and true to his word he braved the icy blasts to take his usual seat in the directors' box just prior to kick-off.

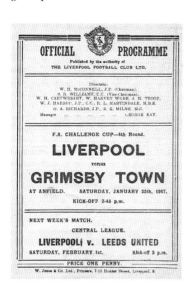

With plenty of space on the terraces and, "cup-tie rattles," being largely conspicuous by their absence there seemed to be a distinct lack of big-game atmosphere about this fourth round tussle. It was reported that, "in no league match this season had the ground been so empty near to the time of kick-off," but still a crowd in excess of 45,000 were in attendance to see if the Reds could win through to the next stage against a side they'd already defeated heavily away from home earlier in the season. With the memories of that emphatic 6-1 rout at Blundell Park still fresh in the memory Liverpool were clear favourites to overcome the mid-table Mariners who, like the Reds, had little previous success in the cup to boast about.

Their best run in the competition had come the season immediately prior to the outbreak of war when they reached the last four. There they met Wolves at Old Trafford where a then record crowd for the ground - 76,962 – saw Grimsby suffer the misfortune of losing their keeper early on through injury and, not surprisingly, they subsequently crashed to a 5-0 defeat. On the only other occasion they'd gone that far in the FA Cup, Arsenal ended their Wembley dreams with a 1-0 semi-final win at Leeds Road in 1936. Grimsby hopes of reaching round five on this occasion where not helped by the unavailability through injury of two key players; centre-half Harry Betmead and full-back Norman Vincent, but they went into the game boosted by a 2-1 home win over Sheffield United the previous week.

Despite a mild thaw the ground remained hard underneath the snow. *Bee* later reported that the famous Norwegian ice-skater of the time Sonja Henie, "would have found her steps faltering at Anfield." As a result of the poor state of the pitch, "great expectations faded through no fault of either side," and, "every man at the start of his movement found his feet sliding underneath him." Indeed, Liverpool almost suffered before the first whistle had been blown when Stubbins slipped and fell heavily on his back while attempting a shot on goal during the warm-up. Fortunately he was fine, but as the action got underway it was patently clear for all to see that, "conditions made every step a lottery."

With both sets of players finding it difficult to turn at speed, the deceiving surface was a great leveller and a cautious opening ensued as a result. With Hughes missing due to the injury sustained against Bolton, the ever-dependable Jones made a seamless transition from left-back to centre-half. Ramsden returned for his first senior appearance in almost seven weeks, while Done replaced a tired Nivvy and, in the only other change to the side that had crashed to defeat against Bolton, Sidlow, not surprisingly, earned an instant recall after his brief flirtation with the reserves.

Jones was quickly in thick of the action and overcame an early uncharacteristic slip to beat inside-forward Billy Cairns in a compromising aerial duel, while down the other end a Stubbins back-heel set up Liddell for a shot that was fired wide. With the game gradually opening up Town keeper Tweedy was forced to punch a Liddell corner clear and it fell invitingly to Taylor who, "ballooned the ball in a half-volley on to the roof of the stand." When it finally came back down to earth, referee Mr T S Norcott of Gloucester examined it and called for another. Maybe it was the change of ball that did the trick but, almost immediately, Liverpool took the lead.

Liddell was again involved, crossing from the left to where an unmarked Stubbins was lurking and Tweedy, rooted to his line, "appeared to miss the curvature of [the] header," as the ball nestled into the corner of the net. Moments later the visitors went close to snatching an equaliser through Horace Wallbanks who got himself beyond the Liverpool defence and into a good scoring position. Fortunately, Ramsden was tailing him all the way and pressured him into a, "weak shot which Sidlow collected easily."

Grimsby threatened again soon after and left-winger Billy Wardle smashed a shot against the bar from the edge of the box, although the whistle had already gone for offside, and the half ended with Liddell thinking he had scored, "with a fine shot from a headed pass by Done," but he too had strayed offside and had failed to hear the whistle.

A mazy dribble down the right wing by Eastham got the second half off to an exciting start. He eventually pulled the ball back to Balmer and his effort was deflected across goal to Liddell who went agonisingly close to connecting for what would have been a certain goal. The all-important second wasn't long in coming however, and just eight minutes after the restart Liverpool all but booked their place in the fifth round. Tommy Blenkinsop was penalised for handball and from the subsequent set-piece Taylor looked to the left but confused the opposition defence by passing low to the right. Anticipating the move, Done made his run and although Tweedy advanced off his line to narrow the angle, "the Liverpool man turned the ball into the net."

It was a well taken effort and one that drew words of praise from *Bee*;

> *"Done's conclusive goal was testimony to a man working hard and willingly and effectively. He pre-judged Taylor's free-kick notion and showed that someone was planning before the game began."*

The busy Liddell, uncharacteristically involved in an ongoing argument with Town's veteran wing-half Alex Hall following an earlier altercation, almost added a third but was denied by some fine goalkeeping from Tweedy that earned the Grimsby number one a round of applause from the home fans. To their credit, the visitors continued to try and play football, "in conditions that were not suited to it," but when they eventually became dispirited Liverpool's passage into round five became a comfortable one and just to prove there was no ill-feeling at the final whistle Hall waited to congratulate Liddell as they left the pitch.

Had the Liverpool forwards performed more as a unit the winning margin could have been a lot more and, although it was Stubbins and Done who'd got the decisive goals, *Bee* believed once again that it was a victory built from the back.

> *"The three half-backs gave the line the key on which to reach top notes. Taylor, outstanding in feint and finely-judged etchings before passing the ball; Jones as pivot (he plays where you care to test him and is always sure in his delivery of the ball) and Paisley (who scours the ball with never-ending energy and still finds time to connect up with his forwards), were superb."*

With neighbours Everton losing 2-1 away to Second Division Sheffield Wednesday, Liverpool were now the city's sole representatives in the competition and with six other top-flight sides, including Wolves and Manchester United also exiting at this stage the twin towers were suddenly starting to shimmer tantalisingly in the distance. But would progress in the cup be to the detriment of their title pursuit?

Everton v Liverpool
Wednesday 29 January 1947

*"Though Everton won, and deservedly, one cannot do other than name Phil Taylor
as chief exponent of control in every facet of the half-back game. So much so that in
his case one felt supernatural skills enabled him to play as though the pitch were gently
yielding and devoid of mischief. His work cried out for the glory of a goal."*

Liverpool Daily Post

As the dust settled on FA Cup fourth round weekend the moods on either side of
Stanley Park couldn't have been more contrasting ahead of the 85th Merseyside
derby. Having dropped down a place in the table to sixth, by virtue of the point
gained by Blackpool at Aston Villa the previous Saturday, the Reds were now being
dismissed as serious title contenders but revelling in the progress they were making
in the cup. Buoyed by the win over Grimsby, Monday's lunch-time draw brought
pre-derby training in Birkdale to a standstill and the prospect of a mouth-watering
fifth round tie at home to either holders Derby County or Chelsea had the players
and staff - all gathered around the wireless to hear the draw - buzzing with
anticipation.

By contrast, Everton were trying to come to terms with their shock exit at
Hillsborough. They were still clearly reeling from the departure of Joe Mercer to
Arsenal the previous month. To make matters worse their new number nine - Jock
Dodds - signed from Blackpool in November and who had netted nine times in his
first 14 games for the Blues, had suffered an injury that would keep him on the
sidelines until early April. Just three points and five places separated them from the
dreaded drop zone and for a team that were champions in the last league season
before the war, not to mention runners-up to Sheffield United in the 1945/46
Football League North, it was clearly not good enough in the eyes of their
frustrated supporters.

The Toffees were a team in crisis. Seen by Evertonians as being more vital for the
Blues than the Reds, this was also a match that the men from Anfield had to win if
their faltering title dreams were to be kept alive. "If they are to regain the
opportunity of making a championship challenge," said the Daily Post then,
"Liverpool must win against their neighbours."

With cup-ties taking preference over league games the Goodison clash, originally
due to be played the previous Saturday, had been rescheduled for a Wednesday
afternoon 2.45pm kick-off, and it was Liverpool, despite having not won in the
league since Boxing Day, who the bookies made favourites. As so often happens
when two local rivals meet though, league positions and current form counted for
nothing.

The adverse weather, which had resulted in the Newsham Park lake being frozen solid for a week, restricted the gate to a surprisingly low 30,000 – one of the poorest in Mersey derby history and a complete contrast to the chaotic scenes witnessed at Anfield when the two sides had gone head-to-head earlier in the season. Those who braved the sub-zero temperatures however, were treated to a spectacle far better than the eventual score-line suggests;

> *"beautifully played and handled, clean, never lacking in interest and generally measuring up to, if not beyond, standards produced with the ground in perfect condition. This proved to be one of the most notable of Liverpool-Everton conflicts."*

Harley for Ramsden was the only Liverpool change to the side that had got past Grimsby in the cup four days previous, while Everton did likewise, replacing Tommy McIlhatton with the impish Republic of Ireland international Alec Stevenson.

"The cold was arctic and the wind whistled through half-empty stands," as play commenced and, "on a brick hard ground," both sides found conditions difficult, with a layer of snow covering the pitch and players constantly struggling to keep their feet. Liverpool adapted, "extraordinary well," and during a bright opening 20 minutes;

> *"did everything one could expect, except master the final barrier of that Welsh mountain of enthusiasm, [Jack] Humphreys, and full-backs who saved a special effort for their neighbours."*

Taylor was the first to try his luck with a, "shot that was not far off the bull's eye," and a powerful strike from Done cannoned back to Stubbins but he fired his long-range rebound high and wide of the target. Done, a long-time target of Everton, had once again been the subject of transfer speculation in the days leading up to the game. This time it was Blackburn Rovers who were reported to have bid a paltry £5,000 for his services and, again, it came to nothing with Reds' boss George Kay swatting it aside with a typical sharp riposte, "I've heard nothing of it. Do Blackburn think we are a Third Division club?"

Having withstood Liverpool's early onslaught the under-fire Toffeemen gradually grew in confidence and managed to raise their game to a level they had failed to reach in recent weeks. Inside-forward Wally Fielding let fly with a venomous drive that Sidlow managed to handle with confidence and McIlhatton shot narrowly over the crossbar as Everton enjoyed a spell of pressure themselves.

"The game was interesting, but naturally had not the bite about it due to the conditions," wrote *Stork*, but the play continued to flow from end to end and, just before the interval, Liddell went the closest yet to drawing first blood. Cutting inside on the right, "he hit the ball hard and true, and [Ted] Sagar had to save at his second attempt."

Jackie Balmer, Phil Taylor and Albert Shelley talk tactics during training at Anfield.

There wasn't much to choose between the two teams but as the second-half wore on Liverpool's earlier lack of potency in front of goal was to prove costly as Everton gained the ascendancy once again. A minute before the hour mark, in what was to be the game's decisive goal, Eddie Wainwright, in his first appearance at centre-forward, cleverly heading home a Fielding corner whilst under pressure from Cyril Done and Sidlow. Liverpool's attempts to salvage at least a point were not helped by the loss of Done, who was badly shaken in a fall when challenging Sagar and, although he later returned at outside-left, he became a passenger, "and a severe handicap to the side a goal down."

Apart from a brief ten-minute Reds' rally, during which time the Everton keeper twice almost allowed the icy ball to slip through his fingers, "without paying the extreme penalty," the Blues' one-goal lead never looked in any real danger and it was the home side who ran out winners to claim local bragging rights and, perhaps more importantly, a crucial two points in their battle against the drop. Despite Liverpool's loss, most of the post-match plaudits went to Phil Taylor for an, "outstanding half-back display."

Victory for Everton lifted them up to the heady heights of 13th (10th would be the highest peak they would scale this season) and left Liverpool seven points off the pace of leaders Wolves, although more worrying now was the presence of Aston Villa, Stoke and Sheffield United creeping up behind them.

"But for Done's injury, Liverpool might not have been beaten," the Daily Post sympathetically noted. "They need not be disconsolate in this defeat." Their FA Cup run aside however, these were worrying times for the Reds. With just eight points now separating first place from ninth it was getting tighter at the top with every passing week. There was no more room for error. As one of the coldest January's on record drew to a close, this fourth straight league defeat had left Liverpool's title ambitions hanging by a thread.

Chapter Nine
Is the 'Double' on?

Leeds United v Liverpool
Saturday 1 February 1947

*"That it would be a freakish game was evident from the way the ball dragged
in the snow...[and] moving the ball the length of the field was a feat in
itself in such conditions. On the wings it was slowed up by the minor drifts
and a ball could scarcely be too hard hit to the winger."*

Ranger, Liverpool Football Echo.

If Liverpool were to keep alive their interest in the title race then their faltering league form had to be arrested. And fast. Four straight First Division defeats had severely dented their once realistic title aspirations and it was widely perceived that another loss would bring to an end all hopes of championship glory. For this reason, the stakes were high as the Reds made their way across the Pennines to take on Leeds United, a team in just as desperate a need for points, albeit at the opposite end of the table. The struggling Yorkshiremen were two points adrift at the bottom and, in the view of many, their fate was already sealed. Their sorry predicament put Liverpool's troubles into perspective but it seemed a tailor-made fixture for the Reds to reignite their championship challenge.

In complete contrast to the weak resistance they showed at Anfield in September however, Leeds belied their lowly position with what was arguably one of their more impressive performances of a dismal campaign.

Liverpool's response to defeat in the derby was to recall veteran winger Nivvy, who returned at the expense of Eastham, and with Fagan back from injury to replace Done it was hoped the forwards could rediscover their scoring touch.

After a week in which much of Britain had been coated in a heavy blanket of frost, two inches of snow covered what was a hard, uneven, playing surface and, although getting the ball under control and passing it just a short distance was difficult, the two teams coped well and managed to put on an entertaining show for the 25,000 crowd who braved the freezing temperatures. Nevertheless, in what was a bright opening there were chances at either end. George Ainsley – yet another player who had pulled on the red shirt as a guest during the war – set the game alight when he unleashed a, "bullet shot," from 35 yards that Sidlow did well to tip over. Then good wing play by the returning Nivvy embarrassed both Tom Holley and Eddie Bannister before the South African lost control at the vital moment when a goal looked certain.

After 12 minutes, and somewhat against the run of play, Liverpool took the lead with a, "good goal." Stubbins was the scorer, his 11th of the season, tapping the ball into an empty net from close-range after Fagan had collided with goalkeeper Jack Hodgson while chasing a loose a ball. After breaking his arm saving a Stubbins penalty back in September, Hodgson had only recently returned to action and must have been sick of the sight of Liverpool's number nine. "The lead so much inspired Liverpool that they did pretty much as they liked for some minutes," with Fagan, "making an appreciable difference to the attack." Despite the hazardous conditions the football being played by both teams was, "fast and quite often thrilling," although the hosts were prone to a more "route one," approach at times.

Balmer went close to increasing Liverpool's advantage with, "a pulled shot from a Stubbins pass," while at the opposite end, although the Leeds attack couldn't be faulted for effort the, "90 per cent enthusiasm and 10 per cent ability," they were showing was one of the main reasons why they found themselves languishing at the foot of the table. Their best move of the match came midway through the first half and only the heroic goalkeeping of Cyril Sidlow, with two stunning one-handed saves in quick succession, denied them two certain goals. The first was from a John Short effort and then, "in an astonishing minute of Leeds superiority," the Wales' number one did it again to keep out a low shot from winger Dennis Grainger.

Bill Jones was an equally impressive performer at the back for Liverpool and his excellent man-marking job on bustling Geordie centre-forward Ainsley did not go unnoticed. Described a few weeks previously as a, "perfectly polished diamond," and, "the world's best," Jones was living up to his blossoming reputation and enhancing his claims for an international call-up.

The Leeds pressure continued though, and after a penalty appeal was, "rightly disregarded," Sidlow again had to be at his best when flicking the ball over the bar with one-hand to prevent Aubrey Powell from registering. At this point it was, "all Leeds," but Liverpool responded with, "one of the greatest shots," Leslie Edwards, "had ever seen." It came via the boot of Liddell and although Hodgson was well beaten it crashed off the bar and out towards the corner flag. Then, in what was another close shave for the hosts, centre-half Holley over-hit a back pass that stopped just short of crossing the line when, luckily for him, it stuck in the snow.

If either chance had gone it may have killed off the hosts, but they began the second period in much the same way as they had finished the first and after a further flurry of attacks they eventually drew level in the 57th minute through Grainger, who raced onto a fine pass, "to take the ball on a few yards and score as he pleased."

The goal was no more than Leeds deserved and it was they who now looked the more likely side to go on and snatch victory. With just over half an hour remaining and with both teams striving for the goal that would clinch a priceless two points, "the game became a bit rough," and the tackles began to fly in recklessly. Taylor was injured and required treatment, "after poking his foot at the ball to clear," and, "Liverpool were failing now because [like Leeds] they lashed the ball upfield in haphazard fashion rather than progress by more thoughtful methods."

With just five minutes left on the clock Stubbins came back to haunt Hodgson once more by popping up to net the all-important winner. Again Fagan was involved, sliding a clever ball through a host of players and Stubbins', "prompt shot on the turn was in the goal before Hodgson fully appreciated what was happening."

In the dying minutes Liverpool's number nine twice went close to completing his hat-trick but a greater winning margin would have flattered the visitors and, "only have emphasised Leeds' bitter regret at having shot too petulantly." In what would become a tim -honoured trait of future title winning teams, Liverpool had, "[come] along, cheekily, near the end to take a leading goal and points as precious as gold."

"Luckless Leeds," were left to bemoan a 16th league defeat of the season and the Reds, although way below their best, left Elland Road more than satisfied with a result that saw them make up some vital ground on the chasing pack – three of whom crashed to heavy defeats on the same afternoon; Preston at Stoke (5-0), Man United at Arsenal (6-2) and Middlesbrough at home to Sheffield United (2-4).

With Wolves' match at Portsmouth falling foul of the weather, sixth-placed Liverpool were now five points off the leaders and had played a game more. Only time would tell if this victory was to be a significant turning point of the season but the win had certainly handed Liverpool a title lifeline and gave them the lift they needed going into the following week's cup-tie.

Liverpool v Derby County (FA Cup 5th round)
Saturday 8th February 1947

"This was an Anfield display of distinction; a cup-tie epic, with spectators unanimous on the verdict and on the view that the winners had not one weak link."

Bee, Liverpool Daily Post

Never before had interest in a cup-tie at Anfield been so great. Relatively easy victories over Walsall and Grimsby in the previous rounds had heightened the belief that this could finally be Liverpool's year to win the FA Cup and the fifth round visit of Derby County was eagerly anticipated.

Such optimism among Kopites was nothing new. "Anfield followers feel convinced that this is their favourites' year and that the cup will find a place in the Liverpool boardroom." Usually, however such optimism didn't last beyond February. On only four occasions in the 20 seasons that bridged the two world wars had the Reds progressed further than this round. Their dire cup record was the source of much amusement among followers of other clubs but if the current cup holders could be overcome then the feeling was the rest of the country would have to take their claims seriously.

Defending a Liddell free-kick.

With Liverpool finally back to winning ways in the league, and Derby desperate to defend the trophy they had won so gloriously beneath the twin towers against Charlton the previous April it was a contest that had captured the imagination of everyone, not just those on Merseyside and Derbyshire. Indeed, such was the nationwide appeal of this - the undoubted tie of the round - that the BBC sent their esteemed radio commentator Raymond Glendenning up from London to cover it.

In the build-up to the game club officials reported an unprecedented demand for tickets and the row which subsequently broke out threatened to overshadow the build-up. Stand tickets, "went like wild fire," and many supporters were left disgruntled. "Liverpool are trying the patience of their supporters too far. We have had a raw deal," wrote W Hall of Agate Street. "This is not playing the game," said another, "regular supporters who pay at the gate have not been considered." With a quote that could be taken from many local supporters today, another added that, "Liverpool are sacrificing a lot of regular and loyal supporters for those who merely go to cup-ties."

As a way to appease fans a decision was taken by the directors to issue 5,000 tickets for the Paddock, 25% of which went to the visitors. These went on sale at 10 o'clock in the morning two days before the match and, not surprisingly, and despite severe snowstorms, they were quickly snapped up. Long queues formed well before the sale commenced with a shipyard worker from Bootle being the first in the queue at 6am! Still there were rumblings of discontent among the Reds' massive fan-base but luckily for them another 400 were made available on the morning of the match due to Derby's failure to sell their full allocation.

With a big crowd expected, the matchday programme urged spectators to pack into the centre of the various terraced enclosures so that the entrances were clear for any latecomers, while a warning was also issued to the young LFC urchins of the day;

> *"Complaints have been received about oranges and other missiles being thrown on the playing pitch from the Boys' Pen. This conduct must stop otherwise the facilities enjoyed by the boys will be withdrawn and the Pen moved to a point where missiles cannot be thrown on the ground."*

Meanwhile, manager George Kay found himself inundated with good luck charms from superstitious supporters but, "magic spats, the rabbits foot or credulous faith in the infallibility of a black cat with green eyes," was not for him and this, "hard-head and phlegmatic unbeliever," while grateful for the gifts, was pinning his hopes solely on football ability.

Unsure of just what state the pitch would be in come Saturday, the directors pondered meticulously over their team selection at the weekly board meeting before eventually opting for just one change; Done for Nivvy. The biggest surprise was the tactical switch that saw Fagan moved to outside-right, a position he played in for Preston in the 1937 Cup Final at Wembley.

As for the opposition, despite not enjoying the best of seasons in the league and having already been on the receiving end of a 4-1 thrashing by Liverpool in October, Derby's reputation as one of the best cup sides of recent times remained intact and they were boosted by the return from injury of centre forward Angus Morrison and big Jackie Stamps, formerly of New Brighton and scorer of two goals in the previous seasons Cup Final.

Noted for their fast, open, and good sporting football the Rams lined up at Anfield with seven of their cup-winning team on show but most notably without Peter, "the Great," Doherty, who had left for Huddersfield in December after a much-publicised falling out with members of the Derby hierarchy. As a consequence, three directors resigned in protest and an even greater burden of responsibility fell on the shoulders of his strike partner Raich Carter, once the youngest player to captain a championship winning side and also the only player to win the FA Cup either side of the war. With 15 league and cup goals already under his belt in 1946/47 the veteran Carter, now approaching 35, was considered the biggest danger to Liverpool's cup hopes.

Many felt that Liverpool's best chance of success would come on heavy ground but the weather was not in Liverpool's favour. Of the eight grounds due to host cup-ties that weekend, Anfield reported the smallest amount of snowfall – just two inches – and after referee Mr Wiltshire passed the pitch as playable Liverpool officials decided not to remove the layer of snow that had already fallen in the hope it would soften the ground by, "acting as a cushion." By kick-off time however, the light covering of snow had turned to crusted ice and, far from being a cushion, conditions were decidedly difficult underfoot.

With a bitter wind blowing in from the banks of the Mersey the crowd was much lower than expected. "Ticket sharks were left outside the ground trying to sell at bargain prices." While congestion on the terraces wasn't a problem several supporters did require medical attention after collapsing as a result of the freezing conditions. It really was that cold! The cry from the majority of the near 45,000 fans who braved the sub-zero temperatures however, was, "if they can play, we can watch," and those of a red persuasion were rewarded for their commitment with a Liverpool performance that warmed their hearts if not their bodies.

Only the magnificent goalkeeping of pre-war England number one Vic Woodley prevented this tie from being a walkover in Liverpool's favour. Veteran Woodley was only in the team because Alec Grant had dislocated an elbow in the Rams' fourth round replay success over Chelsea and he had plenty to do. For the first three quarters of the match, on a surface that, "looked far more dangerous and treacherous than any Liverpool had played on during the cold spell," the Reds totally dominated their opponents but frustratingly had nothing to show for their efforts. Liddell was twice denied by the keeper, while Stubbins had the misfortune of seeing a well-struck shot come back off the bar. So impressive was Woodley's display between the sticks that Liddell went as far as congratulating him as the players left the field for half-time.

The Reds' cause was not helped when Balmer twisted his ankle as a result of the hard ground and was forced to swap positions with Fagan. As the last 15 minutes approached a replay seemed certain but, with the vociferous backing of the Kop ringing in their ears, Liverpool continued to push on and eventually they got the reward their endeavours warranted.

Liddell sent a soaring 30 yard pass deep into the Derby box where Balmer suddenly reappeared unopposed.

> *"His innate sense of positioning showed him the possibility of Liddell's centre landing slightly to the right. A long stride carried him inward and head slightly tucked in, he rammed the ball low to goal."*

It was a, "glorious header," through which to score. Anfield erupted and the "Liverpool crowd roared, roared and roared."

Not content with one goal the Reds immediately went on the hunt for another in order to kill the game off but Woodley pulled off yet more heroic saves to ensure a nail-biting finale. Liverpool's all-out attacking policy could have had dire consequences had Derby been able to hit them on the break, and an animated George Kay could be seen pounding the touchline in a desperate attempt to get his side to play safe.

Balmer's lone effort though, was enough. It was reported that there had been "few better [goals] and none as important," and it kept Liverpool's cup dream very much alive. They were in the last eight for the first time since 1932 and it had been a thoroughly deserved victory. "The prospect of a new name appearing on the FA Cup grows brighter," said *Ranger*, hinting that the fans may be right and this could possibly be Liverpool's year.

> "There is one all Merseyside is burning to see there but I must breathe it not, lest the sorrow and disappointment be laid at my door if it does not pan out that way, for daring to suggest it."

After years of hardship and failure in the cup chairman Bill McConnell was revelling in the success of the current team. As he reflected on what had been a memorable afternoon he added;

"At this stage it does not do to take things for granted, but I think our boys are good enough to advance yet one step further towards Wembley. Our form against Derby County was good enough for anything. There are still difficult obstacles ahead but they will be met with confidence."

This cup run was breathing new life into Liverpool's season. It was all starting to get very exciting once again.

Liverpool v Grimsby Town
Wednesday 12 February 1947

> *"On recent form they must have an outside chance...this may seem outlandishly impossible, but though we may appear to be in sight of the season's end, there is still a distance to be travelled, and the side, on present indications, seem capable of beating anyone."*

Leslie Edwards, Liverpool Daily Post

As Liverpool fans celebrated their famous victory over cup holders Derby the government ordered a widespread industrial shutdown in a desperate bid to prevent the entire country coming to a complete standstill. With coal unable to be transported because of the ever-worsening weather, power supplies were running dangerously low and a stark warning was issued that if such action was not taken now the nation could, within the days, find itself in a condition of total disaster. Emergency powers cuts were immediately put in place and this winter of increasing discontent had just got worse. As a consequence of the 'great switch-off' city streets were plunged into darkness, public transport was severely affected, newspapers suffered a reduction in size - as did match-day programmes, factories ground to a halt and millions of people found themselves temporarily out of work.

Football though somehow continued and in the only game of the day on Wednesday 12 February Cyril Done lit up Anfield with an electrifying performance as Liverpool took advantage of their nearest rivals not playing to firmly re-establish themselves in the title race. In light of the momentous weekend cup win a big crowd had been expected for this rearranged afternoon kick-off but just over 20,000 made it to Anfield – a clear sign of the deepening gloom that was descending over Britain.

On the pitch, with Balmer not having recovered from the ankle injury that forced him to be sent home from Anfield in a taxi on Saturday, Stan Palk came in for his Football League debut - yet another Liverpool debutant this season - and he did so with a glowing endorsement in the local press;

> *"when he returned last autumn it was a surprised manager who discovered that behind the immense beard was the youth who had promised to make good in his first team displays in 1939, 1940 and 1941. Those who have not seen him play since will be surprised to see how much he has filled out. That he has skill and enthusiasm is undoubted."*

With a thick layer of snow covering the Anfield turf, conditions were once again not conducive to playing the precise, clever game that Liverpool excelled at, but the Reds turned on the style here, dominating from almost start to finish against opponents they had comfortably beaten twice already this season.

The biggest surprise of the day was that it took until the 24th minute before Done broke the deadlock, the reason being that veteran Grimsby keeper George Tweedy was - once again against the Reds - in outstanding form. "It was Tweedy and Tweedy only who delayed the opening goal," reported Leslie Edwards. "Then Polk (sic) deliciously brought the ball to earth," and, "Done used his bump of anticipation to take a well-earned, well-placed goal."

The visitors had enjoyed a brief spell of early possession - during which time they twice hit the bar - and twice saw Jones come to Liverpool's rescue with vital clearances. This was all they could muster however, and once behind they retreated into their shell, allowing the Reds to take control. A quick-fire brace of goals from Fagan put the outcome of the points beyond question shortly after the half hour mark. Both goals emanated from, "left-wing spadework," and Fagan's task was to simply, "fire past the goalkeeper." From thereon in it was a procession. Five minutes before the break Done, "glided the ball through with his head beautifully for the fourth," to kill the game off as a contest and take, "all the heart out of the opposition." It remained 4-0 until five minutes from time when Done completed his second hat-trick of the season with what was the undoubted goal of the game – the culmination of a fine flowing move that saw the ball transferred from one penalty box to the other without an opposition player touching it.

Despite his treble goalscoring heroics it was not Done but Stubbins whose brilliant all-round display caught the eye of the watching pressmen. "Again [he] delighted with his subtle touches, telling passes and facility for finding the open spaces." Fellow marksman Fagan was also overlooked when the post-match praise was dished out. Indeed, the harsh assessment of one local reporter was that, "apart from getting those goals Fagan did not do a great deal." Not convinced the talented Scotsman was the answer to Liverpool's outside-right problem, the reporter here showed as much fickleness as the fans.

Perhaps even more strangely, especially after an emphatic 5-0 win, credit was also given to the defence, in particular Jones, whose performance at the back was such that, "the longer he plays there the more surely does he approach international standard." The two men alongside him - Paisley and Taylor - were also equally deserving of the plaudits that came their way and it was this talented half-back line that was later credited with being the foundation on which this latest Liverpool success was built;

> *"What struck me most again about the winners was the back-bone of half-back endeavour. Paisley was best but all were top class, and while they play on these lines the forward job will be made easy. Few clubs enjoy such effective football as comes from Taylor, Jones and Paisley."*

In terms of goal average, five without reply was certainly a boost to Liverpool. What was even more crucial however, were the points. Even though the night before *Ranger* had almost written off Liverpool's title challenge by claiming that, "in terms of league position, neither side is vitally in need of points," this, "solid and encouraging victory," garnered two more points and it sent Liverpool soaring up the table from seventh to second, level with Preston and Blackpool. Was the title challenge back on?

Had it not been for 34-year old Tweedy the Reds could well have ran up a double-figure score. The former England international, who'd won his one and only cap against Hungary at Highbury in 1936, and was now in his 17th season with the Mariners, "saved shots from all angles in wonderful style and dived on the cast-iron surface as if it was a feather bed."

"The side is now working better as a team than at any previous period this season,' concluded *Ranger*. What a difference two weeks make. A fortnight before the vultures were circling, ready to write off Liverpool's championship credentials. Now, as the fans headed home along the freezing cold and dimly lit Anfield streets, title talk was back on agenda.

Liverpool v Huddersfield Town
Saturday 22 February 1947

"Whatever earnest supporters of the Liverpool team may say about the fare served up, the fact remains that Liverpool won and Huddersfield Town stand convicted out of their own misses."

Bee, Liverpool Daily Post

After an enforced ten day break, the Reds returned to action on a day when the fixture list was decimated by postponements and 42,000 shivering fans huddled together at Anfield to see Liverpool turn in one of their poorest displays for some time. In what was a drab encounter - with few clear-cut scoring opportunities - the loyal supporters who made the effort were left far from enthralled by the fare served up in front of a snow covered Kop.

With more than half of the days scheduled Football League games falling foul of the arctic conditions that had now taken a vice like grip on the entire country however, they were lucky to see any action at all. A staggering 23 matches were called off, two more than the previous week and a new record. Luckily, Merseyside had escaped the worst but the weather was starting to seriously affect the nation's sporting programme, with football in particular, being hit hard. The previous week Liverpool's scheduled game away to Charlton had been cancelled. As a result the Reds slipped back to fifth in the table, overtaken by Blackpool, Middlesbrough and Stoke, whose games had all survived and who had all emerged victorious from the snowscape that seemed to cover the whole country.

Only three points separated Liverpool from top spot but, while every game was vital, victory at home to a struggling Huddersfield Town was imperative if they were to maintain their pursuit of Wolves. Despite this, it was clear for all to see that it was the FA Cup - in particular the forthcoming quarter-final tie with Birmingham - that was uppermost on the minds of a Liverpool side that showed just one change with the fit again Balmer returning in place of Palk.

"Liverpool made a voluntary emergency cut in their power," noted *Bee*. "They were not their exuberant selves." With referee Mr J Williams declaring the Anfield pitch playable early in the day, deceivingly clear blue skies greeted the entrance of the two teams onto, "the rink." On what was another treacherous ice-bound playing surface the Reds seemed more concerned with avoiding injury than trying to create chances and very few risks were taken against a Huddersfield side who, despite pulling off the high-profile signing of revered Irish international Peter Doherty from Derby in December, were still battling to avoid the drop alongside fellow Yorkshiremen Leeds United.

A better team than Huddersfield, "could have won this game with ease if they had shown sense near goal," and Liverpool were lucky not to be punished for their light-hearted approach. Given their plight at the wrong end of the table the Terriers appeared too anxious when near goal and wasted several good opportunities with the, "great mystery at Anfield," being, "how Huddersfield could take the ball up to goal so frequently by good workmanlike football and still fail to score."

With Liddell finding it tough against right-half George Howe, and the visitors packing their defence whenever Liverpool went forward, the home side struggled to create any noteworthy opportunities during the early stages. The best chances came at the opposite end where Harry McShane - father of future TV actor Ian - and Doherty were combing well to keep Liverpool's defence on high alert, the most notable coming when McShane fired narrowly over following a flowing two-man move. The bow-legged winger then hit a shot that was deflected for a corner and, moments later, "Huddersfield were most unlucky not to get a goal," when Alf Whittingham beat his man on the right flank and centred for Doherty who, "hitting the ball all too promptly, slashed it wide."

Huddersfield keeper Bob Hesford can do nothing to prevent Stubbins from scoring with a 20 yard shot.

Most of the Reds' best work came courtesy of skipper Fagan but, "the Liverpool attack was playing tenderly and rather erratically, and Huddersfield were making fewer mistakes." Jones roused the crowd with, "one superlatively good series of tackles in front of the main stand," but still it was the visitors who looked the most likely to break the deadlock. A cannon-ball shot from that man McShane ended in another narrow escape for Liverpool and Sidlow was by far the busier of the two keepers. Almost out of the blue Liddell struck the foot of the upright with a low shot and could only stand and stare as the ball rolled agonisingly across the face of goal and beyond the other post.

Lady luck however, was smiling on the Reds just minutes after this nearest of misses. Done, "sailed through from Paisley's throw-in, but instead of shooting himself, [he] unselfishly elected to make a square pass to Stubbins." Huddersfield centre-half George Hepplewhite looked to have it covered but, on the rock hard pitch he lost his footing and, "this left Stubbins with a clear opening, which he accepted," by promptly banging the ball past schoolmaster keeper Bob Hesford to score at the Kop end. It was a goal that came against the run of play but one Liverpool were most grateful for. Until then the supply line to the forwards had been virtually non-existent but;

> "the big leader's long leggy efforts showed him once more the ideal type of centre-forward who is fair as a jewel, graceful in transit and possessing a clinching shot. Stubbins asks but little and snaps up trifles without being selfish."

Shortly after this 37th minute opening goal Huddersfield suffered another blow when the influential McShane was forced to leave the field for treatment after appearing to injure his collar-bone following a collision with Jones. He was attended to by both his trainer and ambulance men but, after a minute, it became clear that he would be unable to carry on and he was led away with the applause of the Kop ringing in his ears. Whilst acknowledging the fine performance he'd put in, the sporting Kopites were also no doubt relieved to see him exit. As he made his way to hospital for further treatment - on what later turned out to be a dislocated shoulder - any hopes Huddersfield had of salvaging at least a point went with him.

Despite his exit Liverpool found it no easier against the ten men he left behind. Genuine efforts on goal remained few and far between, although the visitors went a bit too close for comfort following a misunderstanding at the back between Lambert and Sidlow. Fortunately, neither of the two Huddersfield players who followed it up, Whittingham and Albert Bateman, "could keep their feet well enough to deliver a shot."

Liverpool seemed content with the one goal advantage but, with such a slender lead, they were running the risk of throwing away what could be another crucial two points. Paisley required, "the refreshing iciness of the trainers sponge," to bring him round after getting his head in the way of a fiercely struck free-kick by Howe, while Doherty fired a shot straight at Sidlow after evading the offside trap. In a rare goalmouth incident at the other end Liverpool almost doubled their advantage due to another defensive mishap. Wing-half Eddie Boot was the culprit on this occasion and Balmer was there to seize on it but, unfortunately, his subsequent shot was blocked.

To their immense credit Town did not give up and continued to threaten until the end. *Contact* described the visitors as;

> *"workmanlike in all they did except when they came to the most important phase of the game, finishing off their own good work with a goal...right to the last Huddersfield were poor shooters."*

The relegation-threatened side had been far from disgraced and there's no doubt that had they not lost the services of McShane shortly before half-time they may have well travelled back across the Pennines with more to show for their efforts.

For the vast majority of the Anfield crowd the most welcome sound of the second half was the referee's final whistle, which confirmed not only that another two points were in the bag, but also that Liverpool remained firmly in the hunt for title. With three of the four sides above them also winning there was little change position-wise, but they did move up a place to fourth - ahead of Blackpool on goal average.

Perhaps more importantly in the Liverpool players' minds, especially ahead of the eagerly anticipated quarter-final, was the fact that they had all come through another game on an icy pitch injury-free and, although their performance would have given watching Birmingham boss Harry Storer little to worry about, *Bee* was in no doubt that;

> *"the evidence he takes back to his players will be false...whatever earnest supporters of the Liverpool team may say about the fare served up, the fact remains that Liverpool won and Huddersfield Town stand convicted out of their own misses."*

Chapter Ten
The 'Goal in the Snow'

Liverpool v Birmingham City (FA Cup quarter-final)
Saturday 1 March 1947

"An epidemic of Wembley-itis, a hugely infectious complaint, is imminent among the male population of Merseyside. Fortunately, the disease is not dangerous and causes no anxiety in medical circles, although occasionally it upsets the harmony of some family circles."

Ranger, Liverpool Echo

Wherever you went in Liverpool during the week leading up to the FA Cup quarter-final clash with Birmingham there was only one topic of conversation on everyone's lips. Cup fever had taken a stranglehold on the red half of the city and, try as you might, there was just no getting away from it. As with the previous round, interest in the tie was immense and, with Liverpool aiming to book a first semi-final appearance since 1914, there was once again a huge clamour for tickets. Having learnt their lesson against Derby though, just days after the draw was made Anfield officials declared it the first ever all ticket game in the city before setting the crowd limit at 52,000.

Following the initial sale to shareholders and season ticket holders, a general sale took place on the Sunday after the league game with Huddersfield. The streets around the ground had never seen anything like it and an estimated 50,000 turned up - more than had been at the game the previous day! With thousands of disappointed supporters eventually being turned away it wasn't long before counterfeit tickets, "the latest racket of the black marketers," were in circulation around Liverpool. The Police were called into investigate and club chairman Bill McConnell issued a warning via the Daily Mirror for fans to, "ascertain the source of issue of all tickets before buying."

Another problem ahead of the weekend was the ever worsening weather. Blizzards during the week had covered northern England in a blanket of snow and the game was in doubt until a mid-morning pitch inspection saw it passed as playable. A layer of snow still covered the surface however, and while the morning sunshine had helped to thaw it considerably condition were once again difficult underfoot. In later years, Albert Stubbins, the name that was to become forever synonymous with this game, recalled that;

"it was played on an ice bound pitch and this didn't help us in our efforts to play football. But nevertheless, it was an excellent cup-tie. Birmingham were indeed tough opposition.

They were a good strong team, maybe not a lot of frills, but certainly workmanlike and they weren't easy to beat."

Handily place for promotion in an extremely competitive Division Two, the Blues trailed just Manchester City and Burnley at the top, and were widely regarded as one of the strongest sides around. They were Football League South champions in 1945/46 and boss Harry Storer, the son of the former Liverpool goalkeeper of the same name and a native of West Derby, was adamant that his team were more than a match for the Reds. "Their record is no better than ours," he said with - at a time when the maximum wage put almost everyone on an even playing field - perhaps some justification. "They are just lucky to be in the First Division while we're in the Second."

City had already beaten top-flight opposition in the shape of Portsmouth, 1-0 at St Andrews in round four, and emphatically secured their place in the last eight with a 5-0 thrashing of Second Division leaders Man City. Add to that the experience they had gained during their run to the semi-final of the previous season's competition - when they were only beaten by eventual winners Derby County after a replay - and you had all the makings of a classic cup-tie. The Times certainly agreed and, despite Liverpool and Birmingham being a league apart, they reckoned there wasn't much to choose between the two third-placed sides in their respective divisions "Sound in defence and quick in attack...the game has very much the look of a draw about it."

Birmingham were pinning much of their hopes on lively inside-left Harold Bodle, another player who had slipped through the Liverpool net as a youngster after failing to impress during a trial, but it was future England goalkeeper Gil Merrick who was the rising star of their team, while they could also boast a Welsh international in the form of outside-left George Edwards as well as inside-right Neil Dougall who earlier in the season had won his one and only cap for Scotland.

With such credentials Liverpool certainly left nothing to chance. Jack Balmer and club official Jimmy McInnes had been to see Birmingham in action, while George Kay had, as ever, also done his homework. Showing the tactical acumen for which he has now sadly been forgotten, he was to get his tactics spot on to make a mockery of the pre-match forecasts.

Of the eight teams left in the cup Liverpool were one of five never to have gone all the way, but it was against the backdrop of soaring expectations among fans that the Reds made their way to Anfield from their usual pre-match headquarters in Birkdale. While confidence was high so too was the tension, but any big match nerves were eased on the coach journey to the ground by Barney Ramsden, "a born impersonator," and one of the renowned jokers in the Liverpool pack, as he treated his team mates to an impromptu sing-song. Once inside the dressing room Stubbins and Fagan pulled on a wishbone, Fagan took the bigger half and wished that he would be leading the Reds out at Wembley come April.

174

The team lined-up as it had done for the previous round against Derby, with Harley returning in place of Ramsden, and Fagan again operating at outside-right, the latter having a key, but unsung, tactical role to play.

Bright sunshine and a deafening roar from the Kop greeted the two teams as they ran out and Liverpool kicked-off attacking their favourite end. The all-ticket policy seemed to work well, with little congestion reported at the turnstiles and, despite 4,000 Birmingham fans being stranded in the Midlands due to transport difficulties, the visitors were also not lacking in support. From the very first whistle though, Liverpool appeared too strong for their Second Division opponents and, although the ball was constantly being held up in the snow and some fierce tackles were flying in, the Reds proceeded to outclass the Blues in all departments. When Stubbins opened the scoring on 31 minutes it came as no surprise.

The Geordie capitalised on a slip by Arthur Turner before drilling his shot home from a narrow angle. 47 years later, in an interview with the now defunct XTRA Time magazine, Stubbins reminisced about his career with the Reds and recalled the events of this game as if it were yesterday;

"I remember later reading a report about this match and the journalist who'd written the piece actually thought my first goal that day was the best of the game. I remember collecting the ball on the right wing, Phil Taylor played a beautiful through pass and I floated past one or two defenders before hitting this low ball across the goal to the far post. The way I actually hit the ball, I knew as soon as it left my boot that it was going in. It was definitely one of the finest shots I ever hit.

"An embarrassing incident followed though because Phil Taylor came up and kissed me on the cheek. In those days this was wild extravagance, because usually if you scored a goal you would turn away and maybe get just a handshake off one or two team mates. But with this being such an important cup-tie I think Phil got a little bit carried away."

The lead was nothing less than Liverpool deserved but ten minutes after half-time Frank Mitchell drew the visitors level from 12 yards out after a penalty had been awarded following Harley's trip on winger Jock Mulraney. Stubbins however, attached no blame to the full-back. "With the pitch being so icy it was very difficult for defenders to time their tackles and Jim was a bit unlucky."

The blow of being pegged back after playing so well forced Balmer to make a point of rallying each and every one of his team-mates just as play was about to restart. His actions paid dividends. Within sixty seconds Liverpool had regained the lead through their vice-captain who redirected a Liddell free-kick past keeper Merrick.

A head injury sustained by Paisley saw Liverpool reduced to ten men for a spell and while he was off the field getting treatment the tie was put virtually beyond Birmingham's reach with a goal that those who saw it never tire of talking about.

Liddell, the creator once again, hit a low free-kick across the goalmouth that took the defence by surprise. The ball seemed to be heading out of play until Stubbins suddenly appeared at the far post with an almost horizontal dive across the snow covered surface. Somehow, he managed to connect with his head and score from close-range. It was a goal that has since passed into the annals of Anfield folklore. The Football Echo describing it as a, "wonder goal," but it has since been famously rechristened as the legendary 'goal in the snow'. The legend who scored it remembered it clearly;

"The move that led to that goal actually came about because of something that had happened in the previous round against Derby County. During that particular match Billy Liddell made ground on the left wing and hit a terrific low ball across, which myself and Jack Balmer just failed to get to. I was annoyed because the ball needed just a touch and it would have been in the back of the net so I thought to myself that next time Bill put the ball over I would anticipate him hitting it low and hard.

"Anyway, we won a free-kick on the left and he hit this low ball across the goalmouth. The Birmingham defence was certainly not expecting such a cross but, remembering what had happened against Derby, I threw myself full length at the ball and just managed to get my head to it.

"With the force and velocity of the ball coming over and me heading it, the ball went past the goalkeeper like a rocket. But with the pitch being so icy I skidded along on top of the ice and as I picked myself up my knees were all bloodied. Although at the time I didn't mind in the least."

The roar which greeted the goal almost, "lifted the roof off the Kop," and Stubbins went on to complete an unforgettable afternoon by adding a fourth to complete his hat-trick with another header, this time from a Fagan centre 16 minutes from time.

"The final goal to complete my hat-trick and ensure our progress into the next round was another header. A corner from the right was floated over by Willie Fagan and it was a difficult ball to judge in the sense that it seemed to hang in the air above me and I just managed to get my head to it and loop it into the net.

"We finished the game in great style and in the end Birmingham were well beaten. Thinking back, it must have been a great game for the spectators and I remember the atmosphere around Anfield that day was electric."

According to The Times, "a fine constructive display by their half-backs was the mainspring of Liverpool's convincing win, "while proof of the ease at which victory was secured lay in the fact that Sidlow was, "scarcely trouble," and, "almost workless," throughout.

The Echo thought the victory to be one of Liverpool's finest displays of the season so far, "they had the tools and knew how to do the job." The Reds were deemed, "'worthy semi-finalists," whilst *Contact* wasn't wrong when he wrote that; "The game will be remembered for all-time as the one in which Stubbins got three goals, one of them the most spectacular ever seen on this ground."

Stubbins was the hero, for that there could be no doubt. He concluded;

> *"After the game I was returning to the North East to visit relatives, but before travelling up I called into the old Imperial hotel on Lime Street for a meal. Some of the supporters must have seen me going into the hotel and I remember looking out from this window, about two or three floors up, and there were hundreds of fans outside chanting my name.*
>
> *"It was one of the greatest thrills of my career and one of the most marvellous things that has ever happened to me. Overall it was just about one of the most memorable cup-ties I could have experienced. Scoring a hat-trick was the icing on the cake - it was certainly one of the best I ever scored."*

While it was Stubbins who deservedly hogged the post-match headlines however, the contribution of Fagan went unnoticed. To those at the game Fagan appeared to do very little, isolated on the right he got only a few touches and was even accused in some quarters of being idle. However, as Ray Lambert revealed afterwards, that was all part of the grand master-plan hatched by Kay;

> *"Even though it meant sacrificing the right-wing, we knew Birmingham would have to watch Fagan, and decided to play down the middle for all we were worth. With Balmer*

The legendary 'goal in the snow'

playing well up with Stubbins we always had a spare man in the centre. Birmingham's tendency to play their full-backs wide apart had been noted earlier, and we knew there would only be their centre-half in the middle."

With a place in the last four assured and a first appearance beneath the twin towers now just a possible 90 minutes away, George Kay admitted that; "Our boys are playing with such team spirit and confidence that I don't think we need fear anyone." It was hard to keep a lid on the feverish excitement that was sweeping through the Liverpool fans' ranks. The cup adventure meant Liverpool's pursuit of the league would to have to remain in the background for a little while longer, but it was a thrilling distraction nevertheless. The semi-final draw couldn't come quick enough.

Liverpool v Blackburn Rovers
Saturday 8 March 1947

"Such is the enthusiasm for Liverpool I verily believe the same huge support would turn up of they were playing the blind school at water polo."

Ranger, Liverpool Echo

The feel good factor of reaching a first FA Cup semi-final in 33 years meant that a renewed wave of optimism swept through Anfield. With the prospect of a long-awaited trip to Wembley now more than just a dream, Monday's lunchtime Cup draw had everyone waiting by their wireless with baited breath.

The news from Lancaster Gate however, was that Liverpool would have to wait until the following evening before discovering who their last four opponents would be. While Charlton were drawn to play Second Division Newcastle, the Reds were pulled out of the hat alongside both Middlesbrough and Burnley who had contested a thrilling 2-2 draw at the same time Liverpool were beating Birmingham.

Eager to witness at first hand just who that would be, the entire first team - plus reserves - attended the replayed quarter-final tie at Turf Moor and saw the Second Division Clarets pull off a shock 1-0 win, leaving the Reds clear favourites to progress. With Ewood Park named as the venue club officials and fans alike excitedly began planning their travel arrangements. For the Liverpool players however, it was the pursuit of the league leaders that their thoughts returned to, a chase that, while beginning to gain momentum, was still not looked upon as the most realistic route to success.

Ahead of the weekend visit of the team from Ewood Park *Ranger* wrote that; "The Reds have a lot of leeway to make up to catch the Wolves but they are playing so well just now that they still have a chance if the Molineux lads make any slips." With five successive victories behind them and a cup semi-final place secured confidence was understandably high and Rovers were not expected to blot this fine run of form.

Once one of the wealthiest and most influential clubs in the land, Rovers had fallen on hard times and found themselves languishing in the lower reaches of the division. In a bid to pull away from the drop zone they had splashed out a total of £26,000 on three new signings but it wasn't enough to prevent manager Eddie Hapgood from resigning in mid-February. As so often happens in such cases, Hapgood's successor Will Scott immediately oversaw back-to-back wins - away at Sheffield United and home to Leeds. Although this eased their relegation fears Rovers still found goals hard to come by – a problem that had plagued them throughout the campaign. With just 28 goals from 29 games they were the lowest scorers in the division. In comparison, Liverpool's record of 62 from the same number of games was bettered only by Wolves and Stoke.

Given these statistics, what followed may suggest that this wasn't a vintage Reds performance but in reality the winning margin belied Liverpool's superiority. On a playing surface that was described as, "like playing on a vast sea of porridge," the cup semi-finalists expertly mastered the troublesome conditions. The week leading up to the match brought even more snow and ice, with severe blizzards cutting off towns and paralysing rail and road links the length and breadth of the country. Come Saturday, with an inch of watery snow once again covering the pitch, the lines at Anfield had to be painted blue.

Despite the strange colour choice, man of the moment Stubbins had no problem finding his way through the Blackburn defence. Early on he, "brought the house down," with a long dribble towards goal that ended with him shooting into the side-netting and he also went close with, "a fine low shot, off the mark by only a half-yard." Blackburn's attackers were surprisingly lively themselves at this stage and outside-left Billy Guest wasted a splendid opportunity when opting to try and lob Sidlow instead of choosing to pass.

As in most games for the past two months the ball was being held up in the snow and this was a cause of much frustration for the home side who were constantly discovering that, "it was not running kindly...when they built up moves which were worth goals."

It was soon all Liverpool and Liddell used, "his speed electrically to poke the ball across for Stubbins almost to get a goal." In a similar incident just moments later, Liddell was again the creator - this time for Done - but, as he aimed then fired at an empty net, right-back Les Cook got back just in the nick of time to block the shot. Former Hibs man Jock Weir, one of Blackburn's recent acquisitions, then squandered an even better chance to open the scoring when, from, "not more than five or six yards out," he failed to hit the target.

After a brief spell of playing with ten men while Fagan was off the field receiving treatment on a thigh injury, Balmer and Liddell, "were over the top and into the Kop," with a couple of noteworthy efforts and, "although Fagan [returned and was] was a semi-passenger, Liverpool still threatened to produce goals, even if they were a bit over elaborate." Paisley's constant shackling and expertly timed tackles on Rovers' main danger-man, Jack Smith, "received a due measure of applause," but on a rare occasion that the centre-forward escaped his close attentions, "a glorious shot produced from Sidlow a catch high above his head, with the wet ball well and truly held."

The deadlock was eventually broken eight minutes before half-time and Stubbins - one of the brightest performers on a dull afternoon weather wise - was the scorer, seizing on a through pass from Liddell and veering slightly to his left before, in the same movement, unleashing a well-struck left-footed shot that flew sweetly into the Kop net. It was a, "well earned goal," and one that the Geordie's efforts in recent weeks thoroughly deserved. Done almost doubled Liverpool's advantage with a strike every bit as good as the goalscorer's shortly after, but former Arsenal keeper George Marks pulled off a magnificent save to deny him, while just before the break Stubbins, "smashed the ball in for what appeared to be a certain goal and once again Marks showed just what a good goalkeeper Arsenal had lost."

The poor state of the pitch and the size of the ball for the game against Blackburn can clearly be seen here, with Albert Stubbins bravely attempting a header in difficult conditions.

Contact wrote that, at this stage, "strictly speaking this was not a match as Liverpool at their best were obviously so much better than Blackburn." The second period continued in much the same vein, with, "Blackburn a very uncertain opposition, with more streaks of bad than good, and

Liverpool remained on top." It was a game, "following the pattern of several others at the ground recently, in that although Liverpool should have had it won they led by the barest of margin." In a bid to improve on this, Balmer saw a good shot tipped over by Marks and Done, latching onto a through ball from Stubbins, dragged the ball a few inches past the post.

With Jones coolness personified at centre-half, as, "he made several beautifully executed tackles and clearances," there seemed little danger of Blackburn ruffling the Liver Bird's feathers but on 76 minutes they stunned the home crowd with a goal totally against the run of play. It was a knock-out blow for both the Reds and for Smith - who was temporarily knocked unconscious when solidly heading a long pass onto the right wing. From there, John Oakes picked up the play and cut inside before letting fly with a long-range strike that went in off the inside of the post. Liverpool, "at this stage had gone almost stone cold and appeared to be playing with one eye on the clock, one eye on Blackburn Rovers, and their mind on the cup." The equaliser stung Liverpool into action and the visitors' joy at drawing level was short-lived as, just 60 seconds later;

> *"Done seized his chance at 77 minutes to restore the lead with a low shot in a spell of Liverpool fury, which suggested that they were now really determined to show Blackburn what they could do."*

Apart from a penalty appeal that was waved away when, "Liddell ploughed through and got close to goal," Liverpool failed to trouble the Rovers goal again. Instead they, "tried much pattern-weaving in the snow...nice to watch, without being severely practical," and Done's goal, his 11th of the campaign, proved enough to seal the points. Had it not been for the thigh strain that had handicapped Fagan for most of the game it was generally agreed afterwards that Liverpool would have ran out more comfortable winners and their performance left watching Burnley boss Cliff Britton with plenty to ponder ahead of the cup semi-final.

It was a victory that was enough to lift Liverpool into second on goal average from Blackpool and Middlesbrough, the latter having done the chasing pack a massive favour by holding Wolves to a 1-1 draw in the big game of the day at Ayresome Park. Four points still separated the Reds from top spot and the leaders also had t a game in hand but, while still highly unlikely, what had been previously deemed unthinkable - the league and cup double - was now seen as just improbable.

The ever popular Stubbins again received most of the post-match plaudits, but Liverpool's all-round play was winning new admirers with every passing week.

> *"He [Stubbins] is one of the few stylists who also makes for better team-work. He has transformed Liverpool's attack into a five-point striking force which, with the indefatigable Paisley and Taylor as prompters has few equals today."*

Another reason for Anfield officials to be pleased was that, despite the adverse weather conditions and given the mediocre standard of the opposition, the Liverpool supporters were continuing to pour through the turnstiles in huge numbers, with the attendance of just under 50,000 for the visit of Blackburn being deemed a "great crowd." Liverpudlians were already establishing themselves as one of the most loyal set of fans in the land.

In terms of postponements Saturday 8 March 1947 was widely described as the, "blackest in the history of League football." So bad was the snow, wind and ice, that Liverpool's fixture had been one of only 17 to survive the weather and the number of games called off – 27 – was a new record high, taking the total for the season to 160. With such a serious back-log of fixtures building up there was trouble ahead and widespread calls for the season to be extended.

Portsmouth v Liverpool
Saturday March 15 1947

"The worst conditions I have ever experienced, with a raging blizzard which made it difficult to stand upright, never mind run about."

Jack Balmer

Liverpool's gradual rise towards the top may have be gathering pace but there were growing fears that it could be to no avail as the future of English football hung precariously in the balance in mid-March. The Daily Mirror went as far as describing it as, "the most critical week in the history of soccer,"' and even suggested the forthcoming round of matches could well be the last for some time. The unprecedented number of postponements had thrown the fixture list into chaos. So much so that the entire structure of league football was in danger of complete collapse. Repeated calls for the season to be extended had continually fallen on deaf ears, with the FA Council refusing to budge on their insistence that the campaign must be completed by May 10. To make matters worse, the ban on midweek matches was upheld by the Home Office.

Possible solutions to prevent the season over-running was to operate a pro-rata points system for teams who were unable to complete all their fixtures or play games behind closed doors on weekday afternoons, neither of which were really viable. Without the much-needed income these fixtures would bring many clubs would, even with the increased income high attendances had given them, hav been faced bankruptcy.

If all this wasn't bad enough, with footballers, "not blind to the fat gates which are being banked by their clubs," the long running row between the Players Union and the Football League was threatening to boil over once again and an all-out strike loomed if the players' wage demands were not finally met. At a meeting in Manchester the previous month Jimmy Fay's Union had once again outlined their desire for a wage increase to £12 during the season and £10 in the summer. Once again however, their proposals were rejected, and they were now preparing to submit their case to arbitration by the Ministry of Labour, stating that should this be opposed then strike action will be the only option.

Never before had football in this country faced a such a crisis. With so much strife off the pitch it would have been easy to get distracted from the immediate task in hand on it. Fortunately, the players and officials at Anfield remained totally focussed on the formidable tasks ahead. Of greater concern to all at the club towards the latter part of this turbulent week was whether or not the in-form Phil Taylor would be available for Liverpool's weekend trip to Portsmouth.

Taylor had been in midweek action for the Football League against the Scottish League in Glasgow but severe snowstorms meant all rail and road links out of Scotland were cut off and the Reds half-back was marooned north of the border overnight. Would he make it back in time? This was the question everyone Liverpudlian was asking and the next day, with the help of the local constabulary, he embarked on a long and arduous journey by squeezing himself onto a tightly packed train crawling south. He was hoping to travel direct to Portsmouth but 15 hours after leaving Glasgow's Central station it had only got as far as Preston and Taylor was forced to give up on that idea and return home for the night.

It was late Friday night by the time he walked through his front door but, believing Liverpool had no-one to fill in for him at half-back, he was up bright and early the following morning and on the 5am train out of Lime Street with Fratton Park his ultimate destination. At five minutes to three, Taylor finally met up with his team-mates in the visitors' changing room only to be greeted with the news that Barney Ramsden had been drafted in as a replacement, with Ray Lambert moving to right-half in a re-shuffled Reds' back line. Having hardly slept or eaten since his epic journey began, he was hardly in the best condition to play a gruelling 90 minutes of football anyway, but such dedication to the red cause was typical of the man.

With Fagan suffering from a bad case of lumbago, Eastham was called up for his first appearance since the derby defeat in January. These enforced changes only served to make an already difficult task even harder.

For Portsmouth the 1946/47 season was to be one of consolidation. After their FA Cup win of 1939 they were in the midst of a rebuilding programme – one that was just two years away from title-winning fruition. Boasting a strong defence that contained a renowned half-back line of Jimmy Scoular, Jack Froggatt and Jimmy Dickinson, plus an unbeaten home record since Boxing Day, Portsmouth away was considered to be one of the season's trickier fixtures. A draw at Fratton Park would usually have been considered a good result but if Liverpool's title challenge was to be maintained then nothing less than maximum points were required.

Having lost the toss – the coin having to be spun twice after sticking in the mud the first time – the Anfield men's cause was not helped by the blinding blizzard that blew straight into their faces during a difficult first half. Jack Balmer later described the conditions on the South coast that day as the worst he had ever played in. Pompey officials had used a steam jet to rid the pitch of snow prior to kick-off but in-turn this had transformed the playing surface into a, "farm-yard duckpond," making conditions even more difficult. Not surprisingly, the Reds found themselves on the back-foot for long spells. Portsmouth seemed quicker on the ball and, "there was a verve and spirit about them which was disturbing."

The dogged defending of Lambert, Paisley and the two full-backs was no doubt a big factor in Liverpool weathering the early Pompey storm but with the snow coming down thicker and now sticking they, "were far from functioning in their usual style." It was the same for both sets of players however, although Scoular required medical attention when, after being, "struck hard by the ball when Stubbins tried a long pass, [he] went down like a log."

With the pitch now, "now causing many mistakes and many freakish incidents, Scoular, with a surprise long-distance shot, almost caught Sidlow napping." Luckily for Liverpool the ball was going wide otherwise the keeper, "would have been hard put to reach it at the angle."

In what had so far been a fairly, "undistinguished game," Stubbins, "with one of his cutest back-heel passes," fed Liddell and only for full-back Harry Ferrier getting his body in the way of what was a terrific goalward bound drive, the Scottish winger would surely have opened the scoring. Having already pole-axed one Pompey player with the power in his boots, Stubbins, "again hit a hard ball in an attempted pass and caused injury, this time to [Reg] Flewin, who got the full force on to his head and went down as though shot."

Luckily for the home side, the raging snow storm had petered out slightly by the time the two teams swapped ends for the second half and within just two minutes of the restart it was they who drew first blood. Froggatt shot from outside the area and, with his feet seemingly rooted in the deep Fratton Park mud, Sidlow could only look on motionless as the ball rolled into the net off the inside of the post. "An enlivened Pompey," had given, "the crowd something to shout about," but for the second week running Liverpool responded in the best possible fashion. Where before the break it had been the defence that caught the eye it was now the turn of the attackers to silence the famous Pompey chimes, and they did just that through Stubbins four minutes later. Although winded after being struck in the midriff by a goal bound Balmer effort, Stubbins, "pivoted immediately and slammed the ball [into the goal] for an equaliser."

After receiving some pitch-side attention from trainer Albert Shelley the injured goalscorer was soon back in the thick of the action and in the 57th minute was on hand again to put Liverpool ahead, this time, "hitting a spectacular shot past Butler for a good goal," after the keeper had expertly blocked his initial volley. Liverpool were now on top for the first time and, "every attack was matching the excellence of the work done by the defence in the first half," noted *Contact*.

The match continued to be fiercely contested and Portsmouth replied to this quick-fire Stubbins' double with a late rally of their own. "Paisley and Harley were the defensive heroes now in a sea of mud," while the hosts;

> *"had chronic luck when [Fred] Evans got in the way of a shot which seemed certain to beat Sidlow. Almost a repetition of the Balmer-Stubbins experience, except that there was no goal to round off the move."*

With the home crowd roaring their heroes on, Jones had to make a vital headed clearance to deny Dickinson and Sidlow made a fine save to keep out a Bert Barlow free-kick. The Reds number one was by far the busier of the two keepers at this stage and, "earned his bonus in one minute's work near the end," when flicking a Reid effort over the bar with one-hand. "Liverpool had to fight hard to hold their lead," and the fact that they did was thanks in no small part to their solid defence.

This was, unmistakeably, a crucial win for the Reds - Portsmouth's first loss for 15 games. At a venue where many were predicting they would come unstuck - almost literally given the atrocious state of the pitch - Liverpool had, "produced the best football of the season." It sent out an ominous warning to their fellow title challengers. Leaders Wolves may have continued their winning streak with a routine home defeat of Charlton, as did Blackpool against Sheffield United but it was clear for all to see that Liverpool were not going to be shaken off so easily. With Manchester United, Middlesbrough and Preston all crashing to defeats away from home Liverpool had overcome adversity on the south coast and proved they had the mental strength required for this particular battle. Could their run continue?

Liverpool v Derby County
Saturday 22 March 1947

> *"The Reds chances of the League Championship are fairly slender at best.*
> *Their prospects of lifting the cup are much brighter.*
> *You can indulge league aspirations every season. Cup chances come but seldom."*

Ranger, Liverpool Echo

With the cup semi-final just a week away, it was hard for the players and fans to concentrate on the upcoming league visit to Anfield of Derby County. The age-old cliché of taking one game at a time was trotted out on countless occasions ahead of the clash with the Rams but it didn't fool anyone. Despite the First Division summit now being within realistic reach, the FA Cup - and getting through to a first

Wembley final - was the players' and fans' number one objective. There could be no denying it. At a time when even the famed FA Cup is often seen and referred to as a secondary competition when compared to the Premier League or European glory, such a view is difficult to entertain. *Bee* however, put it succinctly. "Liverpool believe they can win the FA Cup...It is a glittering prize. League consistency or the championship has no corresponding glamour."

Despite this view, a near capacity crowd packed into Anfield to see if the Reds could make up more ground at the top of the table and keep alive hopes of a dream double. With seven successive victories confidence was high and Anfield's fourth highest league gate of the season – 50,848 – turned up to see if their heroes could sign off in style in the league ahead of the much-anticipated semi-final.

The big talking point prior to kick-off – aside from the forthcoming cup tie and the breaking news that the Football league had finally bowed to pressure from all sides and had agreed to extend the season to June 14 – was the fact that for the first time since the turn of the year Anfield's playing surface was devoid of snow or ice. The big freeze had finally ended. The widespread floods caused by the thaw had also subsided, and these rare, "pleasant conditions," no doubt contributed to the impressive gate.

A weaving run and shot from Liddell, which was deflected behind off the shoulder of centre-back Leon Leuty, and Fagan's left-footed snap shot from the resultant corner, which was turned splendidly around the post by keeper Vic Woodley, contributed to a bright start by the hosts. Having beaten Derby twice already this season nothing less than another two points were expected. It soon became clear however, that, "Liverpool were playing this League game with a laissez faire indicating that their feet were tramping the League road while their minds were wandering towards the cup."

Sensing this, the mid-table visitors quickly gained the ascendancy and. despite having little else but pride and their win bonuses to play for, looked the far hungrier team. Having been involved in a long and ultimately successful cup run of their own twelve months previous, seven members of the Derby team no doubt sympathised with the predicament their red-shirted opponents found themselves in. Should they go all out for league title success - even though few gave them a chance? Or instead focus all their efforts into the upcoming semi-final against Burnley - for if they won that they would be just 90 minutes away from securing their place in Kop folklore. The same sympathetic outlook could not be said of the home fans however, and it wasn't long before, "they began to get a little irritated at the non-success of their favourites." It was a subject that *Bee* pragmatically broached in his Monday match analysis;

"The public calling upon the side to exert itself, failed to consider the margin of financial gain as between the Cup and League. This carried a bonus of £2 for victory; the Cup match a week hence offers £20 per man. It is natural players shall not risk injury, but the public

goes to support their belief in the team and the somewhat nonchalant method adopted in some quarters caused the crowd to lose a little faith."

With Bill Jones deemed unfit, John Easdale had been brought in for his first senior appearance since the Christmas Day defeat at Stoke and, "did his best," against a Derby side that, even without star man Raich Carter, posed a constant threat. "Rat-a-tat-tat went Liverpool shots in a burst of enthusiasm raised by Liddell's inspiring and enthusiastic effort," but the bulk of the action was in the opposite goalmouth where only poor finishing, especially by the "entertaining and enterprising," Stamps, let the Rams down.

As the interval approached this, "clash between cup holders and potential cup holders," was swinging in favour of the visitors and Liverpool were fortunate to still be on level on terms. "Here and there, notably with Liddell and Stubbins and Easdale, there was an intensity of effort; elsewhere there was not the urge to go into the task with tenacity."

Having netted five times against Derby in this season's two previous meetings Balmer was one of the players who looked, "completely out of sorts," and he should have done better when presented with a gilt-edged scoring opportunity midway through the second half. A delightful through ball found him perfectly placed but his shot was tame and straight at Woodley.

"Only when Liddell joyfully soared in his left wing work did Liverpool show signs of life," so it came as a major surprise when, totally against the run of play, Phil Taylor broke the deadlock with a rising, "Busby-esque," strike after Fagan and Done had both had shots blocked. "It was a high flyer, and in the sunshine Woodley never had a real chance," reported *Ranger*, and with only 11 minutes remaining it looked likely to seal maximum points.

Unfortunately, another morale boosting pre-semi final victory was snatched from their grasp just sixty seconds later when big Jackie Stamps, scored, "one of the flukiest goals imaginable," to draw Derby level – netting from a seemingly impossible angle courtesy of a wicked deflection off Sidlow. In the dressing room afterwards a despondent Liverpool keeper admitted; "There was no one more amazed than I was," but vowed, "it won't happen next week...not with the cup at stake. I'll make up for that miss."

As the game drew to a close, "a rainbow spread its arc over the ground," but Liverpool's performance had been, "not nearly so colourful." On the balance of play the Reds could have few arguments about the end result but, just to prove that fickleness among football fans isn't a new phenomenon, minor murmurs of discontent continued to be heard from a small section of the Anfield crowd with the Daily Post reporting that, "one or two players receiving an unkindly 'raspberry' on occasions," for failing to maintain their winning streak.

Like its sister paper, the Echo was quick to defend the lacklustre display, arguing that, given the magnitude of the occasion that awaited them at Ewood Park the following week, the Liverpool players could be forgiven for this rare off day and that the performance was no indicator as to what to expect against Burnley. As for the supporters who vented their feelings, they were branded foolish and reminded that, "it was patent to all what lay behind their [the players] motions."

With Wolves losing 2-0 at Sheffield United this was clearly a missed opportunity for Liverpool to greatly improve their championship chances and the dropped point meant they relinquished second spot to Blackpool, who were 3-2 victors over Grimsby at Blundell Park. For the time being at least however, the league was of secondary importance. This game was never going to live long in the memory and, although it had been, "a not very satisfying dress rehearsal," the phoney war was now over and all energies could be correctly channelled into the build-up to what was one of the most eagerly anticipated matches in Liverpool history.

Liverpool v Burnley (FA Cup semi-final – Ewood Park)
Saturday 29 March 1947

"The century's worst floods flushed the country out of its long hibernation into the 'deafening' roar of 29 March: 'the greatest day in British sporting history.'"

Thomas Taw, Football's War and peace"

It was a weekend for sports enthusiasts to savour. The Grand National, the boat race and two FA Cup semi-finals all on the same day. But while the eyes of the nation were on Liverpool and the first ever Saturday running of the world's greatest steeplechase at Aintree, the eyes of Liverpool were on events 30 miles up the road in Blackburn, where eleven men in red were aiming to do what no other team from Anfield had achieved – to book their place in a Wembley Cup Final.

Excitement among Liverpudlians ahead of their club's first appearance in the last four of the FA Cup for 33 years could hardly have been any greater had it been the final itself. Think Istanbul 2005 and that's no exaggeration. For these success starved fans winning the Cup was the holy-grail and

OFFICIAL SOUVENIR PROGRAMME 6ᴅ.

F.A. Cup. Semi-Final Tie.

BURNLEY versus LIVERPOOL

EWOOD PARK, Blackburn Saturday, March 29th, 1947 KICK-OFF 3-0 o'clock.

now, after years of mediocrity, they could almost reach out and touch it. In Kopite's eyes, George Kay's men - if they could at last make their long-held dream come true - stood on the verge of immortality and with Liverpool's class of 1946/47 already being hailed in the local press as, "one of the finest sides ever to wear the Red of Anfield," there was an air of quiet confidence among the supporters.

So too however, was there a sense of nervous tension. Summed up on the morning of the match by Daily Express reporter Henry Rose who, while of the firm belief that, "on their day Liverpool can win the FA Cup, Grand National and the boat race," was also of the opinion that, "on an off day the Gasworks team could beat them."

This 'Jekyll and Hyde' form meant fans never knew which Liverpool team was going to turn up and so there always remained a nagging doubt in the back of their mind. Would it be the swashbuckling Liverpool that surged to the top of Division One on the crest of a 12 game unbeaten run earlier in the season? Or would it be the mild and meek Liverpool that suffered four successive League defeats at the turn of the year? At this most crucial juncture in the club's history, fingers, arms, legs, feet, toes and whatever else could be crossed were crossed in the hope that it wouldn't be the latter.

Such was the hype surrounding this match that the team escaped to the sanctuary of a 17th century coaching inn - high in the hills of Clitheroe - to prepare, and the travelling party consisted of the squad that had been on duty against Derby plus Jones and reserves Minshull, Palk and Ramsden. Previews to the game dominated the sports pages of every newspaper and while most were tipping Liverpool to meet Newcastle in the final their Second Division opponents were certainly not to be underestimated.

Like Liverpool's quarter-final opponents Birmingham, Burnley were also chasing promotion to the top-flight. They had occupied a position near the top of the table for most of the season. Managed by Everton's 1933 FA Cup winner Cliff Britton - this was his first season in the job - the Clarets had also shown their mettle in the previous round by eliminating Middlesbrough, a team Liverpool had failed to beat on two occasions earlier in the season.

They had also lost just one of their previous 32 league and cup matches - keeping clean-sheets in 16 of their last 22. With only seven goals conceded in their last 28 games there was no doubt that Burnley were going to prove a much sterner test than Birmingham. Even accounting for the difficult task they undoubtedly faced, *Ranger* set his anticipated scene - the, "mouth-watering prospect," of a first visit to Wembley - in the previous Saturday's Football Echo.

"I think they can but it will be a hard task, for Burnley are a well-balanced side, just as much on the crest of a wave as Liverpool and – on paper, at least – there is little to choose between them. I am pinning my faith in a Liverpool victory on the superior skill of the Reds in attack.

"Burnley's defence is brilliant, but, from what I saw of them in the replay against Middlesbrough, I don't think their forwards have the same finishing power as Liverpool's. With a front line of five players who have all had centre-forward experience, who all know where the goal lies, and can hit the ball with terrific power, I bank on Liverpool's attack to win the day."

It was to be the first time Liverpool and Burnley had met in the cup since the final of 1914 - when Bert Freeman's goal settled the issue in favour of the men from Turf Moor - and it was difficult to argue with those in the press who billed this semi-final as the biggest game in the club's history since that meeting at Crystal Palace.

The only Liverpool player to have experienced the unique atmosphere of a FA Cup semi-final before was Willie Fagan, who had been a member of the Preston side that defeated West Brom at Highbury in 1937. His experience was considered vital, as was that of fellow veteran Jack Balmer, whose build-up to the match was disrupted during the week when he was forced to rush home from training after receiving a message from his wife that 18-month old son Colin had scalded himself on a kettle. Manage Kay hurriedly drove Balmer to his West Derby home but luckily it was nothing too serious and their semi-final preparations were not affected.

Given the club's record of misfortune in the competition since their one and only final appearance, Reds' fans were taking nothing for granted. It was a tense travelling Kop that converged on Blackburn bedecked with rattles, rosettes and red ribbons and scarves of every size. Liverpudlians lucky enough to get their hands on

The Liverpool squad leave Anfield ahead of the FA Cup semi-final.

tickets travelled in their thousands with some leaving Exchange Station as early as 1.50am. By midday the town was reportedly a mass of red and white, with visiting fans from Merseyside easily outnumbering those who'd made the much shorter journey from Burnley.

Like a modern day European away game, it was a Scouse invasion of colour and noise. "A tornado of football frenzy," was one apt description of the pre-match scenes in Blackburn where, "'Burnleyites' felt strangers in a strange land."

"Everywhere was a blaze of colour with red and white represented in almost every form of garb. Liverpool had come to town in force, and their supporters made themselves heard with their sirens, klaxons, horns, motorcar hooters, rattles etc."

An hour before kick-off Ewood Park was, "seething with excitement and noise from the vociferous crowd," and even a torrential down-pour just before the teams emerged failed to dampen their enthusiasm. But while the fans had no problem getting in the same couldn't be said of the Liverpool team who, because of a misunderstanding over tickets, were denied admission by an over-zealous gateman. Only after a long and protracted discussion did he relent and allow them through but the reserves carrying the kit bags were forced to endure a further wait before common sense prevailed.

With Jones fit enough to return in place of Easdale and no fresh injuries to report Liverpool, once through and changed, were able to field their, "first choice cup eleven.' This was the same team that had beaten Derby and Birmingham in rounds

Liverpool fans leave Anfield ahead of the FA Cup semi-final.

five and six respectively and the one that was obviously deemed by the selection committee to be their strongest. Burnley were also at full strength for this eagerly awaited, "Lancashire Hot-Pot," but with so much at stake the fear of defeat hung heavily in the air and both sides proceeded with caution.

Liverpool at their Clitheroe hotel prior to the FA Cup semi-final.

That the two teams were not eager to overcommit and they duly cancelled each other out was not to be unexpected. Indeed, with two sides so strong in defence it was never going to be much in the way of a spectacle. Having won the toss for choice of colours Liverpool sported their traditional red while Burnley wore white. When the action got underway it was the men in white who made the early running. The men from Turf Moor, appeared to be a lot more relaxed and, "showed First Division craft," in their play, while Liverpool, it seemed, were awestruck by the sense of occasion and took their time to find top gear.

With goalmouth incidents few and far between Sidlow - who had been demobbed the previous day - and his opposite number Jimmy Strong had little to do during the tentative opening stages. Both sides gave a fine demonstration in the noble art of tackling and Clarets captain Alan Brown's close marking job on Stubbins ensured the Reds number nine endured one of his quieter games.

With the crowd so densely packed together in certain sections of the ground it wasn't long before fans started encroaching onto the pitch, most notably when right-winger Jackie Chew tried taking a corner. "Extra police were rushed there and ambulancemen with stretchers were kept busy. To avoid a repeat some fans were allowed to move to more spacious parts of the terracing.

As expected, it was renowned amateur winger Peter Kippax - who had scored in his one guest appearance for Liverpool during the war and who move to Anfield two years later - who posed the greatest threat for Burnley. In a bid to stop him the Liverpool defenders were guilty of conceding several free-kicks. It was his impressive left-footed shot, "after turning Harley on a sixpence," that came closest to breaking the first-half deadlock. Fortunately for the Reds it flew just inches over.

"When half-time came it was Burnley who were ahead on points," but it wasn't all one-way traffic and fellow left-winger Liddell was equally as dangerous when in possession. Fagan had an angled drive saved at the foot of the post but, according to The Times, it was Liddell, "who all through the game looked the one man capable of winning the game on his own." Liverpool's rising star later switched wings in an attempt to unlock what was proving to be a stubborn Burnley rearguard and 20 minutes into the second half a rare clear-cut scoring opportunity fell his way from a Fagan corner. The ball landed at his feet just 10 yards from goal then as, "he moved forward, perfectly balanced and controlled, the goal that looked a certainty was shouted home, but his shot sped past the far post."

Speaking to journalists immediately after the game Liddell moved a comb across his hand to describe just how close he'd come to firing the Reds to Wembley.

"The ball moved just that much. I'd actually picked my spot for a right-foot shot. Then as the ball moved away, I had to pull it quickly on to my left foot. I knew my chance had gone as I hit it."

Billy Liddell can only raise his arms in anguish as his shot goes just wide of the Burnley goal.

Watching the British Pathe newsclip of the chance today proves just how close Liddell came to a goal. It was an agonising moment and one Liverpool were left to rue. After 90 goalless minutes the game drifted into extra-time and it was Liverpool who once again came closest to ending the stalemate. Liddell beat Woodruff for pace and delivered a teasing centre across the Burnley goalmouth.

"Stubbins was left, slightly off balance, with an open goal and Liddell's lobbed pass bouncing awkwardly in front of him. The next moment all that remained of the scene was Mather lying injured in the goalmouth, where his superb and desperate tackle of Stubbins saved the day for Burnley."

Exhaustion set in during the second period of extra-time and although both defences were guilty of mistakes late on no goals were scored. Despite carving out the two best chances Liverpool were never really on top until near the end but their efforts came too late and the tie "was left in a state of suspended animation," with honours deservedly even. Although it had been a "fierce two hours," Pat Collins of the Daily Mirror was not impressed. "In a grim 120 minutes, in which two iron defences compressed the game into a negative midfield battle, Liddell's was the only real chance." The draw meant that a replay was required - so Liverpool's potentially pivotal game away at Wolves was moved to a date even later in the season.

Clearing the danger from a Burnley corner.

But while incident and action was thin on the ground in Blackburn, elsewhere the Great British public revelled in what had been an epic sporting Saturday; 100/1 shot Caughoo romped home in the Grand National; Cambridge crossed the line first in the Boat Race; and Charlton Athletic demolished Newcastle 4-0 at Elland Road to clinch a second successive appearance in the FA Cup Final. Unfortunately, all the thrills must have got lost somewhere on the way to Ewood Park. For the 53,000 present it had been a bit of an anti-climax and, with the Easter holidays approaching, it would be another fortnight at least before Charlton would discover who they would be walking out with at Wembley.

Chapter Eleven
Easter Cup of Woe

Preston North End v Liverpool
Friday 4 April 1947

"Gratifying as it would be to see the Reds bidding for the double of League and Cup I'm afraid we may have to wipe off their championship hopes in view of the semi-final replay. The cup is their main aim and I think the general body of supporters would count the league well lost if the former could be assured. To make up the leeway of five points on Wolves at the present juncture seems to be an almost impossibility."

Ranger, Liverpool Echo

The Easter holiday meant a return to league action for Liverpool and three games in four days that George Kay's men could well have done without ahead of the FA Cup semi-final replay with Burnley. Often viewed as a defining moment in the season as far as the league is concerned, Liverpool still had ten games to play and trailed leaders Wolves by five points so on paper there was still plenty to play for. However, it was the cup that remained uppermost in their thoughts and, when selecting the team to play Preston, Liverpool's directors made it perfectly clear where the club's priorities lay.

With more than an eye on the upcoming replay, three games in four days was considered far too big a risk and a total of 19 players were called upon over the course of the holiday weekend, three of whom were Football League debutants. Indeed, as key men were rested in readiness for the eagerly anticipated cup-tie, only one player – Eddie Spicer – played in all three Easter games. Such actions today would see the club in question crucified by the press but ahead of Liverpool's trip to Preston - the only side thay had not yet met in the league - on Good Friday, most commentators firmly agreed on their cup-only approach.

The team showed five changes to the one that had drawn with Burnley with the big news being the return of Laurie Hughes - after a ten-week injury lay-off - at centre-half. There was also a first senior appearance for youngster Tommy McLeod who, although wearing Stubbins' number nine shirt, occupied the, "problem position" of outside right, a role he'd impressed in for the reserves.

Just three points and four places separated Liverpool and Preston in the table, but a 4-1 defeat to Wolves the previous weekend had severely dented any aspirations the Football League North champions of 1940/41 may have had of clawing their way into the title race. Their side included Scottish international inside-left Bobbie Beattie who'd won a Lancashire Cup winners medal with Liverpool in 1944, while at half-back they had a man who also represented the Reds during this time (against Everton in May 1942 - won 4-1) and would later become the most idolised of all Anfield legends – Bill Shankly.

Capped five times by Scotland, Shankly had won the FA Cup with Preston in 1938 but, like many players of his generation, his career was cruelly interrupted by the outbreak of hostilities the following year. 33 years old at the start of 1946/47 his best days were now considered to be behind him but he remained a vital member of the Preston side. North End's best hope for future success was said to rest with their then up-and-coming star Tom Finney. A time-served plumber who had been demobbed from the forces early in order to join the in-demand ranks of building tradesman, Finney had only made his league debut in August 1946 but was already seen as a tricky and two-footed forward of some repute.

The Reds found themselves under pressure for much of opening 45 minutes and, "early moments suggested Liverpool might be used as chopping blocks." The hosts however, were guilty of missing several good opportunities and with Hughes showing no ill-effects on his comeback he fully justified his recall to a back-line that, "was able to stand firm against the Preston attack." While inventive enough, the North End forwards lacked the necessary power to seriously trouble the Liverpool rearguard, in which;

> "*Lambert has rarely played better; Hughes, far from appearing to be having his first game in for weeks, shaped as though he had never been absent. Spicer's defence was good and Phil Taylor was characteristically sound in possession.*"

When Finney picked up an injury and started to limp the danger posed by Preston was severely reduced and Liverpool gradually forced their way back into the game. Cyril Done was unlucky not to break the deadlock with a header that, "only Fairbrother's best effort could keep from goal," while McLeod, om his debut, showed that, "his football ideas are first-rate." Twice during the early stages of the second half he delivered pinpoint centres into the Preston area, "which literally begged to be put into the net," and generally, "did enough to suggest that when he appreciated the speed of Division One, he will make the grade."

In one late moment of drama a well-earned point was almost snatched from Liverpool's grasp when, with Sidlow well beaten, Ramsden - in only his fourth outing since the turn of the year - had to get back to make a crucial goal-line clearance. A 0-0 draw may have done little to change the pre-match opinion of *Ranger*, but the point gained was generally considered to be a good one and Leslie Edwards noted afterwards that, "in so far as goalless matches can be satisfactory this was a good performance." Although Liverpool failed to score for the second successive game, with Wolves not in action the gap at the top was at least reduced by another point.

Liverpool v Blackpool
Saturday 5 April 1947

"With Wolverhampton Wanderers beaten, Liverpool may well pin down this sorry occasion as the one on which their League hopes, if any, were laid to rest."

Leslie Edwards, Daily Post

Just 24 hours after the draw with Preston, Anfield played host to the, "Battle of the Pools," as second-placed Blackpool visited Anfield in the second of three Easter fixtures, looking to inflict upon Liverpool a first double loss of the campaign. It was the second game on Merseyside in as many days for the Tangerines who had come from behind with just six minutes remaining to snatch a 1-1 draw with Everton at Goodison the previous afternoon but, like Liverpool, nothing less than a victory would suffice if they were to remain genuine title challengers.

Although their position near the top may have been slightly misleading due to the fact they'd played more games than any other club, Blackpool's high-level of consistency had seen them drop no lower than sixth in the table all season and with just three points separating them from the third-placed Reds it was easy to see why this was viewed as a crucial clash for both teams.

Liverpool continued their Easter rotation policy and the directors shuffled their pack once again to make a total of six changes, the most notable being a first League appearance in a red shirt for wing-half George Kaye who replaced Taylor. Harley, Jones, Stubbins, Palk and Liddell all returned and the influx of fresh legs paid immediate dividends with the Reds taking the game to their opponents from the first whistle and edging in front on 15 minutes.

Liddell stepped in to take a short pass from Palk out on the wing near the corner flag and, "his centre beyond the far post was met by the head of Fagan, who did well to get there first." The Reds' captain managed to out-jump both keeper Jock Wallace and full-back Eric Sibley and diverted the ball into the net for his sixth goal of the season. While Anfield celebrated what was a well-worked opening goal Stan Mortensen, Blackpool's match-winner in the season's first meeting between the two sides, almost drew the visitors level straight away but, "with the easiest of chances he completely kicked over the ball when not more than four yards out," and Liverpool were let off the hook.

The early action was frantic. A strong wind didn't help matters either but with Palk and Done showing, "unexpected spirit and ability," it was the Reds' attack that posed the greater threat. Stubbins, with an angled drive, forced Wallace into an impressive double-handed save at full-stretch, but the Liverpool forwards were generally, "too hurried," in their approach.

"It was hard football in a strong wind," reported that night's Football Echo, "and there were moments which suggested that there might be too much bite about the game," such as when Liddell was fouled by Sibley. Tempers became frayed as a result and an orange was thrown from a disgruntled home fan in the direction of referee Mr Prescott!

"The side with the gusty wind behind them, always had a big advantage," and so it came as no surprise that Blackpool started strongest after the break. Indeed, they had the ball in the back of the net within minutes of the restart only for Munro's effort to be disallowed for handball. The large Anfield crowd breathed a collective sigh of relief once more but they were soon celebrating for a second time as a swift counter-attack, against the wind, split the visitors defence wide open and from, "a lovely pass by Spicer," Done, "cut through to score at ease."

That should have been job done for the Reds. With Spicer and Kaye, "doing nobly," in defence there seemed no danger of Blackpool getting back into the game, especially as their, "ineffective front line seemed incapable of scoring once, much less three times." With Liddell playing much better than he had before the break and starting to get the better of tough tackling full-back Eddie Shimwell, the most likely outcome at this point in time was further goals for the home side.

The tide began to turn 21 minutes from the end however, when Tom Buchan converted with a simple low shot past a, "blinded," Sidlow. It seemed little more than a consolation for the visitors but it planted a seed of doubt in Liverpudlian minds and just two minutes later they could only look on in horror as Mortensen silenced the Kop with an equaliser by correctly anticipating, "the swirl of the ball round Jones," and nipping in to fire past Sidlow. Blackpool, now, "full of fire," and looking for a winner, had Liverpool on the back-foot and Sidlow had to be at his best to tip a shot from winger Alex Munro over the bar. The prospect of having to settle for a point after leading two-nil was galling but the home fans would have gladly taken just that at this stage.

The Reds were visibly rocking and it was to get worse in the 80th minute when Mortensen again, just like he did at Bloomfield Road back in November, scored what was to prove the decisive goal, drifting, "the ball beautifully, by flick of the head, over a goalkeeper who had only just got back to his line after a clearance which Munro returned with admirable promptitude."

Liverpool's misery - and Blackpool's heroic comeback - was complete and there could be few complaints from the shell-shocked hosts. They had carelessly tossed away more vital points in their pursuit of the title, although in his post-match analysis Leslie Edwards reasoned that the capitulation wasn't as shocking as it seemed.

"It may be argued that there must be something drastically wrong in a team which loses after being so far ahead. The explanation I think was that in a half-gale the side which had the

elemental advantage was always liable to find opposition weakness."

One positive aspect to emerge from the match was the form of Stan Palk at inside-left, a youngster described as, "quite the best post-war discovery his club has made," and, "an inside-forward who must soon measure up to Division One standards." Although on the losing side Palk linked up effectively with both Stubbins and Liddell thus allowing Done to operate more freely at inside-right and thereby aiding the Liverpool attack forward line. Unfortunately, this wasn't enough to maintain an unbeaten streak which had run to ten games, two short of the sequence that took them to the top earlier in the season. Ironically, it was Blackpool who also ended it then and this result was enough to send the Tangerines to the top of the table for the first time since Liverpool had knocked them off their perch back in mid-November.

On the same afternoon the biggest league crowd of the season – 66,947 – saw morning leaders Wolves lose 3-1 to Manchester United at Maine Road, and Liverpool now trailed behind in fifth place, five points off the summit but with four games in hand on the new table-toppers. It had been yet another missed opportunity for the Reds to drag themselves back into the title picture. Despite their loss, Wolves remained favourites for the championship. The big question now was how Liverpool would respond to this latest setback.

Liverpool v Preston North End
Monday 7 April 1947

"The spring saw England's matches against European opposition, as usual preceded with anxiety about the potential loss of prestige...England needed a magician to cast his spell, but which one, Matthews or Finney? The choice between them was a season-long controversy, one that captured two images of football. Matthews represented the individual par excellence, but also the slower tactical game of the 1930s. Finney was more evidently a team man, and his direct style reflected the faster post-war football."

Thomas Taw, Football's War and Peace

Thankfully for Liverpool, there wasn't much time to dwell on the second-half capitulation against Blackpool and just two days later - on Easter Monday - the Reds set about the task of trying to reduce the widening gap between them and the new League leaders. In a re-run of their Good Friday fixture, Preston provided the opposition but with just five days to go until the much anticipated semi-final replay it was again a much changed Reds' eleven that took to the field from that which had lost to Blackpool and drawn at Deepdale.

Whilst Preston made only two changes, Liverpool astonishingly made six, the most notable being that of veteran Tom Bush who, 13 years after making his debut for the club, ran out for what was to be his 72nd and final game in a red shirt. Now 33, and with only two previous senior appearances to his name that season, Bush came in to replace rookie half-back George Kaye. Elsewhere, goalkeeper Minshull was also brought in for what was to be his sixth and final appearance of the campaign. On his last outing in January he had conceded three against Bolton, but he was to memorably make amends in front of the Kop late in this game.

Without the injured Finney, who hadn't recovered from the knock he'd sustained on Good Friday, Preston were a pale shadow of the side that had led the table for a spell early in the season and they were unable to stem a rampant and fresh Reds' side tide.

With gale force winds again swirling around Anfield, inside-left Palk was in inspired form. "Once he fastened onto the ball he was extremely difficult to move from it," and showing, "splendid football ideas," he provided a constant supply line to Stubbins and Liddell. Both forwards, "found from Palk provision for the ball and an inner link to their liking. For a heavily built man he has the knack of the feint which opens up immediate avenues." It was from one of Palk's, "judicious passes," that Stubbins swung a shot just wide after 10 minutes, while it was following a foul on him that Liddell stung the fingers of keeper Fairbrother with a venomously struck free-kick.

It was from another, more debatable, set piece that Liverpool opened the scoring in the 24th minute. There were, "very hearty protestations from Preston," that the free-kick should not have been given but their appeals fell on deaf ears and Spicer, "who in the three games over the holidays has begun to show the form expected of him early in the season," picked out Stubbins with a great delivery. Stubbins' initial shot was saved but, showing, "first-rate opportunism," he stooped low to head in the rebound.

Palk remained at the heart of everything that was good about Liverpool's offensive play and;

> *"his 'dummying' was never better illustrated than a moment later, when he opened up a clear way for himself with a swerve of the body and hit a fine shot, which the imperturbable Fairbrother saved magnificently."*

The Reds were dominating the game and it came as no surprise when they doubled their advantage just a minute before half-time. Taylor and Liddell combined down the left flank and from the latter's centre Balmer headed home despite the best efforts of keeper Fairbrother, "who appeared to get his hands to the ball, but could not prevent it passing into the net, near the post." Despite the one-sidedness of the game, "the play ebbed and flowed," but Preston, just as they had done at Deepdale, lacked the necessary firepower to trouble Liverpool and the final outcome was, "an issue which was almost never in doubt."

With the Reds in total control, the third and final goal duly arrived on 70 minutes, "the result of individual effort crowned with a fine shot," earning scorer Stubbins a deserved standing ovation. Collecting the ball out towards the left he cut inside two players and, evading two tackles, unleashed an unstoppable shot into the roof of the goal at the Kop end. A fitting strike to seal a thoroughly deserved victory.

All that was left now was for Minshull to round off the day with, "as fine a penalty save as one could wish to see." It denied Bill Shankly a goal at his future home and came about somewhat controversially after Ramsden was adjudged to have fouled his opponent in the box. Despite his obvious, "aggravation," at the award, referee Mr Mortimer of Huddersfield stood by his decision and up stepped the future Reds' boss to try and add a touch of respectability to the scoreline.

Netting for Preston at Anfield was nothing new to Shankly. He had managed it once before, during a 2-2 draw back in February 1938, but there was to be no repeat here as Minshull heeded the pre-match words of advice from stand-in skipper Jack Balmer and dived correctly to his right to make the save from what was a, "low, truly hit shot." Albert Stubbins recalled the incident in his newspaper column the following week;

"Before our Easter Monday game with Preston Jack Balmer commented that Bill Shankly, visiting wing-half, always placed penalty kicks to the left side of the goalkeepers. During the game when Preston were awarded a spot kick, the wily Shankly ran at the ball as though to slam it – instead he attempted a place shot. Ray Minshull was prepared, and his clever save ended any hopes Preston had of saving the game – and proved Jack Balmer to be correct."

What the authors believe to be - although poor quality - a rare photograph of Bill Shankly's penalty miss for Preston against Liverpool that kept the Reds in the title picture.

The painful memory of Saturday's late collapse had been banished and, "a Liverpool taking things nonchalantly won with something [to] spare." While their superiority had been hammered home in emphatic style, it left fans and journalists alike pondering, "what could have been if they had not faded out so rapidly against Blackpool."

With the leaders crashing to a 3-0 defeat at home to Everton and Wolves losing their second successive match, 2-1 at Derby, it was a good day for the Reds. They were now just three points off the top and seemingly back in the title chase.

However, it was still the cup that remained uppermost in everyone's thoughts and as the countdown to the semi-final replay began in earnest the Liverpool directors, in light of this impressive win over Preston, were left wondering, "whether to stand by the team that has brought them thus far or to drop the pilot and make the bold choice which might make all the difference in attack." Team selection now, rather than commitment, was the major Reds' talking point for the next five days.

Burnley v Liverpool (FA Cup semi-final replay - Maine Road) Saturday 12 April 1947

"I think we should win through this time.
We will certainly do our best and hope to improve on the Blackburn display."

George Kay

After what had been a taxing Easter schedule, Liverpool's focus was now firmly fixed on securing a first trip to Wembley. Nothing was being left to chance. The squad left for their pre-match base in Buxton on the Thursday afternoon and, with no injury concerns, manager George Kay was full of confidence. To avoid any distractions journalists were banned from travelling with the team to the Peak District. Total relaxation was the target as the big game approached; a gentle stroll; a few games of snooker; and a trip to the local cinema before an early night for the Wembley hopefuls.

Just had been the case a fortnight previous, demand to cheer the Reds on in this most vital of games was immense and 27 special trains left Liverpool for Manchester on the Saturday morning. It was estimated that Liverpool's travelling supported numbered at least 30,000 and, as well as the trains, thousands of private cars and buses left Liverpool carrying supporters wearing rosettes and fancy hats decorated in red and white. On the East Lancashire Road thousands straggled along trying to, "thumb a lift," and although most private cars were full, it was reported that, "motorists on the whole were invariably willing to squeeze another one in."

One of the first fans to arrive was 49-year old Joe Wilson of Alfred Street, Wavertree. He was spotted sitting outside the player' entrance at one o'clock in the morning! Maine Road's greater capacity meant even more Reds' fans were able to make the journey to Manchester than had been at Blackburn but tickets were once again like gold dust to obtain.

Six days before the big match one Liverpudlian was hospitalized with crushed ribs and 30 people injured when tickets went on sale at Anfield. Queues began forming at 7.30 the night before. By midnight the numbers had swelled to around 200 with many coming well prepared for the all-night vigil with blankets, flasks and sandwiches. Hundreds more joined them during the early hours and by the time the turnstiles opened it was estimated that up to 50,000 fans were in the queue that now stretched for over a mile around the ground.

With so many people heading to Anfield Liverpool Corporation even took the unprecedented step of putting on extra trams and tickets sales were temporarily suspended and all turnstiles closed as mounted police were called to restore order.

All 15,500 tickets were sold within two hours and, with the tie a complete sell-out there were, not surprisingly, lots of forgeries in circulation. A large squad of officers from the Manchester CID were deployed at the Maine Road turnstiles to deal with any problems, although the counterfeit tickets, originally discovered in Liverpool where it was believed they had been printed, were easy to spot as the conmen had spelt the word 'competition' wrong!

In an attempt to prevent a possible second replay which, in turn, would add to the increasing fixture congestion, it was requested by the Football Association that 60 minutes of extra-time rather than the standard 30 be played if the scores were tied after 90 minutes. Both clubs objected however, with Liverpool Chairman Bill McConnell confident his team, "will not need more the ninety minutes to complete the job at the second time of asking."

Liverpool were again the team favoured to win by most pundits but *Ranger* explained that it was still a close one to call.

"It would be a brave man who was confident either way. The first meeting in which Burnley showed the craft and Liverpool made and missed chances, proved that both defences are

above ordinary and that only unusually good opportunism by the forwards will produce goals.

"Personally, I have the feeling that Liverpool at their best could win more handsomely than their most optimistic fan might even expect; on the other hand everything depends on whether this is to be one of the Liverpool front line's better days. The nervy, hasty finishing and general comportment at Blackburn, if repeated, could lead only to another draw or defeat."

In terms of national press coverage the semi-final replay was forced to play second fiddle to the big England versus Scotland international at Wembley, a match that would have seen rival wingers Billy Liddell and Peter Kippax line up for their respective countries rather than opposing semi-finalists had it not been for the goalless draw at Ewood Park a fortnight before. Had he played in the international Kippax would have become the first amateur to be capped by England since 1911, but, as with Liddell, such was the importance of his role at club level, special permission was granted by the FA and SFA so that both could play in the replay.

Relaxing before the big game.
Bob Paisley and Jim Harley enjoy a game of snooker (above)
while the team share a meal at a hotel (below).

With Liddell available, Liverpool named the same eleven that had played at Blackburn and this meant disappointment for Eddie Spicer - whose performances in the three holiday fixtures had earned him high praise - and the in-form Stan Palk. According to the football correspondent of the Daily Mirror however, the directors' decision to rotate their squad over Easter - thereby focusing all their efforts on the Cup - was the correct one and could be enough to swing the tie Liverpool's way;

"George Kay and his boys are not worried about League success. Their only concern is that the Cup should rest on the Anfield table for the first time. Burnley, on the other hand, have had a strenuous week. League points are vital to them and promotion is possibly their most cherished ambition."

Two wins and a draw over the holiday period had left the Clarets well placed for promotion, three points off leaders Manchester City but six - and with a game in hand - ahead of third-placed Birmingham. By fielding their strongest eleven throughout though, they were now forced to make one change with Jack Billingham brought in to replace the injured Jackie Chew.

On the eve of the big game the 48 hour 'no soccer talk' ban that Kay had imposed on the players in a bid to help ease the tension that clearly affected them in the first game, was lifted and, using empty ashtrays to illustrate team tactics, he and his coaching staff explained the plan that they hoped would finally end Burnley's brave resistance. Before retiring for the night Kay, keeping his cards typically close to his chest but still retaining the faith he placed in his players, told Leslie Edwards that; "We shall just wade in as we have done in all our matches."

Conditions at Maine Road were, "almost mild and dry enough for cricket. The pitch was firm and, "the general atmosphere of good humour made it a gala occasion…with excitement at fever heat."

When the Liverpool players came out to test the turf they did so, "to an ovation which would have done credit to a Wembley gate," and it was amid a crescendo of cheers that play eventually got underway. A relaxed looking Liverpool seemed to get off to a brighter start than they had done two weeks before and, with the forward line, "functioning a little better," they applied some early pressure on the Burnley goal. Just like in the first game however, both defences were on top and clear scoring opportunities were almost non-existent. After 20 minutes Ray Harrison was the first to force a save when he tested Sidlow but the Reds number one was fully alert and he turned it behind with one hand.

In what was developing into another, "hard, dour match," Paisley required medical attention after being accidentally kicked behind the ear by Harrison, while Stubbins also found himself in the wars following an aerial collision with goalkeeper Jimmy Strong and Alan Brown. The force of the challenge was such that the Liverpool man was knocked out for a few minutes until revived by the magic sponge of Albert Shelley.

Although playing the, "better class of football," Liverpool were again unable to find a way past Strong. Liddell went close with a long-range shot that whizzed just past the post and then he tried his luck again with powerful strike from a similar distance that Strong tipped over the bar with a, "million-to-one," save. From the subsequent corner, Liddell swung the ball over and to the Liverpool fans at the opposite end of the ground it looked as though it had just crept in and they celebrated what they thought was the opening goal. Unfortunately, the ball had landed on the roof of the net and their joy was short-lived.

At half-time, *Ranger* noted, "no side so far can claim any tangible superiority." More worryingly for Liverpool was the fact that their attack was, "still not the dominating force we know it can be." By the high standards he'd set himself since joining the club in September Stubbins was to endure another disappointing afternoon against Clarets' skipper - and future manager of Sunderland - Brown, a player many felt was the country's, "greatest uncapped centre-half."

Paisley and Taylor were the main creative forces in the Liverpool side but, with man-of-the-match Strong continuing to thwart any advances on his goal – he handled a 30 yarder from Fagan with, "perfect judgment," and successfully punched a Liddell corner clear – frustration began to set in, especially after Balmer went agonisingly close to a breakthrough.

"The longer the game went it looked more likely there would have to be a third meeting," recalled Liddell in later years but, just when thoughts started turning towards a second replay at Villa Park the following week, Burnley, slowly but surely, "began to take control," and 11 minutes from time, "a tragic trip," was to have dire consequences. As Kippax attempted to sail through the Liverpool defence towards, "an easy shooting chance," Jim Harley unceremoniously brought him crashing to the ground. A free-kick was awarded and, as Reg Atwell floated the ball in dangerously, Sidlow had no option but to concede a corner.

"From this the ball hung dangerously in the Liverpool penalty area until Harrison fastened on it, after one shot had been blocked out, and spun round to slash the ball to the top of the net for a fine goal."

After 197 minutes of, "nervous strain," the deadlock had finally been broken. Liverpool's players were dejected. Their thousands of fanatical followers silenced for the first time in the tie. A jubilant Harrison could scarcely believe what he'd just done and described the goal as, "the greatest thrill I have ever known. It still doesn't seem true. There was a slight opening in the crowd of Liverpool players when I shot, and the ball found it."

Aside from a Stubbins shot that was saved at full-stretch by Strong, "there was no response to this mortal blow," from Liverpool. With two minutes remaining everyone bar Sidlow was pushed into attack in a desperate attempt to force extra-time. It was to no avail. For the eleven deflated men in white, the final whistle brought the greatest disappointment they had known. Tears were unashamedly shed and hearts were broken as the realisation sunk in that their Wembley dream was over.

Stubbins recalled that defeat was difficult to take, especially considering none of the Liverpool squad, from the Chairman to the manager to the players, felt they would not reach Wembley.

"It was a bitter disappointment to us because we were confident we were heading to Wembley. We were very confident. In fact right through our cup run that year we thought we were good enough to get to Wembley and win the cup.

"I still believe that if we played them ten times, we'd have beaten them on about eight or nine occasions. But that's cup football. There was a period in the first half-hour when a goal to Liverpool might have demoralised the compact Burnley defence so much that we might have added to our score but the men from Turf Moor held out and we could not quibble at the final result."

"L'Pool's Wembley Bid Fails," was the solemn headline that ran across the front page of that night's Football Echo. *Contact* was in doubt as to the reason why the Reds' had lost. "The Liverpool defence cannot be reproached," he wrote, "nor can the half-backs. The fact remains that the front line as a whole was not good enough on this occasion."

In Monday's Daily Post, *Bee* agreed;

"The lesson of Blackburn had not been learned. Forward should have been the watchword. Loyalty to the fetish of 'Never change a winning side' led to the selectors giving the line another chance. Such loyalty was strained to breaking point. They played neither better nor worse than they had played at Blackburn, which means the Liverpool attack had quite forgotten the necessity for combination. Not one single round of passing; hardly a centered ball from extreme wingers; every forward in his turn trying to do too much by individualistic method. Manchester may leave a heritage to the club, if it is used to advantage."

Upon their return to Anfield Liverpool's devastated players were naturally a, "trifle downcast," but the post-match banquet, while not being the celebration that everyone had hoped for, turned into a, "cheery soccer funeral," with Chairman Bill McConnell helping to lift flagging spirits with an emotional, heartfelt address to the players that proves just what a fan of the club he was;

"I want to thank-you most sincerely for what you have done this season. You have put up a splendid show in the league and cup and we are grateful to you. I am sorry you are not going to Wembley, because I know how much you had been looking forward to it but don't be downhearted. We are proud of you and thank each and every one of you."

Liverpool's best and most exciting cup run for 33 years was over but, while it may not have eased the excruciating sense of emptiness at the time, there was one positive to take from the semi-final defeat to Burnley – it meant the Reds were now free to concentrate all their efforts on League matters once again.

Chapter Twelve
The Reds are coming up the hill...

Liverpool v Sunderland
Saturday 19 April 1947

*"Ardent Kopite, deciding to hang himself last Saturday night, was in the
final stage of passing out when his small son said, 'Dad you're going all blue,'
'then cut me down quick,' retorted Pop."*

Liverpool Echo

A lesser team may have crumbled in the face of such an agonising defeat but this Liverpool team was made of much sterner stuff and in the difficult days that followed the cup defeat to Burnley a steely determination emerged from deep within the club that roared, "the Reds are still in the running for League honours." The 'holy grail' may have slipped from their grasp but there was no time for worrying about it. Any flagging spirits within the dressing room were quickly lifted in time for their return to league action at home to Sunderland the following week.

In his weekly newspaper column Albert Stubbins stressed the need for everyone to focus on the league now that cup glory was gone;

"Although the last few weeks of a football season often appear to be without interest when a team is eliminated from the Cup competition the fact that Liverpool still has a lively interest in the League Championship adds spice to the remaining games. Our programme is a stiff one but a fresh winning streak at this stage will see us well up among the leaders, and give satisfaction to supporters whose loyalty has been unwavering throughout the season."

Billy Liddell similarly recalled;

"In the League we had seven games left, only two of them at home, and the championship seemed out of reach. But we were not a team to give up on anything and everybody was determined to have a go at it."

If players and fans needed any extra motivation to put their Maine Road heartache behind them by launching a serious assault on the title, it appeared right before their eyes when they picked up Friday's edition of the Echo. Since the Reds were last in league action, Wolves had regained the leadership from Blackpool courtesy of a 7-2 hammering of Derby. *Ranger's* consensus was that the Midlanders, "have the championship in their pocket," and that, "Liverpool's chances of overtaking Wolves are so slender we can ignore them." So much for local reporters backing the local team!

With seven league games still to play Kay's men sat fifth in the table, a four point gap separating them from top spot but, with the distraction of the cup sadly gone, for the first time since January, all their energies could now be channelled into their pursuit of the title. Liverpool were certainly handily placed and the mood among the players was that they had a point to prove. There was a nagging feeling within the squad that they didn't get their just desserts from their Easter fixtures and there was now a renewed resolve to put this right. Stubbins wrote that;

> *"Results over the holidays have left us with the feeling that we might have five points instead of three out of a possible six. However, the Reds' championship hopes are good and the Wolves versus Liverpool game will be a vital one. Our League rivals are a well-balanced side and will fight hard for honours which once appeared to be in their grasp. With Stoke, Manchester United and Blackpool also making big efforts, indications are that the struggle for the First Division Championship will be grueling."*

Failure to find the back of the net in two games against Second Division Burnley - albeit a side with one of the best defensive records in the country - meant scapegoats in an under fire forward line were sought and changes were made for the visit to Anfield of 10th placed Sunderland. After much deliberation by the directors Done and Fagan were the unfortunate duo to be dropped, replaced by Palk and McLeod respectively. However, it was Stubbins - ironically the man guilty of spurning one of the best chances in the first semi-final - who was to get

The Liverpool dressing room.

Liverpool's season back on track with a predatory piece of attacking play, the very sought that had so frustratingly eluded him against the Clarets.

In what was a keenly fought contest, illuminated by rare rays of bright sunshine and warm temperatures, the visitors gave a decent account of themselves in terms of possession but didn't have the, "necessary punch," to match their grace. If they had then the chances are that they could well have returned home with more to show for their efforts.

Liverpool's cause had not been helped by the fact Balmer, who unfairly bore the brunt of the crowd's criticism, was forced to play 75 minutes of the match in, "great pain," after straining himself when stretching for the ball. The fans' treatment of him was described by the Daily Post as, "partisanship cloaking unjust hatred," and it prompted *Bee* to launch an impassioned attack on the Anfield spectators for their lack of respect for such a loyal club servant.

> *"They levelled their laughter (the worst form of barracking) on Saturday at Balmer. I hate them for it. If they had half-sensed what had happened they must have known Balmer was bruised and in agony from the first fifteen minutes. Barracking home players has become a disgrace. Perhaps the Anfield enthusiast is never so happy as when he is miserable."*

Such a hot topic of conversation did this become that the club felt it necessary, in the following matchday programme, to politely remind these critics of their duty as so called supporters of the team.

> *"It is regrettable that a certain section of our supporters so far forgot themselves as to barrack players at a previous home game. Players are only human – not machines, and it is inevitable that on occasions they may be slightly below form, but as sportsmen it is up to supporters to encourage and not discourage. A player is fully conscious of his failings and it does not assist to improve his game with gratuitous advice."*

Fortunately, this sorry incident failed to overshadow what was a welcome return to winning ways against Sunderland - a win that hopefully helped to lighten the mood of the demanding Liverpool fans. While not the free-flowing victory that had taken Preston apart in their last League outing, there were still many positives to take from the performance of the recently beaten cup semi-finalists.

Sidlow may have seen plenty of the ball, which suggests the Reds were under pressure, but only two of the many saves he had to make were what could be classed as difficult, while in front of him the solid Hughes, on his return to the team after a four game absence in place of the injured Jones, and the almost faultless Taylor caught the eye.

Taylor in particular, was rapidly establishing himself as a, "real touch of class," and his fine form continued, with the Echo commenting that, "[he] is adding style and polish to his consistent half-back work week by week. Some of his cunning flicks, back-heel touches and body swerves were in the real Busby tradition." Recognition of his ever improving form came when called up as a reserve for England's looming international clash with France at Highbury, while alongside Jones and Stubbins he was also named in the squad selected to represent the Football League in their forthcoming clash with their Irish counterparts in Dublin.

Inexperienced inside-forwards Palk, "of the [Harry] Chambers mould," and McLeod who, "could be mistaken for [Willie] Fagan in his hair, build and stance," also drew praise for, "linking well with their fellow attackers," but it was Stubbins who hogged the headlines, his 23rd goal of the season the icing on the cake of another impressive all-round display. From a free-kick deep inside the Liverpool half Lambert's hopeful punt into the Sunderland box resulted in a race for possession between the centre-forward and goalkeeper. Luckily Stubbins just managed to get there first, poking his right foot out and deflecting the ball over the advancing Mapson.

Some journalists reported the goal as a fluke; others described it as the perfect example of being in the right place at the right time. Luck or opportunism? The newspapers were undecided. But it didn't really matter as it was a goal good enough to see off the doughty challenge of the Mackems. It was the second time that season Stubbins had netted against the club he had once represented as a junior and, while not one of his best, it was certainly one of the most important as it was enough to clinch a narrow victory and another priceless two points.

His quick thinking and intelligent use of the ball had once again proved decisive. "Stubbins played Sunderland by himself in a series of runs, personal and private, and all engaging, making the first half-hour his own special niche and triumph."

But still the pain of the previous weekend's cup defeat was not forgotten and for those still suffering a semi-final hangover – and there were plenty of those among a subdued crowd of just over 40,000 – his goal had, "come a week too late." For the more optimistic Liverpool fans the goal had breathed new life into the season. With six games left to play and a title still to fight for, to them, there was little point reflecting on 'what if's'.

With the four teams above them also winning it was a case of as you were at the top of the table but, while victory over Sunderland was never going to make up for the bitter disappointment of so narrowly missing out on a first ever trip to Wembley, it did manage to bring a smile back to some Liverpudlian faces and restored belief that there could yet be a silver lining to this most amazing season.

Aston Villa v Liverpool
Saturday 26 April 1947

"With a home fixture against Manchester United and a visit to Wolverhampton to come, the winners are now looking ruefully, on home failings which seemed unimportant at the time, but which now begin to tell a tale on League hopes."

Leslie Edwards, Daily Post

On what should have been the biggest day yet in Liverpool's history, a date that had been pencilled in the diary since early January, the colour of the opposition shirts served as a stark reminder as to why the Reds were not at Wembley to take on Charlton Athletic in the FA Cup Final. Time may be a great healer and a fortnight had now passed since Liverpool bowed out of the cup but, as the focus of the nation turned to English football's showpiece event of the year beneath the twin towers, the men from Anfield could be forgiven for thinking it could have been them. Instead, hoping to exorcise the Claret and Blue demons that had haunted them for the past two weeks, it was off to Villa Park in the continued - and many thought vain - pursuit of vital league points.

Ahead of the game the club received a tremendous boost when it was announced that Billy Liddell had been selected to represent a Great Britain XI in the prestigious, "match of the century," to be played at Hampden Park against the Rest of Europe on May 10. Arranged by Stanley Rouse to celebrate the return of England, Scotland, Northern Ireland and Wales to football's governing body FIFA, the squad was chosen by a panel of selectors from the four home countries and the inclusion of Liddell alongside greats such as Stanley Matthews, Wilf Mannion and Tommy Lawton, and ahead of players such as Raich Carter and Peter Doherty, was viewed as a huge honour for the club and proof of Liverpool's status as one of the top post-war club's in Britain.

The imperious Billy Liddell.

Of greater importance however, was the ongoing quest for points in the race for the title. The prospect of collecting two more at Villa Park, a venue where Liverpool had not won since 1929, wasn't helped by the news that Balmer was unfit due to the injury he'd sustained against Sunderland the previous week. The news may have delighted his detractors - but it was clearly a blow for the Reds.

Balmer's injury meant a recall for Fagan, while Prescot-born Bill Watkinson - with just two Lancashire Senior Cup games (and one goal) - under his belt, came into the side for his league debut at the expense of McLeod. Having impressed in the three games he had recently played McLeod could count himself unfortunate to drop out but the call-up of Watkinson was to prove inspired - as was the return of Fagan.

Villa, a side plagued by inconsistency and who had spent most of the season hovering between mid-table and the fringes of the title race, also fielded a debutant in the shape of diminutive local discovery Bill Evans. "Born within a penalty kick of the ground," it was his header after just five minutes that opened the scoring on a pleasant Spring day in the Midlands.

The goal came as no surprise. Villa had started brightly and Evans in particular, "a midget centre-forward of real value," was already proving a handful. Before netting he had hooked a teasing ball deep into the heart of the Liverpool box and but for no other forward being up with the play the hosts could have been ahead even earlier. His goal a few moments later came via a cross from the left by wing-half Dickie Dorsett. Evans and Jackie Martin both went up for it, as did Sidlow, but slight hesitancy on the part of the Reds' number one allowed the debutant to get his head onto the ball first and he glanced it into the back of the net.

What a start to his top-flight career. But anything Evans could do so could his fellow debutant in the opposition ranks. Just three minutes later Watkinson latched onto a through ball from Stubbins and proceeded towards goal, "at his leisure," before expertly picking his spot in the far corner of the net to stun the home crowd. Those watching in the press box were instantly impressed - Watkinson, "has the speed and spirit to ensure a further run in the outside right position." The Liverpool directors were certainly in agreement and the 25 year old did enough here to retain his place for the remainder of the season.

An eagerness to build on his equalising goal saw the new boy twice caught offside soon afterwards, " through his natural desire to be up and doing," but it wasn't long before the hosts began reapplying pressure on the Liverpool defence where, "Hughes was doing the bulk of the work in the centre." Dorsett went close to restoring Villa's lead, "when he took up Evans' inside pass and hit a good shot to scrape the outside of the post," and as the hosts, "swarmed around the Liverpool goal at this point," Dorsett again, and then Evans, both had shots that Sidlow , saved with his feet. The Welsh stopper was certainly busy and he had no time to rest before having to punch clear a free-kick whipped in by Bob Iverson.

Under so much pressure it was a total surprise Fagan fired the visitors in front on the half hour mark. Liddell's free-kick near the far touchline was volleyed towards goal by Stubbins. The ball fell to Fagan who drifted by his marker to convert past keeper Joe Rutherford with what was described as a real opportunist strike.

Thankfully for Liverpool this was the end of the scoring. On the balance of play that followed Villa were unlucky not to come away with more to show for their efforts. At times they laid siege to the Liverpool goal with Evans and Leslie Smith an almost constant attacking threat. Sidlow pulled off two great saves in quick succession to deny Smith and although the visitors were under the cosh for long periods of the second half the football on both sides, "was first-rate even if there was a general lethargy about the 40,000 present."

Liverpool's work rate was exemplary and it was because of this that they were deemed fully deserving of their win. The fact they managed to come away with maximum points owed much to the defensive brilliance of Lambert and Hughes, and the goalkeeping heroics of Sidlow, especially after the break when Villa piled on the pressure in an attempt to redress the balance. So good was Sidlow's second half showing that many observes rated it his best ever performance for the Reds.

When Harley suffered a knee injury with 20 minutes remaining, forcing a positional reshuffle that saw Fagan moved to right-back, "Liverpool were hardly well placed to retain the lead," and Holte End hopes rose. Amid a frenzied end to the game Paisley was temporarily knocked out when bravely putting his head in the way of a George Edwards centre and, "Liverpool finished gasping."

A hard-earned two points it was and – on the day Charlton beat Burnley 1-0 after extra-time in the first ever FA Cup Final to be televised in its entirety and Leeds became the first club in the country to be relegated – it kept Liverpool in the title picture.

With just one game out of their remaining four at home however, the local papers were once again playing down their title chances. "Anfield is bewailing the losses of home fixtures," wrote *Ranger*, "the winning of which would have given them a fair chance of overhauling Wolves in the league race." According to the Echo, second or third was the best the Reds could hope for but what he failed to take into account was Liverpool's impressive away form.

The reporter's view also differed greatly from that offered by Albert Stubbins. "While it was mathematically possible for the Reds to catch Wolves," he wrote, "then hope remained."

On the same afternoon Blackpool - despite not playing - saw their faint title aspirations finally extinguished courtesy of the leaders' thrilling 6-4 victory over Chelsea at Molineux. Just four teams could now win the title – Wolves, Manchester United, Stoke and Liverpool – and two of them were to clash in a pivotal game at Anfield the following week.

Liverpool v Manchester United
Saturday 3 May 1947

"Although they have little hope of overtaking Wolves
they are certain to be in the first four."

Ranger, Liverpool Echo

In terms of stature it may not have been quite the biggest domestic fixture on the English football calendar that it is today, but when Liverpool went head-to-head with fellow title challengers Manchester United at Anfield on the first Saturday of May 1947, the stakes could not have been much higher. On what should have been the last weekend of the league season Liverpool still had five games left to play and this was their final home game. An afternoon of high tension was expected.

Much had changed at Anfield since the 5-0 hammering at the hands of United back in September. But with Liverpool still trailing their fellow north-western Reds by two places and three points - although they had played a game less - anything other than a victory would signal the end of their gallant bid for top spot. While Liverpool's form was the cause of growing optimism among fans on the Kop, United were in the midst of an even more impressive run of form – unbeaten since mid-March - and tipped as the most likely of the chasing pack to catch Wolves should the Molineux men falter.

Adding extra spice to an already vitally important occasion was Matt Busby's first return to the venue he had called home for nine years prior to him accepting the role of manager at Old Trafford in October 1945. Such was the high esteem in which Busby was held by Kopites of the time many still regarded him as the 'King of Anfield' and he duly received a reception you could never imagine being afforded to future men in charge of United.

Of the Liverpool side selected to face their title rivals, five – Lambert, Hughes, Paisley, Palk and Liddell – had played alongside Busby for the Reds during the war while Balmer had been a team-mate of his in the two seasons prior to the outbreak of hostilities. Two of Busby's other pre-war Anfield colleagues were missing however. With speculation again mounting about his future, club captain Willie Fagan - the previous weekend's match-winner - was a notable absentee, while Phil Taylor was on stand-by duty for England in the international friendly against France at Highbury.

With Spicer and Jones returning to the team, a defensive reshuffle saw Paisley move to right-half and, after impressing against Villa the previous week, there was also a home debut for Watkinson, who was to again impress at inside-right with his, "splendid notions of a ground pass, and a through pass, together with a wholehearted endeavour that must be encouraging." As kick-off approached the ground appeared to be nowhere near full but supporters continued to pour in as play got underway and eventually close on 50,000 crammed inside to witness a classic 'four-pointer'.

United - who had adopted a similar warm-up approach to that which Liverpool displayed on the opening day of the season at Bramall Lane - started strongly in their changed strip of, "vivid," blue shirts with red numbering and white shorts, and a promising run by Scotland winger Jimmy Delaney was let down by a finish that flew high into the Kop. Although bright and sunny there was a,"gusty wind which curled the ball awkwardly under the big stands," and with Liverpool playing against it in the first half, the defence at times found it difficult to clear their lines.

There was a let off for the hosts when a great volley by Jack Rowley was fortuitously deflected behind for a corner with Sidlow looking well beaten. It was, "counter-balanced," however, just moments later when Liddell, "took the ball into the centre and, ploughing through on his own, hit an immensely strong shot over the bar."

One of the more interesting duels of the day was Liddell against United's esteemed Irish full-back Johnny Carey. The two were due to face each other again in seven days time at Hampden Park in the eagerly anticipated Great Britain versus the Rest of the World clash and, as a pointer to that, all eyes were on them here. Up until this point Carey was perhaps edging it, but in the 12th minute Stubbins, amid a frantic goalmouth scramble, struck what was to be one of the most important goals he would ever score - and Liddell played a vital part in it..

The move began when Spicer expertly dispossessed a United forward and played a neat ball to Liverpool's flying Scot. With several members of his family having travelled down from Scotland and looking on from the Main Stand, Liddell treated them to a sudden burst of pace that left Carey trailing in his wake. As he raced upfield United's defence was forced onto the back-foot and, with the goal getting closer and closer, the crowd braced themselves for one of his trademark thunderbolts. Unselfishly however, the Scot, "took the ball within five yards of goal before putting across a square centre to Stubbins." The big number nine saw his first effort deflected and Balmer then took a pot-shot that was blocked by the keeper before Stubbins seized quickly on the rebound. At the second attempt, he managed to, "net through the ruck," to break the deadlock.

For *Contact*, 'it was a goal which gave almost as much joy as any this season." It was to prove a priceless strike. With leaders Wolves a goal down at Portsmouth the realisation swept around the ground that, for the team that emerged victorious from this clash, a genuine chink of light could be shining down on them from the First Division summit. As a consequence the pace of the game became even more frenetic. The action flowed from one end to the other with Liverpool, "surprising the natives by their bright and able artistry."

But, as United had proved back in the earlier meeting between the two sides, they boasted a, "forward line of great penetrative power," and it required, "some stern work," by Hughes to keep them at bay as they threatened an equaliser. Indeed, as time wore on it was the visitors who started to play more, "fine on the floor football," and although Liddell continued to have the beating of Carey, there could have been no complaints had an equalising goal been scored at this point. It was famous fighting spirit to come to the fore and, knowing their title aspirations depended on it, they battled to preserve their precious one goal lead with relentless, "tenacity and enthusiasm."

Never was this more evident than during the last quarter when the visitors lay siege to Sidlow's goal. Unsurprisingly in a game of such magnitude, tempers became frayed, with the Football Echo reporting that, "there was more than a shade of spike and spirit about the game at the present time." With decisions going against both sides and United beginning to, "take umbrage against what they considered were wrong," the fervour of the crowd threatened to boil over. It was gripping stuff. Typical of what we've now all come to expect from a Liverpool v United clash. With so much riding on the end result a nail-biting finale ensued with the visitors, "battering away for a goal which their approach play deserved." Fortunately for Liverpool, a certain Mr A Ferguson was only five years old and living in Scotland in 1947, and with no fourth official on the sidelines to order the now statutory playing of 'Fergie time', the Reds held on to celebrate a crucial win and gain sweet revenge on the team that inflicted upon them their heaviest defeat of the season.

Victory over United took Liverpool's points tally for the season to 50 – their best since 1924/25. The only downside to the afternoon was the news that Wolves had fought back to snatch a draw at Fratton Park. Still, the gap at the top had been reduced and just three points now separated the leaders and the fourth-placed Redmen. Stoke's 2-1 win away at already relegated Leeds saw them leapfrog United into second place. The Potters were two points ahead of Liverpool but with them and United having played a game more, Liverpool had played themselves back into serious contention

Match-winner Stubbins was hailed as, "the finest centre-forward ever to wear these colours." Few who saw the genial Geordie in his pomp would disagree but while the identity of Liverpool greatest ever centre-forward is a debate that could rage forever there can be no doubting that the record fee paid for him in Autumn was now looking more and more like the bargain of the season. Back in September - , when Liverpool crashed to their heaviest defeat of the season at the hands of United, they did so without him. On this occasion, it was he who proved the difference between the two sides – proof, if it was needed, that their record outlay had been money well spent.

Charlton Athletic v Liverpool
Saturday 10 May 1947

"Stubbins' display was a revelation to the vast crowd...besides his scoring feat, his position play, his impartial distribution of his passes, and the uncanny way he had of always being in the right position had the Charlton backs and half-backs guessing time after time."

Daily Post

It was against a backdrop of rumours surrounding the future of captain Willie Fagan that Liverpool prepared for the visit to FA Cup holders Charlton Athletic. With speculation sweeping the city that Fagan had asked for a transfer, manager George Kay made the unprecedented step of taking time out from his team's preparations for the weekend and issuing a firm denial that anything was afoot. Stories linking the Reds with a swoop for Greenock Morton's Billy Steel only served to heighten the belief that Fagan's Anfield days were numbered, especially when one national newspaper ran with a report that, "a secret First Division club," had offered Morton a, "well-known Scot" in part-exchange for Steel.

After attending the club's weekly board meeting however, Kay told reporters that;

"The matter was not discussed for there was nothing to discuss. I had a talk with Fagan who said there was no truth in the story and that he is perfectly happy at Anfield."

To quash these rumours further, it was then announced that Fagan would be back in the team for the trip to The Valley.

For the first time in many years both Merseyside teams were playing away from home on the same Saturday. Amazingly, both games were of vital importance to the Red half of the city. While Liverpool were playing the first of three games in as many weeks down in the capital, Everton had travelled to Wolves with the best wishes of every Liverpudlian ringing in their ears.

Liverpool journeyed south minus Billy Liddell who was otherwise engaged in his native Scotland as a member of the Great Britain side that was taking on the Rest of Europe at Hampden Park. The hype surrounding this game had been building for weeks and, according to the Daily Mirror, "on the shoulders of our players lies the responsibility of proving to the Soccer world that the teachers of the game are still better than the pupils."

It was a contest that largely overshadowed the first weekend of rescheduled league games and a crowd of 135,000 crammed into Hampden Park to see the Brits totally overwhelm their opponents in an emphatic 6-1 victory. Despite not getting on the scoresheet, Liddell gave a good account of himself in a star-studded side, but a pulled muscle just before half-time reduced his effectiveness after the break and would force him to sit out Liverpool's next two games. Despite picking up an injury his participation in the game was an immense source of pride for everyone connected to the club, so much so that four directors journeyed north to support him.

Their presence in Glasgow set transfer tongues wagging again for lining up alongside Liddell in attack was reputed Liverpool target Steel, scorer of the third - and best - goal of the afternoon. So impressed by his performance where the Liverpool delegation, that on their return to Merseyside they immediately reported back to Chairman Bill McConnell and from the hospital bed - where he was under observation after recently falling ill - it was revealed that, "everything possible is being done to bring Steel to Anfield."

One player heading away from Anfield, seemingly never to return, was Barney Ramsden who was reported to be, "somewhere on the high seas...en route for the United States," after finally fulfilling his promise to quit the game to start a new life on the other side of the Atlantic. The full-back had informed the club of his plans back in November and, after starting the first 18 games of the season, he had only figured in five since, the last against Preston on Easter Monday. Liverpool were far from happy at the timing of his departure but this wasn't the end of the matter.

Of more immediate concern to manager George Kay and the selectors was the team to face Charlton at The Valley. With Liddell injured, his place went to red-headed South African Bob Priday, while the only other changes to the line-up saw Taylor return from international duty in place of Spicer and the recalled Fagan taking the place of Palk.

Buoyed by their FA Cup triumph of a fortnight before and playing in front of their home fans for the first time since victory over Burnley, Charlton's need for points was just as vital as Liverpool's as they were hovering perilously close to the relegation zone. No team had ever won the cup and suffered relegation in the same season but they started the day fourth from bottom, just six points clear of the bottom two, and their quest to avoid an unwanted place in the record books was not helped by the late withdrawal through injury of their captain, future Reds' boss and war-time Anfield favourite, Don Welsh.

The absence of Welsh was one of several changes to the side which had lifted the cup. Prior to kick-off the trophy was proudly paraded around the ground amid loud cheers from the home crowd and thoughts of 'what might have been' among the watching Liverpool players. The visitors knew though, that victory would take them a step closer to a prestigious prize of their own and, rather than inspiring the hosts, the pre-match display of silver served only to spur the visitors on. Liverpool burst out of the starting blocks and, once in front, the destiny of the points was never in doubt with the recently crowned cup winners brought back down to earth with a bump.

For the third game running the ever improving Stubbins was the match winner, his stock rising to even greater heights with a sublimely executed, "glorious hat-trick," that left the Addicks anxiously looking over their shoulder in the fight to beat the drop.

In what was, "a rousing start," dominated by two long punts upfield, Bill Johnson almost scored for the hosts before;

> "a minute later the whole Liverpool forward line engineered a beautiful attack. At the right moment, and at the right height the ball went to Fagan, who sent in an oblique shot, which Bartram saved finely in the corner."

Jones then, "distinguished himself by making two smart clearances," but this was the prelude to, "some determined forward play by Liverpool," that led to the opening goal. Watkinson and Priday both tested the keeper and the latter also got himself into a good scoring position but, "shot wide with only the goalkeeper to beat."

When the breakthrough goal finally arrived it was more than deserved. "From a long kick on the left Stubbins got the ball in the centre, and running strongly, the centre forward drew Bartram out and cleverly shot a spectacular goal." With Liverpool clearly the better team, "Charlton were always made to appear as playing second fiddle," and, "Sidlow had an almost idle afternoon in goal." The one save he was forced to make however, during the second half, was later deemed, "the best in the match."

With the visiting forwards always threatening another goal it came as little surprise when Stubbins notched his second in the 59th minute. It owed much to the, "clever scheming of inside-forward Balmer," whose astute through pass presented Stubbins with an opportunity that was, "food and drink," for a goal-getter of his quality.

Prior to the game's first goal, play had been halted for five minutes while repairs were made to a shattered upright following a fiercely struck shot by centre-forward Bill Robinson and due to this delay it was only 2-0 when that evening's Football Echo went to print. For the majority of Liverpool supporters therefore, it was not until they picked up the next morning's newspapers that they discovered Stubbins went on to complete his hat-trick and that Robinson managed to pull a consolation goal back for the home side.

So late in the game did Stubbins' last goal come that reports of how he scored it are sketchy but having already netted with both his left and right foot it has to be assumed that the one which clinched the match-ball came via his head to complete what was widely described as the, "perfect hat-trick." It was his second treble of the season, taking his tally for the Reds to an impressive 23.

On their return to the dressing room the Liverpool team were greeted with the news that near neighbours Everton had done them an almighty favour and pulled off a shock 3-2 victory at Molineux. With Manchester United also failing to win - they had to settle for a 1-1 draw away at Preston - the day couldn't have turned out any better. In the boardroom afterwards;

> *"Charlton boss Jimmy Seed and his directors, were very sincere in congratulating Liverpool officials on their victory. They, and the 40,000 spectators, recognised that Liverpool, if not a super team, showed teamwork, cleverness in controlling a lively ball and opportunism to accept chances."*

It had been a, "fine display of football," and the Echo was, at long last, in no doubt that it was, "championship stuff." Fast, clever, forceful and productive being *Ranger's* assessment of a win that left the Reds breathing down the necks of their title rivals, with just a point now separating them from top spot.

Brentford v Liverpool
Saturday 17 May 1947

"Liverpool are having the league championship almost thrown at them."

Ranger, Liverpool Echo

Of the three remaining league games Liverpool had left to play it was the trip to Griffin Park for the game with Brentford that, on paper at least, seemed to be the least daunting. The Bees had endured a difficult season. They had dropped into the bottom two in early March and only a mathematical miracle could now save them from the drop. They were six points from safety with six points to play for so anything but a win over the title-chasing Reds would see the seemingly inevitable confirmed.

Even if they won it would require a massive turnaround in terms of goal average to save them. Despite the view it would be another away win for the Reds, this, "easy looking," fixture turned out to be anything but.

Almost twelve months to the day since they set sail for the USA, Liverpool's leg weary squad were starting to feel the pace and for many the seasons' end couldn't come soon enough. "The elongated season, plus the American trip has made the players' last 12 months a solid, unending task and many of them undoubtedly feel in need of a rest." But with long time leaders Wolves showing signs of cracking under the pressure - just as they had done in the last pre-war Football League season of 1938/39 - the jaded Redmen entered the home straight in the knowledge that one final push now could reap the ultimate reward.

However the season ended, Liverpool were already making plans for the future and every day it seemed that a new player was linked with the club although prior to the game at Brentford , manager George Kay announced that the Reds had suddenly pulled out of the race to sign Morton inside-forward Billy Steel. After having a club record £15,000 bid accepted, Kay held long talks with Steel in Glasgow but reported back to the club's directors that the Scottish international would still not put pen to paper on the deal and, "so far as Liverpool are concerned the deal's off." Instead, it was reported that the Reds had switched their attentions to Rangers' famous winger Willie Waddell, while Hearts of Midlothian pair Alex McRae and Tommy Sloan were also muted as possible new arrivals.

With all this talk of fresh faces Liverpool's forgotten forward Cyril Done, who had not featured in the first team since the cup exit, let everyone know that he had not disappeared completely by banging in a hat-trick as the Reds finally clinched a cup final place - albeit in the Liverpool Senior Cup. Done's midweek treble came in a 5-3 Anfield victory over South Liverpool, a club that was making great efforts in trying to justify its claims for a place in the Football League and for whom ex-Red Alf Hobson kept goal.

It was a tie that, while not registering high on the Richter scale of interest among Kopites, certainly aroused plenty in Garston, whose inhabitants provided a large contingent of the Anfield crowd. Despite giving a decent account of themselves however, South were undone largely by Done, although his three goals were not enough to earn him a recall to the first eleven for the match at Griffin Park.

Just a week after victory over Charlton, Liverpool returned to the capital in good spirits but were forced to do so without the ever dependable Bill Jones, who was left at home to rest after failing to overcome a troublesome back injury. Jim Harley was recalled to take his place and, with Taylor away on England duty, there was also a return at left-half for Spicer. These changes prompted a defensive reshuffle that saw Paisley move to right-half and it was to be an eventful afternoon for the for the Liverpool number six. His tenacious tackling was a major feature of a lacklustre first-half and, despite suffering a knee injury that was to severely reduce his effectiveness as the game wore on, he also found time to pose a threat at the other end, most notably with a lob that Joe Crozier in the Brentford goal did well to push over with his finger-tips, following a, "a classic long dribble against the odds," by Hughes.

Sidlow was also in the thick of the action during what was, "a rather dull, go-as-you-please start," and at one point, "had to throw the ball away as though it were a piece of hot coal when [Len] Townsend threatened to charge the goalkeeper and ball over the line." Liverpool's use of the offside trap had the crowd on tenterhooks and, much to the dismay of the home fans, their cleverly devised system worked a treat as they gradually drew the sting out of the Bee's early enterprise.

With Priday enjoying, "a fair innings against old man [Bill] Gorman," Liverpool were soon on top and were clearly the better team - "playing beautiful crisp stuff at their best." Indeed, most observers were of the opinion that, "Brentford looked certain to be beaten." During the visitors' period of dominance before the break, Stubbins (twice) and Priday went close but *Contact* still felt that their, "finishing was not punishing enough."

Invigorated by the interval and inspired by their red-headed skipper Archie Macauley, Brentford enjoyed their best spell of the match shortly after the restart and their hopes rose when a limping Paisley had to leave the field for treatment. He was off for ten minutes before returning to the fray at outside-left. During his absence Hughes, "set the seal of greatness on his work," with two magnificent defensive headers.

With Brentford full-back Harry Oliver also struggling with an injury and pushed out onto the wing it was virtually ten against ten with both of the walking wounded of little use to their respective sides. Paisley managed to bravely soldier on until the 70th minute when, barely able to stand, he reluctantly hobbled off for good.

> *"With Paisley on the field they were confident and equal to rather finicky Brentford attacking. Minus, Paisley, who seemed set for an outstanding display, they were shaken but never thoroughly upset."*

As so often happens however, the team with the numerical disadvantage went on to break the deadlock just moments later. Watkinson, now operating from right-half to cover the loss of Paisley, did well to make in-roads along the right hand edge of the box and, although his subsequent centre was scrambled clear by a Brentford defender, the ball fell to an unmarked Priday, "who bore through and hit a fine shot to give Liverpool the lead." The points looked safe and, had it not been for a, "million-to-one," save by Crozier from a Fagan header shortly afterwards, then victory would surely have been assured;

> *"Stubbins put over the most acceptable last centre. Fagan's head hit it truly and with great speed and only the chance positioning of Crozier in the only spot in which he could have saved prevented a goal."*

It was, "an extraordinarily fine chance," and just how crucial a stop that was to be only became apparent seven minutes from time when Brentford snatched a deserved equaliser via the head of inside-forward George Stewart. "It was cruel misfortune that the side that had been minus Paisley for almost the whole of the second half should build a lead then lose it so late in the game," lamented Leslie Edwards,before adding that, "it would have been an injustice to Brentford if they had lost."

A dropped point could have had a catastrophic effect on Liverpool's title bid but the news awaiting them as they dejectedly trooped off the pitch was music to their ears – both Wolves and Stoke had also drawn and they were very much still in the race. The biggest winners on the day though were Manchester United who cantered to a 3-0 win at home to Portsmouth, a result that took them level on points at the top.

Despite Liverpool's obvious disappointment at failing to maintain their winning run the point gained at Griffin Park was generally considered to be a good one given that they were not at full strength and that Brentford's performance was widely rated as one of their best of the season. It may not have been enough to save them from the drop but the Daily Mirror was typical of most newspapers in their post-match assessment that, "only bad luck deprived them of both points for they were unquestionably the better team." The Echo was in agreement that lady luck was smiling down on the Reds and, in light of the other results, suggested that, "Liverpool are having the league championship almost thrown at them."

Arsenal v Liverpool
Saturday 24 May 1947

"A beaten side had came out winners. As a chestnut-rescuing effort it was the team's best, and keeps them interested in the championship until the last kick of the last match at Wolverhampton on Saturday."

Leslie Edwards, Daily Post

With the tension at the top mounting, the last thing Liverpool needed now was a serious injury to one of their key players. With the finishing line in sight every last reserve of energy was required to help drag the worn out Reds over it, but in the run-up to their penultimate league outing the news everyone at Anfield feared was confirmed; Bob Paisley would play no further part in the campaign as a result of the knee injury sustained against Brentford.

With Taylor still away with the FA touring party and Liddell not yet recovered from the injury he picked up in Glasgow, it was a bitter blow that couldn't have come at worse time. Two games remained and to be in with a chance of snatching the championship, nothing less than maximum points were required from both. "It is a bleak prospect," said *Bee*, "yet there is sufficient spirit in the side and reserve talent available to make the challenge to Wolverhampton Wanderers a real one."

In light of their predicament Liverpool, the reserve members of the squad were given a timely opportunity to stake their first team claims in the Lancashire Senior Cup semi-final at Anfield. Five players with previous senior experience were selected for the team to take on Burnley and, before a crowd of 18,000, "a splendid evening's entertainment," was settled by a man still waiting for a competitive call-up - local lad Arthur Shepherd - whose well taken first half strike proved to be the only goal of the game. It was hardly consolation for defeat to the Clarets in the FA Cup semi-final but it secured a place in another final nonetheless and kept everyone at the club in high spirits ahead of the all-important trip to Highbury.

With the situation at the top so tight – just one point separated the top two from those in third and fourth – and with their fellow title rivals not in action until the Bank Holiday Monday this was a chance for Liverpool to lay down the gauntlet by taking over at the top of the table with just one game to play.

Arsenal away was by no means the dreaded fixture it once was. By their lofty pre-war standards it had been a season to forget. At one stage the Gunners had hovered perilously close to the trap door and, although they had long since secured their proud top-flight status, they had little left but pride to play for as Liverpool arrived at the famous Marble Halls. In what was an unexpected pre-match boost Bill, "play anywhere," Jones passed a late fitness test and was promptly named as a direct replacement for the stricken Paisley in what was the only change to the Liverpool eleven that had drawn in London the previous week.

Like Liverpool, Arsenal were also forced to field a much depleted team. Leslie Compton was unavailable due to his cricket commitments – he was a wicket-keeper with Middlesex, record signing Bryn Jones was injured, whilst former Everton favourite Joe Mercer - an audacious transfer target of the Reds earlier in the season - lined up against his old adversaries for the first time in Arsenal colours.

With manager George Kay amazingly, "away on business," - it was believed he was scouting for transfer targets - it was left to captain Jack Balmer to give his team mates tactical instructions but, with the sun in their eyes, Liverpool struggled early on and his plans to, "keep the ball on the floor," quickly dissipated.

Sidlow had to be at his best when turning Rooke's powerful low shot round the post for a corner but that was a rare moment of anxiety for the visitors. In general the defence was playing, "so well and with such consistency that Arsenal's flowing moves invariably came to an end long before danger loomed." As the home side continued to apply pressure, concentration among the Liverpool back line was paramount. *Ranger* noted that, "they tackled well and made some timely interventions," while it was said that Lambert had rarely played better, "extra-ordinary in positional sense and timing."

Watkinson's, "judicious and prompt use of the ball," made him the most notable of the Liverpool forwards. He was, "never guilty of the crime of trying to do over

225

much, live and capable and surprisingly often too good for full-back Barnes." Fellow, "reserve winger," Priday was again on form too and, brimming with confidence after getting off the mark the previous week, stood out with some eye-catching forays down the left flank."

Genuine goalscoring chances though were few and far between. Stubbins tried his luck with a speculative effort that went high and wide, while Spicer's goal bound, "cannonball," effort was deflected behind by an Arsenal defender. There was a let-off for the visitors when Lewis went down in the box and Arsenal's players claimed for a penalty. Fortunately, their appeals were ignored and play was waved on by referee Mr Tedds of Nottingham.

As the strong afternoon sun continued to beat down the intense heat and the effects of a long, hard season, combined to make the second half a gruelling slog. As time ticked by on the famous Highbury clock Arsenal regained the ascendancy and it seemed only a matter of time before Liverpool's stubborn rearguard was worn down. Indeed, it came as no surprise when, just after the hour mark, they took the lead through the Scottish right-winger Ian McPherson, a decorated war hero who had won the Distinguished Flying Cross while serving in the RAF.

At this point Liverpool looked a beaten team and it was only following a positional switch that they managed to turn their fortunes around. In a game they simply had to win the Reds found themselves a goal down with just over 20 minutes to play. It looked like their title hopes had gone. The Liverpool directors then, "by a snap-vote," decided to move Jones to inside-forward in place of Fagan. Showing that even the Liverpool directors knew a thing or two about the game, within a minute of their switch the white shirts had drawn level. "Watkinson went on to earn and take a beautiful full-length corner," from which Balmer, having expertly evaded his marker, leapt like salmon to beat George Swindin in the Arsenal goal with a well placed header.

Highbury fell silent and although, "a draw would have sufficed this was Liverpool's lucky day." The home supporters barely had time to recover when Priday, for the second week running, proved his worth yet again when he;

> "wriggled through to deliver a shot or centre for which Swindin, Balmer and Barnes all went to together. Balmer may have touched the ball but it was Barnes, caught on the wrong foot when trying to clear, who unmistakably put the ball over the line."

The goal stunned the North Bank and, with just 11 minutes remaining, turned out to be the winning strike. Whether the directors' 'switch' was the cause of the sudden upturn in Liverpool's fortunes we will never know, but the fact remained that, "a beaten side had come out winners."

Liverpool's strength in depth was now apparent. The contribution of raw recruits Priday and Watkinson was widely acknowledged, but there was no doubting that

Jackie Balmer heads the equaliser against Arsenal with just 14 minutes remaining.
Former Everton star Joe Mercer looks on.

the foundations for this latest victory had again been built on a rock solid defensive performance. "Without being unfair it can be said of the Highbury surprise that the supreme defence of goalkeeper, full-backs and half-backs was the true basis of success."

For the first time since November Liverpool, with just one game to go, were back in pole position and, "having their victory on the record makes it vastly more difficult," for their rivals who would now have the pressure shifted back to them.

On Whit Monday, while Liverpool took a well earned rest – and relinquished top spot in the process – Manchester United, Stoke and Wolves were all in action. On another pendulum swinging afternoon, four became three in this greatest of title races. Despite rounding their season off in style with an emphatic 6-2 demolition of Sheffield United at Maine Road that took them joint top on points, their four-goal winning margin was not enough to overhaul new leaders Wolves on goal average. It was now impossible for United to win the league.

Ted Vizzard's boys from the Black Country had regained the lead by a point from Liverpool with a narrow 1-0 win away at Huddersfield. Stoke won by the same score at Aston Villa. The results meant that the Reds had dropped three places to fourth but, with the top of the table the tightest it had ever been, they still had a chance. With fate decreeing that they should travel to Wolves for their final game the following Saturday however, the stage was set for the most dramatic of finale's.

Chapter Thirteen
They think it's all over - but not for a fortnight!

Wolverhampton Wanderers v Liverpool
Saturday 31 May 1947

"I had a word with Bob before the game and I told him if he received the ball in a deep midfield position to knock it straight down the middle for me to chase. The first opportunity he got he did exactly that and it took the Wolves defence completely by surprise."

Albert Stubbins

Not even the greatest of Hollywood film producers could have scripted a more thrilling climax to the most tumultuous and longest ever Football League season. Exactly nine months since the opening day of the inaugural post-war Football League campaign, at a time when thoughts should have been turning to sunny days out in New Brighton or listening to cricket on the wireless, Liverpool and Wolves ran out at Molineux for their 42nd and final league game. Had it been played in the modern era then you can rest assured TV executives would have been salivating at the prospect, hyping it up beyond belief and rebranding it 'the big grand slam super Saturday face-off' or something similarly banal.

Back in 1947 however, football fans had only the newspapers to turn to for their daily fix and even then, unless it was a big international or FA Cup tie, the nationals offered little in the way of column inches. Thankfully, there was always the local paper to fall back on. "The Championship had never been in a more entangling position," wrote *Ranger*.

The mathematics though, couldn't be simpler. Victory for Wolves would see them crowned champions. A Liverpool win or draw would take it to the wire and ensure the destiny of the title hung in the balance until mid-June - when Stoke were scheduled to complete their programme at Bramall Lane.

Defeat for either team would end their aspirations and so the countdown began to what was arguably the most important match ever in the history of both Liverpool and Wolves. The latter, having finished runners-up in successive seasons prior to the outbreak of war, were seeking their first title success, while Liverpool were aiming to upset the odds by landing their fifth, and most unexpected, of triumphs.

Understandably, interest in the match was enormous and with thousands of Liverpudlians expected to travel to the Black Country for this potential title-decider an official request by the Reds to Wolves that the game be made all-ticket was surprisingly rejected. This didn't deter the massed ranks of Redmen - the grandfathers of those who 29 years later would make the same journey for a game of almost equal significance - from making their presence felt in the Midlands.

So important was this game that Billy McConnell went as far as getting special leave of absence from hospital to attend. "If Liverpool win, as I think they will, I simply could not be absent," he said. Sadly, it would be the last game the popular Liverpool Chairman would ever attend. For older Liverpudlians it also brought back painful memories of 1899 when Liverpool and Aston Villa clashed in a winner-takes-all battle for the championship at Villa Park. Although that was a trip to the Midlands to forget as the Reds crashed to an emphatic 5-0 defeat!

Four days before the eagerly anticipated clash, Liverpool's directors met for their weekly board meeting but, owing to injuries, they were unable to select a team for the trip and postponed their decision until later in the week. The home side were treating the game with the intensity of a Cup Final and their players spent the week in strict training at a secret base in Blackpool. Liverpool on the other hand, didn't leave home until Friday - when they travelled to Bridgenorth to finalise their big match preparations. Remarkably, they did so without manager George Kay who was away again, this time in Ireland on a pre-arranged five-day scouting mission. The architect of what could be the Reds' most tumultuous title winning season ever would not even be at Molineux - a scenario unthinkable in today's game.

In the build-up to the match plenty of attention was focussed on the duel between Stan Cullis and Albert Stubbins but *Ranger* had no hesitation in revealing who he thought would come out on top in this particular battle, believing that, "Stubbins' speed will be a sore trial to him (Cullis)." Prior to kick-off a shock tannoy announcement revealed that this was to be Cullis' last game. It was explained that the revered Wolves' skipper was hanging up his boots to take up a position on the Molineux coaching staff. He was only 31 but, having suffered a number of serious head injuries earlier in his career, he had been warned by doctors that another blow could prove fatal and he promptly heeded their advice.

Born in Ellesmere Port, Cullis was one of the inspirational figures behind Wolves' pre-war rise to prominence. He skippered the side when just 19 and three years later became the youngest ever captain of England. In total he won 12 caps for his country and was once famously dropped for refusing to perform a Nazi salute in front of Adolf Hitler prior to a friendly against Germany in Berlin in 1938. One of the finest defenders of his generation, his was another career halted by the outbreak of war and during the hostilities he made eight guest appearances for Liverpool.

Cullis' pending retirement ensured all neutrals, if they weren't already, were rooting for Wolves and it was they who the bookies made clear favourites. Not that this worried a Liverpool team that was by now fully accustomed to battling against the odds. In fact, the belief among those at Anfield was that the timing of the game had worked in their favour for there was a lot more pressure on the hosts and long time leaders of the division now than there would have been had the game taken place as scheduled in mid-April.

Since winning so emphatically in front of the Kop in December, Wolves had stamped their authority on the league to such an extent that, but for two brief spells - one over Easter and one just the previous week - they had topped the table throughout and had it not been for a number of high-profile defensive mistakes in recent weeks then the title race would surely have been done and dusted. Unbeaten in the league since Easter Saturday, and with only one point dropped in the process, Liverpool however, went into the game as the form side. The momentum was with them but in the team selected for this most vital of matches two players knew that whatever the outcome they would not be getting a medal. They were wingers Billy Watkinson and Bob Priday, who hadn't figured in the required number of games. Speaking ahead of the game however, Priday typified the unique team spirit within the Liverpool dressing room when he said; "So long as the club wins, it suits us."

Having performed so well in Liddell's absence, Priday kept possession of the number 11 shirt and the outside-left berth for the match versus Wolves, despite the fact that Liddell had now recovered from the muscle he pulled when playing for Great Britain three weeks before. Instead, Liddell took the place of Fagan who had joined Paisley and Taylor on the injured list, the latter having been crocked while away with England in Portugal - some things never change! This was the only alteration to the Liverpool team that had beaten Arsenal seven days previous.

Much to the relief of the Reds defence, Wolves were without Denis Westcott, their chief destroyer when the two clubs met at Anfield in December. Westcott had suffered an injury in the game against Blackburn a fortnight before but the 38 goals he'd already scored that season is a Wolves record that remains unbeaten to this day. Joining him on the treatment table was inside-forward Tom Galley but the hosts were able to welcome future England captain Billy Wright back from international duty, while Jimmy Dunn - a Liverpool fan whose father was a star of the Dixie Dean inspired Everton team of the 1930s - also played. The game in the Black Country was one of four First Division fixtures played that day but there was only one match that mattered and as Stubbins later recalled; "Everyone was very tense during the build up to the game at Molineux because so much rested on it."

With the pitch-side temperature at a sun-baked Molineux high in the 90s conditions were more suitable for cricket than football and the match officials certainly agreed because they sported unfamiliar white shirts. For the spectators, shirt sleeves, summer frocks and handkerchiefs on heads were the order of the day

Jackie Balmer and Stan Cullis shake hands prior to the kick-off.

and over 50,000 of them crammed into the ground with thousands more locked outside. It wasn't long before casualties started spilling out onto the cinder track that surrounded the pitch and several fainting cases were reported due to the intense heat. High up in the stands Billy Liddell's wife Phyllis remembers it getting, "rather messy," when she and fellow 'WAGS' of the day tried eating chocolate under the glass roof, while in keeping with the cricket theme one newspaper described it as, "hotter than the Melbourne Cricket ground," had been during the recent Ashes series.

When Liverpool and Wolves ran out for the final time in the league the pace of the game was not as frantic as would be expected of a contest with so much riding on it - not surprising given the Mediterranean conditions. Wolves enjoyed the greater share of possession but Liverpool's, "speed, stamina and classic football," was to ultimately, "sweep them off their pedestal."

The Reds drew first blood after 21 minutes with a, "beautifully worked goal'. Captain Jack Balmer was the scorer, showing, "mental coolness in plentiful ration," to finish off a superb passing move. For *Ranger* it was a goal right out of the, "football as it should be played," manual. Four Liverpool players were involved without a gold shirt getting a, "smell at the ball." Liddell crossed to Balmer, who then played a one-two with Priday, before eventually firing the ball home with a shot that was described as, "an object lesson in how goals should be taken." *Bee* described it eloquently as, "a picture goal that should be drawn and framed and hung in the dressing room."

Jackie Balmer opens the scoring at Molineux.

Wolves hit back immediately with a flurry of attacks. So much so that the Echo was in no doubt that, "'if games were won on territorial advantage Wolves would be champions today." The statistics certainly backed up their theory but Wolves, with four shots on target to every Liverpool one, paid dearly for their profligacy. In the 37th minute Sidlow pulled off a stunning save to deny Dunn and from the resultant corner came the game's - and perhaps the seasons' - decisive moment.

Liverpool suddenly broke on the counter-attack and Stubbins, having dashed half the length of the pitch, raced clean through on goal after latching onto Priday's through ball. Keeping it, "under control admirably at top speed," he accelerated beyond the chasing Wolves defenders before finally steering it past Williams.

Albert Stubbins races clear to score the second.

It was a great individual effort but, as Stubbins explained years later, one that owed much to a conversation that had taken place prior to kick-off;

"I had a word with Bob before the game and I told him if he received the ball in a deep midfield position to knock it straight down the middle for me to chase. The first opportunity he got he did exactly that and it took the Wolves defence completely by surprise. Anticipating what he was going to do I had already set off and I left Stan Cullis and Billy Wright trailing in my wake. As I closed in on goal the keeper Bert Williams came rushing off his line but I just managed to get my toe to the ball and poke it past him into the corner of the net.

"That goal put us in the driving seat but it was one that was to haunt Stan for many years. He wasn't allowed to forget it. People always asked why he hadn't pulled me back but that was never Stan's style, he was too much of a sportsman and he deserves credit for that."

Cullis himself, admitted immediately afterwards, "I'd no idea Stubbins was so near and then I saw this red head flash past. He's got amazing speed." In later years Cullis rarely spoke about the build up to the second goal when, for an instant, he could have brought Stubbins down and prevented a goal even though it would have seen him almost certainly sent off. Eventually however, the Wolves' legend gave two simple sentences to explain why he hadn't;

"A lot of people have since asked my why I didn't bring him down or pull Stubbins back by

his shirt - and I suppose I could have done. But I didn't want to go down in history as the man who decided the destiny of a championship with a professional foul."

In a desperate attempt to salvage their season Wolves responded by throwing everything at Liverpool. Eventually, after 65 minutes, their efforts paid off when they pulled a goal back through Dunn who lobbed the ball over Sidlow after Spicer had failed to clear a corner. Suddenly it was, "game on," once again. Just one more goal would see the pre-season favourites crowned champions.

As the pressure on Liverpool's goal intensified, the watertight Reds' defence held firm. Dunn remembers former Wolves keeper Sidlow, back on his old stomping ground for the first time since leaving to join the Reds in February 1946, "playing a blinder," and that, "we hammered them after we scored but we couldn't find a way past him for the second time." Raymond Glendenning in the Sunday Graphic agreed, remarking ironically that;

"If they [Wolves] hadn't transferred Welsh international goalkeeper Sidlow to Liverpool he wouldn't have been there yesterday to make several masterly saves that made all the difference."

With Harley and Lambert not putting, "a foot wrong," and the half-back's doing, "all that anybody could have desired - plus a spot extra for full measure," Wolves' title dream wilted in the Molineux sun.

Relief and elation were the overriding emotions among the Liverpool players when the final whistle eventually sounded. Skipper Balmer was triumphantly carried shoulder high from the pitch as the celebrations commenced. "A great day and a great feeling," was his immediate post-match reaction and for a loyal club servant, who'd found himself on the receiving end of so much unfair barracking from the crowd during the course of the campaign - despite ending it as the club's joint top scorer alongside Stubbins, this was a moment for him to savour and one he thoroughly deserved. While Sidlow, Harley, Lambert, Jones, Spicer, Hughes, Liddell, Watkinson, Priday and Stubbins all played their part in this thrilling victory it was the experience of Anfield veteran Balmer that shone through.

For the beaten skipper Cullis it was a heart-breaking end to an illustrious career as he bowed out of the game without a winner's medal in either the league or cup. "It's been the hardest season I've known and it's ended in the second greatest disappointment of my career," he solemnly reflected afterwards. "This was as big a blow as our defeat by Portsmouth in the 1939 Cup Final."

It was to be another 42 years before Liverpool fans experienced the pain Wolves must have felt that afternoon and, as anyone present at Anfield on that ill-fated night of Friday 29 May 1989 will tell you, losing the league on the last game of the season is not a feeling you would wish on your worst enemy.

Wolves though, sportingly, took this most devastating of defeats squarely on the chin and boss Ted Vizzard admitted to having no complaints about the end result, "We had our chances and failed to take them," he said, while an emotional Cullis took time out to applaud the victors - as Stubbins later recalled;

"When I shook hands with Stan at the end of the game he had tears streaming down his face. I commiserated with him and he congratulated me. We had the utmost respect for each other, there was never any ill-feeling."

Back in the dressing rooms the contrast in moods couldn't have been starker and although knowing that this victory would count for nothing if Stoke went on to win their final game Stubbins remembered there being, "wild scenes," as the players allowed themselves a few celebratory lemonades to toast a job well done. Victory away to Wolves, while making up for the pain of the 5-1 home defeat earlier in the season, was Liverpool's sixth on the road since the end of January, an impressive run that prompted the Echo to declare it, "Championship form if ever there was."

Ranger lauded the individual attributes of every player but put this latest win down to a supreme collective effort.

"More than in any other match this season, success was due to Liverpool's grand team-work. No one player stood out by comparison with his colleagues. All were excellent - eleven determined workers, pulling out their last ounce with victory for their side the only aim."

And so the Championship trophy, which was all ready to be presented to Cullis had Wolves done what was expected of them, was hurriedly packed away and taken back to League headquarters. When it was to next appear one thing was for sure - red and white ribbons would adorn it. Whether they were the red and white of Liverpool or the red and white of Stoke City remained to be seen. All would be resolved in 14 days time and for everyone involved it was to be the longest fortnight of their lives.

Sheffield United v Stoke City
Liverpool v Everton (Liverpool Senior Cup Final)
Saturday 14 June 1947

"We have had some wonderful players in the club's history but never have we had a finer lot of gentleman, sportsmen and 100 per cent triers than we have today. That, plus the good work of the manager and trainer, has put us where we are."

Bill McConnell - Liverpool Chairman

After ten months and 42 games, Liverpool looked proudly down on the rest. It was now mid-June but still the destination of the first post-war league title was undecided. In what the longest season on record just one more game remained and the Reds could yet be overtaken at the top on goal average by Stoke City. The Potters final game was away to Sheffield United and, not surprisingly, wherever you went in Liverpool during the agonising two week wait that ensued between victory at Wolves and the grand climax at Bramall Lane this was the only topic of conversation.

The Liverpool players and management were deservedly praised for their efforts in taking the title race this far with *Ranger* writing the following day that;

> *"While waiting with what patience we can muster, we can say right now, whatever happens, that this has now been the finest season in the history of Liverpool FC. They have been within an ace of lifting the coveted double of League and FA Cup - a really glorious effort."*

The 'Crazy Gang' stood on the brink of greatness but their fate now lay in the hands of Sheffield United and all they could do was hope and pray.

Sandwiched in between the game at Wolves and their forthcoming date with destiny was the Lancashire Senior Cup Final against Bury at Anfield. It may not have been the most glamorous of competitions but there was a trophy at stake nonetheless and it also helped take their mind off the pending title issue. The team selected to face the Shakers, who had recently finished 17th in Division Two and defeated top-flight opposition in the form of Blackburn and Bolton to reach this final, was a surprisingly strong one - the same that had finished the league campaign at Molineux a week before.

Reflecting on the previous weeks heroics the matchday programme stated;

> *"The hearty congratulations of all our supporters must be tendered to the team for its magnificent display at Wolverhampton last Saturday. The whole team played delightful football and thoroughly deserved their victory. Those who were unable to be present certainly missed an epic match and the two goals scored were the acme of perfection."*

A crowd of 23,018 turned up as much to congratulate the players on their fine win over Wolves as to see them hopefully lift their first silverware of the season. In a strange replaying of the Wolves' game, they witnessed another goal apiece from Balmer and Stubbins to clinch another 2-1 victory. It was the club's seventh success in the competition and hopefully the first leg of a treble.

Anfield was the venue for another cup final the following week as the Reds played host to Everton with local pride and the Liverpool Senior Cup at stake. For once, a Merseyside derby, in which both sides fielded full-strength teams, had to take a back seat in terms of importance because this was also the day that the destiny of the First Division Championship would be decided in South Yorkshire.

Billed as, "the most important match Stoke City have ever played," in Liverpudlian eyes it was the most important match Liverpool *never* played and interest in events at Bramall Lane were such that a reporter from the Echo was sent across the Pennines to cover the game, while kick-off in the Senior Cup Final was put back by 15 minutes so as the Stoke result could be relayed to the nerve-stricken Anfield crowd on what they hoped was to be a momentous afternoon.

Over in Sheffield, *Contact* spat on the ball for good luck, while United trainer Duggie Livingstone promised to, "snaffle it," for Bill McConnell should the Blades triumph. The absence through injury of Jimmy Hagan, United's, "conductor-in-chief," did not augur well for Liverpool but the return of veteran England international Jack Pickering, a 38-year old inside-left who hadn't played competitive first team football for eight years, was to prove inspired.

By the time the Anfield game kicked-off Pickering had amazingly already made his mark, scoring after just two and half minutes of his post-war bow. The title pendulum was swinging in Liverpool's favour but, minutes later, it was Stoke's travelling fans that were, "waving their rattles," with joy as an equalising goal from Ormston meant they would be champions if there was no further score. It was a sensational start but one that was surpassed back on Merseyside where the fans witnessed three goals inside the first 15 minutes. Liverpool, "who had opened in tearaway fashion," went ahead through Balmer's, "beautiful right-foot drive from the edge of the area which scraped in between Sagar's outstretched hands and the far upright."

Alec Stevenson quickly levelled for the Blues with a lobbed effort and the fans were enthralled. "Two goals in fourteen minutes was a tasty morsel for the big crowd," wrote *Ranger*, "but more was to follow." Straight from the restart Liverpool swept upfield to force a corner. Liddell floated it across and Watkinson rose high above the Everton defence to head home and restore Liverpool's advantage. Any concerns that this local Scouse spat would lack a competitive edge because of more important goings on elsewhere were quickly dispelled. "It might have been a Wembley Cup final not a Liverpool Senior Cup final."

The atmosphere was also what you'd expect of a clash between two such fierce rivals and, "the cheering throughout all the first half had been almost without cessation... it is a long time since a match in this city kept the crowd on such tenterhooks without a hardly a moments respite."

The loudest roar however, was reserved for just before half-time. Three minutes of the second half in Sheffield had been played when Walter Rickett raced onto a through ball by Pickering before unexpectedly firing home from a tight angle. It was to be the most significant goal of the entire season and at Anfield, "the biggest cheer of all rent the skies when the scoreboard was changed to show Sheffield United beating Stoke 2-1."

What had seemed so impossible just a month ago was now looking more than likely. Liverpool - the team many had written off before a ball had been kicked - were less than 45 minutes away from being crowned champions. Given these circumstances the players at Anfield could have been forgiven for taking their foot off the pedal and allowing their minds to wonder elsewhere as the second period got underway. Indeed, Billy Liddell admitted afterwards that, "our minds were more on what was happening there than our game," but you would not have known. "The longer the game went on one marvelled at the enthusiasm, stamina and fighting spirit of both sides. After ten months of football it was almost unbelievable."

The same could be said of the goings on at Bramall Lane. Although with there being a much bigger prize at stake for Stoke nothing less would have been expected. Shortly after conceding, the visitors were guilty of spurning a gilt-edged opportunity to draw level once again, while Blades keeper Jack Smith then pulled off a stunning save to keep out a Neil Franklin header - but almost put through his own net with the subsequent clearance that cannoned off a Stoke forward.

"Never can there have been a more thrilling league match. Drama in every moment," wrote *Contact*, while a more reassuring message being sent back from Sheffield was that;

> *"Liverpool's fate is in good hands - United are fighting like the Tykes they are...playing as though their lives depended on the result. If Liverpool were in their red and white colours they could not do more."*

With Liverpool and Everton still, "going at it hammer and tongs," although without any further goals, the final minutes of the league season were being played out and, "Anfield hopes look rosier every moment."

As the Kop anxiously awaited confirmation of the final whistle from Bramall Lane, the crowd's nerves were becoming more frayed with every passing second. The majority were unable to concentrate on what was happening right in front of them but then, five minutes from time, came the moment everyone had been waiting for - Sheffield United had hung on for victory! Stoke's gallant bid for their first-ever title had floundered at the final hurdle. Liverpool were champions once again!

The news was relayed to the Anfield masses over the loud speaker system by director George Richards.

> *"The roar which greeted this announcement made the Hampden Park one sound almost like a childish whisper. The crowd threw their hands in the air, many lost their hats and did not bother to look for them after they had tossed them high up in a burst of joyful celebration."*

As mass elation swept through the ground the players politely embraced and congratulated each other on a, "'job well done," and play was temporarily held up for both match officials and Everton players to also offer their best wishes. When it restarted Liverpool held on to beat Everton 2-1 - thus winning their second trophy of the day - a unique occurrence. This Liverpool Senior Cup triumph also completed the third leg of a triple trophy haul for George Kay's men and moved *Ranger* to exclaim;

> *"Three cheers for the Great Unpredictables, whose potentialities none can ever foretell, for pulling off the seemingly impossible. No side mixes glorious uncertainty with uncertain glory more than Liverpool. Alternately alluring and vexatious, gratifying and grieving, we now forget the occasional gall and wormwood and remember only the bright fulfillment of their hat-trick of successes - the League Championship, the Lancashire Cup and the Liverpool Senior Cup."*

The referee's final whistle was the cue for the real celebrations to begin and Liddell remembered the fans came, "swarming over the pitch from the Kop and Kemlyn Road to carry us off the field. It was a scene of amazing enthusiasm."

It was ironic that Bramall Lane should be the venue where Liverpool were crowned champions for it was on that same ground on the opening day of the season that they got this most remarkable of campaigns up and running. From Len Carney to Walter Rickett it had been a roller-coaster of a ride.

Reflecting on the triumph in his later years, joint top goalscorer Albert Stubbins recalled;

> *"It was an amazing finish to the season. If you'd read it in one of the old comic books you wouldn't have believed it. So many players in that side reached their peak that season. We were the best team in the country and deserved to win the league. There have been many great Liverpool teams since but I'd like to think that we could have held our own against any of them."*

The style in which this success was achieved was to set a precedent for future Anfield title winners. While many more triumphs followed during the glory-laden days of the 1960s, 70s and 80s, never did the drama come close to matching that of the inaugural post-war season.

For the victorious Liverpool players, their reward for the heroic part they had played in this most momentous of seasons was a share of the £275 prize fund, while the official trophy presentation had to wait until late that summer - given to Bill Mac and taken to the ground in an open-topped taxi amid much cheering from fans who awaited its arrival in Lime Street. Again, the differences between the modern game and the so called, "golden age of football," is pronounced. The players were not even given the opportunity to display the spoils of their victory before the adoring Kop and even their winners' medals were handed over behind the scenes - in the sanctuary of the Anfield dressing room.

But that's just how it was back then - a million miles away from the razzmatazz and hype of the Premier League. The players of the time would have had it no other way however. After the trauma of the war years they were grateful for small mercies. As Stan Palk remembers; "We used to get a turkey from the club at Christmas though!"

Following the long, barren, trophyless years of the pre-war era the good times had at last returned to Anfield and on the night of 14 June 1947 the Higsons flowed like never before as the success starved fans lapped it up in the pubs, clubs and dance halls of Liverpool.

It had been the ultimate triumph against adversity, an achievement to rank alongside any in the illustrious history of this great club and one that should never be forgotten. What a day, what a season, what a team. "Hail the champions!"

To the Liverpool class of 1946/47 - we salute you.

THE GRAND FINALE—BY GEORGE GREEN

Epilogue

Charlie Ashcroft

Remained at the club for a further eight seasons but it wasn't until the early 1950s that Charlie Ashcroft enjoyed what could be deemed a decent run in the senior side. After his two early appearances in the title-winning campaign he dropped down the pecking order to third behind, Sidlow and Minshull, didn't feature again until October 1950. Even then he had Russell Crossley to contend with and over the next two seasons they shared goalkeeping duties as the club slid towards the dreaded drop, although he was considered good enough to be awarded an England 'B' cap against Holland in March 1952. He played in just the opening six games of the 1953/54 relegation campaign and a further 14 times during the club's first season back in Division Two but struggled after suffering a slipped disc. With the arrival of Dave Underwood and then Doug Rudham increasing competition for places even more Ashcroft eventually decided to seek a new challenge elsewhere and left to join Ipswich in June 1955. While at Portman Road he broke his arm in a match against Coventry and left after just seven appearances, ironically to join the Sky Blues, for whom he turned out 19 times before drifting out of the professional game. Built his own house in Eccleston, just outside Chorley, where he still lives today and remains a keen follower of the Reds.

Total LFC appearances: 89   Total LFC goals: 0

Jack Balmer

1946/47 was the undoubted peak of Balmer's distinguished playing career. He was appointed captain on a permanent basis the following season, a position held for two years, during which time he missed only two games and the goals continued to flow, although not at the prolific rate he'd netted them in the title-winning year. Forever remembered for his famous hat-trick of hat-tricks, Balmer never did hit another treble and it's sad to say that his popularity with the crowd didn't improve as the club embarked on a steady decline. On the opening day of the 1949/50 campaign he reached the milestone figure of 100 goals in a red shirt as Sunderland were defeated on the opening day but lost his place in the team soon after and played no part in Liverpool's run to a first-ever Wembley Cup final later that season. At 34 years of age he manage to regain his place and made 36 appearances, scoring a further 10 goals, during the course of 1950/51. The end was nigh though and in May 1952 he hung up his shooting boots for good. His long association with the club continued as a member of the coaching staff for a further three years before he eventually turned his back on the game to work at his family's West Derby-based joinery business. He died, aged 68, on Christmas Day 1984.

Total LFC appearances: 312 Total LFC goals: 111

Tom Bush

A fine club servant, Tom Bush dedicated the best part of his life to the Reds. He didn't play again after the 1946/47 season but a brief spell coaching in Holland, returned to Anfield in a youth development capacity, working closely with the scouts and helping to nurture some of the players who would take the club on to even greater glory during the sixties, such as Hunt, Smith, Byrne, Callaghan and Lawrence. He also became an integral figure on the administrative side of things at Anfield and was a hugely popular figure at the club until his death in December 1969, aged 55.

Total LFC appearances: 72   Total LFC goals: 1

Len Carney

Following his brief cameo appearance at the very start of the 1946/47 campaign, amateur player Carney reappeared in the first team for a four-game spell in October 1947 but was unable to repeat the goalscoring heroics of his debut and left the club in April the following year. Carney later played for Crosby-based non-league outfit Marine and captained them against the barefooted Nigerian national team in a friendly at College Road in August 1949. Eventually entered the teaching profession and became headmaster at Chadderton Grammar School in Oldham. Died in Liverpool in 1996.

Total LFC appearances: 6   Total LFC goals: 1

Cyril Done

Despite finishing the 1946/47 season as the club's third highest goalscorer big Cyril never managed to establish himself as a first team regular. During the campaign that followed he played only six times and although fortunes did improve he faced a constant battle to impress the selectors. His best season, in terms of appearances and goals, came in 1948/49 when he started on 28 occasions and netted 13. But even a prolific purple patch of eight goals in seven successive games, while confirming his goalscoring credentials, failed to establish him as a regular. Like fellow forward Balmer, he played no part in the 1950 FA Cup run and finally cut his losses with the club in May 1952 by completing a move across the Mersey to Tranmere. A two-year stint at Prenton Park yielded an impressive 61 goals in 87 league appearances and earned him a £2,000 transfer to Second Division Port Vale. Just four months later he lined up against some of his old Liverpool team-mates, including Ray Lambert and Billy Liddell, and marked the occasion by sensationally scoring all four home goals in a valiant 4-3 victory at Burslem Park. Done topped the scoring charts at Vale that season and again in 1956/57 before leaving on a free transfer to join non-league Winsford United, where he saw out the final two seasons of his playing career. In 1959 he took over the managerial reigns at Skelmersdale United, a position he held until 1962. Upon retirement from the game Done worked tirelessly to raise awareness of cancer and passed away in Formby on the same day as England World Cup winning captain Bobby More in February 1993. He was 72.

Total LFC appearances: 111 Total LFC goals: 38

John Easdale

Didn't play again for Liverpool after 1946/47 and eventually left to join Stockport County in September 1948, for whom he made only a handful of appearances before drifting out of the game for good. He passed away in 1998.

Total LFC appearances: 2 Total LFC goals: 0

Harry Eastham

Failed to figure in the first team at all the following season and was allowed to join Tranmere Rovers on a free in May 1948. Spent five years at Prenton Park, where he clocked up over 150 appearances, and later moved on to Accrington Stanley for a single season. In 1963 his nephew George brought about the end of the maximum wage and the retain and transfer system. Ended his career with non-league Netherfield and died in Bolton in September 1998.

Total LFC appearances: 68 Total LFC goals: 4

Willie Fagan

Injury problems restricted his appearances in the two seasons that immediately followed the triumph of 1946/47 but despite having lost the captaincy he was back to his best in 1950 and played a starring role, scoring four goals en route, as Liverpool went all the way to a Wembley FA Cup Final for the first time. Aged 33, the end of his career was drawing close and following the disappointment of defeat to Arsenal he played just seven more first team games the Reds before leaving on a free to join Irish club Distillery in January 1952. Returned to England just months later and took up a player-manager position with Weymouth but after three years in that job Fagan turned his back on football and went to work as a prison officer. Passed away in Wellingborough, nine days after his 75th birthday in February 1992.

Total LFC appearances: 185 Total LFC goals: 57

Jim Harley

Lost his place in the team after just two games of the next season but fought back to finish the campaign with 21 appearances under his belt. Was dislodged from the right-back spot on a permanent basis by the emergence of Bill Shepherd the following year though and never played for the club again, his last senior outing being a 1-1 draw at home to Manchester City in April 1948. Retired, aged 32, in February 1949 and died in Liverpool 40 years later.

Total LFC appearances: 134 Total LFC goals: 0

Laurie Hughes

Served the club with loyalty and distinction for a further 13 years, and made history in 1950 when he became the first Liverpool player to appear in the World Cup Finals, while that the same year, despite not playing in the semi-final victory over Everton, he was on the losing side in the FA Cup Final against Arsenal. Scored his one and only goal for the club in a home draw with Preston in December 1951 but was unable to halt the steady decline in Liverpool's fortunes after their first Wembley appearance and played 27 times in the relegation season of 1953/54. Captained the club during the following season and played on at Anfield until the 1957/58 campaign, his last appearance coming in a 5-1 drubbing away to Charlton. Despite rumours linking him with a move to Manchester United in the wake of the Munich air crash he played out the remainder of his career in the Liverpool reserves and was still at the club when Bill Shankly arrived as manager. Hughes eventually hung up his boots in May 1960 and had several local business interests near his home in Waterloo where he still lives.

Total LFC appearances: 326 Total LFC goals: 1

Bill Jones

Deemed by Sports Spectator Magazine to be Liverpool's, "outstanding player," of the 1946/47 title triumph, Bill Jones went on to establish himself as an almost permanent fixture in the side during the years that followed but continued to be used in a variety of positions and never got rid of his utility man tag. Finally gained belated England recognition in 1950 when awarded his only two caps but was kept out of the World Cup squad by club-mate Laurie Hughes, this just a month after he had been controversially selected ahead of Bob Paisley for the FA Cup Final against Arsenal. Jones scored one of the goals that saved Liverpool from relegation in 1953, but had the unfortunate distinction of captaining the side that lost its top-flight status the following season. Aged 33, he left Anfield in the wake of that bitter disappointment and became player-manager at Ellesmere Port Town but never cut his ties with the club. Later worked as a scout and was responsible for spotting, among others, Liverpool's all-time record League goalscorer Roger Hunt. The grandfather of Liverpool and England full-back of the early 1990s Rob Jones, Bill is now long retired and living in Cheshire.

Total LFC appearances: 277 Total LFC goals: 17

George (Harold) Kaye

In the face of such stiff competition for places in the Liverpool half-back line 'Harry' Kaye submitted a transfer request in the immediate aftermath of the 46/47 title success and found there to be no shortage of interested suitors. He opted to join Third Division South Swindon Town and despite some bad luck with injuries, including a broken ankle, went on to put in six years good service at the County Ground, making 189 appearances and scoring five goals before hanging up his boots in 1953. Remained in the Swindon area until his death in 1992.

Total LFC appearances: 2   Total LFC goals: 0

Ray Lambert

Remained a first choice full-back, predominantly on the left but occasionally on the right, for the next eight and a half years. Played in the FA Cup Final of 1950 and was also in the team that suffered relegation four years later. Scored just two goals for the Reds, both from the penalty spot, and won a total of five international caps for Wales. After 20 years at the club, Lambert eventually retired in May 1956, just a few weeks short of his 34th birthday and later worked as a newsagent in his native North Wales. Passed away in October 2009 during final preparations for this book.

Total LFC appearances: 341   Total LFC goals: 2

Billy Liddell

One of the greatest players ever to play for Liverpool, older fans who remember Billy Liddell will forever argue he *was* the greatest. Served the club with distinction throughout the barren years of the 1950s and was such an influential figure that the club became widely known as 'Liddellpool' in his honour. Had he not been kicked-off the park by Arsenal's Alec Forbes in the 1950 FA Cup Final then Liverpool's long wait for what was then the most-coveted trophy of all may have ended 15 years earlier than it did. Many Reds' fans felt that the presence of the King was the only that prevented the Arsenal defender from becoming the first man sent off in a cup final. As the club's fortunes dipped alarmingly his unswerving loyalty was admirable and in 1951 he rejected a lucrative £2,000 offer to play in Columbia. After the Reds were relegated in 1954 Liddell played out the rest of his career in Division Two but such was his star status he was selected to represent Great Britain for a second time in 1955, a feat emulated only by the great Stanley Matthews. Was the natural choice to succeed Laurie Hughes as captain the same year and led by example. Topped the Anfield goalscoring charts for three successive seasons in the mid-1950s, played in every outfield position and in 1957 became the club's record appearance holder, an accolade he would hold until Ian Callaghan's longevity saw it surpassed in the 1970s. Remained a big favourite of the crowd throughout this time, so much so that when he was controversially dropped from the team during the 1958/59 season the fans demanded he was recalled. Bill Shankly's arrival as manager in 1959 unfortunately coincided with the end of his career and he played just a handful of games under the new manager before finally bowing out in August 1960. Was awarded a testimonial by the club the following month and almost 40,000 were in attendance to pay tribute. Later served as a Justice of the Peace and continued to be a regular in the stands at Anfield until his death in July 2001.

Total LFC appearances: 534 Total LFC goals: 228

Tommy McLeod

Wasn't called upon at all during the 1947/48 season but reappeared for a four-game spell in December 1948. A 2-0 home defeat to Manchester United however, was to be his last first-team outing and after failing to fulfil the early promise he had once shown, left Liverpool to join Division Three North Chesterfield in July 1951. Scored three goals in 25 appearances during his one and only season with the Spireites and he wound down his career with a spell at non-league Wisbech Town between August 1952 and April 1954.

Total LFC appearances: 7   Total LFC goals: 0

Ray Minshull

Added another 25 appearances to the six he made in 1946/47 but eventually conceded defeat in his battle to dislodge Cyril Sidlow from the number one spot in 1951 after Russell Crossley moved ahead of him in the pecking order. Joined Southport, who were then in Division Three North, in June that year and made over 200 appearances for the Sandgrounders before moving on to Bradford Park Avenue in 1958. He then embarked on a career in coaching and, after working abroad in Austria and Gibraltar, he took up a position as a regional FA coach before becoming Youth Development Officer at Everton where he was responsible for bringing through the likes of future Red Steve McMahon, Gary Stevens, Kevin Ratcliffe, and Kevin Richardson. Passed away, aged 84, in February 2005.

Total LFC appearances: 31   Total LFC goals: 0

Berry Nieuwenhuys

As expected, Nivvy hung up his boots for good at the end of the 1946/47 season and finally returned to South Africa where he became assistant coach to golfing great Bobby Locke at the Transvaal Country Club. Retained an involvement in football through coaching several South African teams, including former club Germiston Callies, and later acted as a scout on behalf of a number of English sides. Retired from active sport in the 1970s and passed away in June 1984.

Total LFC appearances: 260 Total LFC goals: 79

Bob Paisley

A virtual ever-present in the team over the next six seasons, Paisley hit the headlines in 1950 when, after famously scoring in the FA semi-final win over Everton, he missed out on a place in the final against Arsenal at Wembley. In the immediate aftermath he seriously contemplated quitting the game and it required the persuasive powers of Albert Stubbins to convince him that his future belonged at Anfield. While still a player he studied physiotherapy and, after the club suffered relegation, he accepted the offer of a position on the backroom staff. In 1957/58 he guided the Reds' reserves to their first-ever Central League title. He gradually worked his way up through the ranks, becoming an original member of the much-fabled 'Bootroom', and when Bill Shankly stepped down as manager in 1974 Paisley was the automatic choice to succeed him. Accepted the challenge reluctantly but, it's fair to say, didn't look back. Over the course of the nine years that followed he oversaw the accumulation of 13 major trophies, won six manager awards and received an OBE in 1977. Retired in 1983 but acted as an advisor to Kenny Dalglish during the double-winning season of 1985/86. Remains the most successful English football manager of all-time. Another former player who suffered with Alzheimer's disease in later life, Bob Paisley passed away on Valentine's Day 1996 and has since been honoured at Anfield with the Paisley Gateway outside the Kop.

Total LFC appearances: 277 Total LFC goals: 12

Stan Palk

Played in six of the first nine games in 1947/48 but afterwards made only one more senior appearance for the Reds. In search of regular first-team football Palk joined Port Vale in the summer of 1948 in a £10,000 deal that also involved the transfer of Liverpool reserve Mick Hulligan. At Vale Park he played under Anfield goalscoring legend Gordon Hodgson and spent four years in the Potteries. Was an ever-present for two seasons, skippered the club and netted 14 goals in 169 appearances before embarking on a nomadic spell on the non-league circuit where he turned out for Worcester City, Northwich Victoria, Prescot Cables, Pwllheli, Flint Town, Oswestry Town and finally Maghull. Passed away in October 2009, during final preparations for this book and just a couple of weeks short of his 88th birthday.

Total LFC appearances: 13   Total LFC goals: 0

Bob Priday

Appeared in just over half of Liverpool's fixtures the following season but lost his place after a FA Cup fourth round defeat to Manchester United and afterwards struggled to win it back. Played his last game for the club away to Chelsea in March 1949 and later that month was sold to Blackburn Rovers for £10,000. Scored 11 goals in 44 league appearances at Ewood Park but was involved in a serious car accident during this time. Brief spells at Clitheroe and Northwich Victoria followed before Priday returned to the Football League with Accrington Stanley and then finished his career playing for Rochdale.

Total LFC appearances: 40   Total LFC goals: 7

Barney Ramsden

Within just nine months of Liverpool clinching the inaugural post-war title Barney Ramsden left to join Sunderland. Unable to win back his place from Ray Lambert, he made ten appearances in 1947/48 after he returned from America and played his last game for the club on Christmas Day that season - a 3-1 home defeat to Arsenal. Didn't enjoy the best of spells at Roker Park, making just 13 first-team appearances in two years, and brought the curtain down on his career with a five-month stint at Hartlepool United before finally emigrating to America for good. Made a nostalgic return to Liverpool in 1972 but was back in California when he passed away in March 1976.

Total LFC appearances: 66   Total LFC goals: 0

Cyril Sidlow

Was Liverpool's undisputed number one for the next three seasons and played every game en route to the club's first Wembley Cup Final appearance in 1950. Was helpless to prevent Arsenal running out 2-0 winners that day but later that year conceded four goals in a disastrous ten minute spell and was never picked for the first team again, replaced by Russell Crossley – a keeper he himself had recommended to the club. Ended what had been a distinguished association with the Reds in August 1952 by signing for New Brighton and later served his former club Wolves for two years as a coach. Retired from the game altogether in May 1955 and worked in the building trade as a carpenter. Died in Codsall, near Wolverhampton in April 2005, aged 89.

Total LFC appearances: 165 Total LFC goals: 0

Eddie Spicer

Finally established himself as a permanent fixture in the Liverpool first team during the 1949/50 season and played left-back in the FA Cup Final defeat to Arsenal. A broken leg, sustained against Malmo on a summer tour of Sweden in 1951, ruled him out of the entire next season but he battled bravely back to regain his place before suffering the misfortune of another broken leg in December 1953. It occurred at Old Trafford following a collision with his own goalkeeper, debutant Dave Underwood. So severe was the injury that, in all, his leg was fractured in 19 places and following a lengthy spell in hospital it took almost 12 months before he could walk properly again. Unfortunately, it also signalled the end of Eddie Spicer's football career. There was to be no comeback from this second break and, aged 31 he was forced to retire. Was awarded a well deserved testimonial in 1955. In later life he ran a village pub in North Wales. Died, aged 82, in December 2004.

Total LFC appearances: 168 Total LFC goals: 2

Albert Stubbins

After his goalscoring heroics of 1946/47, Stubbins repeated the feat by top scoring for the Reds the following season, with four of his goals coming in one game against Huddersfield Town - despite a pre-match threat from an unknown source that his legs would be broken if he scored! Exploits such as this helped maintain his hero status among the fans. In their eyes he could do no wrong, even when he went on a much publicised, self-imposed, strike prior to the 1948/49 campaign. Unfortunately, injuries then prevented him from scaling the heights of his first two seasons at the club and after he'd helped the Reds reach Wembley for the first time in 1950, he finally returned to his native Tyneside for good in 1953, finishing his career with non-league Ashington. A Liverpool scout in the 1950s in 1960, he coached in America before embarking on a full-time career in journalism. Was famously chosen as the only footballer to appear on the cover of the Beatles' Sergeant Peppers album and, such was his popularity at Anfield that half a century after hanging up his boots a fan club was formed in his honour - the 'Albert Stubbins Crazy Crew'. Continued to live in his native north-east until his death in December 2002.

Total LFC appearances: 180 Total LFC goals: 83

Phil Taylor

Remained an integral member of the team for the next six years, and won three England caps in the process, but was unable to stop the sudden decline in Liverpool's fortunes following the title-winning success of 1946/47. Succeeded Jack Balmer as captain and proudly led the Reds out at Wembley in the Cup Final of 1950. Retired at the end of the 1953/54 relegation season but took up a position as a coach, working under manager Don Welsh. When Welsh was relieved of his duties in 1956 Taylor stepped up to the plate to succeed him. Three successive near misses in the quest to secure a top-flight return eventually took its toll and his managerial fate was virtually sealed after an infamous FA Cup third round defeat away to non-league Worcester City in January 1959. Before the end of the year he'd resigned, stating that he'd took the club as far as he could and that, "the strain of trying to win promotion has proved too much." His departure paved the way for Bill Shankly's arrival but Taylor continued to wholeheartedly support the club and was regular in the Main Stand at Anfield for many years after.

Total LFC appearances: 345 Total LFC goals: 34

William Watkinson

Started out as the Reds' first choice number seven in 1947/48 but failed to make the same impact as he'd done towards the end of the previous campaign and lost his place within a couple of months. Played the first six games of the following season, scoring one, but was soon replaced by Jimmy Payne and Watkinson went on to make only one more senior appearance in a red shirt, away to Portsmouth a week before the Cup Final in 1950. In January 1951 Accrington Stanley paid a club record £3,100 to sign him and he enjoyed a successful three years at Peel Park, scoring 45 league goals in 105 matches. Moved on to Halifax Town for £2,500 in September 1954 before winding down his career where it all began, with his local side Prescot Cables. Eventually hung up his boots in May 1958.

Total LFC appearances: 24   Total LFC goals: 2

George Kay

After leading Liverpool to their fifth Championship George Kay's health suffered as the stress of trying to keep the Reds at the forefront of the English game took its toll. In 1950 he became the first manager to guide Liverpool to a Wembley FA Cup Final but, although he travelled with the team, illness overshadowed the big day and after collapsing on the morning of the game he was unable to lead the team out, that honour going to Albert Shelley. Was able to watch from the stands as his team lost 2-0 but suffered a relapse afterwards and it came as little surprise when, in January the following year, he stepped down from his managerial duties after being advised on medical grounds to retire. After a long spell in hospital he eventually died 18 April 1954, aged 62. His passing was mourned by all those who had played under him - Billy Liddell remarking that; "He had no other thought but for the good of Liverpool. If ever a man gave his life for a club, George Kay did so for Liverpool."

Bill McConnell

After failing to recover from the illness that struck him down during the run-in to the 1946/47 season, Bill McConnell sadly passed away that summer but not before receiving the ball from the Wolves' game in his hospital bed and proudly attending the official League Championship presentation party in London. His brother Tom McConnell joined the Anfield Board in 1948.

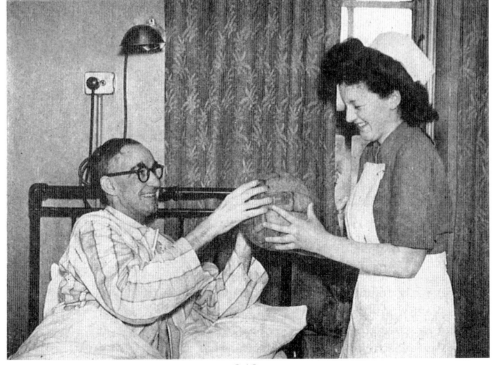

Statistics

Final League Table

	P	W	D	L	F	A	W	D	L	F	A	Pts
Liverpool	42	13	3	5	42	24	12	4	5	42	28	57
Manchester United	42	17	3	1	61	19	5	9	7	34	35	56
Wolves	42	15	1	5	66	31	10	5	6	32	25	56
Stoke City	42	14	5	2	52	21	10	2	9	38	32	55
Blackpool	42	14	1	6	38	32	8	5	8	33	38	50
Sheffield United	42	12	4	5	51	32	9	3	9	38	43	49
Preston North End	42	10	7	4	45	27	8	4	9	31	47	47
Aston Villa	42	9	6	6	39	24	9	3	9	28	29	45
Sunderland	42	11	3	7	33	27	7	5	9	32	39	44
Everton	42	13	5	3	40	24	4	4	13	22	43	43
Middlesbrough	42	11	3	7	46	32	6	5	10	27	36	42
Portsmouth	42	11	3	7	42	27	5	6	10	24	33	41
Arsenal	42	9	5	7	43	33	7	4	10	29	37	41
Derby County	42	13	2	6	44	28	5	3	13	29	51	41
Chelsea	42	9	3	9	33	39	7	4	10	36	45	39
Grimsby Town	42	9	6	6	37	35	4	6	11	24	47	38
Blackburn Rovers	42	6	5	10	23	27	8	3	10	22	26	36
Bolton Wanderers	42	8	5	8	30	28	5	3	13	27	41	34
Charlton Athletic	42	6	6	9	34	32	5	6	10	23	39	34
Huddersfield Town	42	11	4	6	34	24	2	3	16	19	55	33
Brentford	42	5	5	11	19	35	4	2	15	26	53	25
Leeds United	42	6	5	10	30	30	0	1	20	15	60	18

LFC appearances 1946/47

	League	Cup	Total
Jack Balmer	39	6	45
Ray Lambert	36	6	42
Albert Stubbins	36	6	42
Phil Taylor	35	6	41
Cyril Sidlow	34	6	40
Billy Liddell	34	6	40
Bob Paisley	33	6	39
Bill Jones	26	6	32
Laurie Hughes	30	1	31
Bernard Ramsden	23	1	24
Cyril Done	17	6	23
Willie Fagan	18	4	22
Jim Harley	17	4	21
Harry Eastham	19	2	21
Berry Nieuwenhuys	15	0	15
Eddie Spicer	10	0	10
Robert Priday	9	0	9
William Watkinson	6	0	6
Stan Palk	6	0	6
Ray Minshull	6	0	6
Tommy McLeod	3	0	3
Tom Bush	3	0	3
Len Carney	2	0	2
Charlie Ashcroft	2	0	2
John Easdale	2	0	2
George Kaye	1	0	1

LFC goalscorers 1946/47	League	Cup	Total
Jack Balmer	24	4	28
Albert Stubbins	24	4	28
Cyril Done	10	2	12
Billy Liddell	7	1	8
Willie Fagan	7	0	7
Berry Nieuwenhuys	5	0	5
Robert Priday	2	0	2
Bill Jones	2	0	2
Len Carney	1	0	1
Phil Taylor	1	0	1
William Watkinson	1	0	1

Miscellaneous

On the road Liverpool were the division's highest scorers with 42, an average of two goals per game.

They managed the same total at home - but eight other sides netted more.

Liverpool used a total of 26 players in the 1946/47 season. 17 were Football League debutants.

Blackpool was the only team to complete a league double over Liverpool.

In turn, the Reds did the double over eight teams – Bolton, Leeds, Grimsby, Huddersfield, Portsmouth, Arsenal, Sunderland and Aston Villa.

Only one team prevented Liverpool from scoring against them in the league – local rivals Everton.

Preston were the only team not to score against Liverpool in the league.

Liverpool were involved in the highest scoring game of the season – 7-4 v Chelsea, and had the biggest away winning margin – 6-1 v Grimsby.

Liverpool won the most number of away games (12) in the division.

The lowest league position Liverpool occupied during the season was 12th (fourth match)

Liverpool finished the season with the highest average attendance in the First Division - 45,732.

The aggregate attendance in league matches was 960,368. The highest home attendance was v Wolves, the lowest v Grimsby. The highest away attendance was v Chelsea, the lowest v Huddersfield.

The highest attendance of all was in the FA Cup semi-final replay at Maine Road - 72,000 watched this game.

The club received only 13 League Title winners medals. At a Board meeting on Tuesday 24 June 1947 it was decided to give these to Sidlow, Harley, Lambert, Taylor, Hughes, Jones, Paisley, Balmer, Stubbins, Fagan, Liddell, Shelley (trainer) and Key (manager). At the same meeting the Board decided that an application would be made to the Football league for permission to purchase four additional medals - for Eastham, Nivvy, Done and Ramsden. As a further reward the players were treated to a club holiday - to Keswick in the Lake District and a picnic in Llandudno.

At the end of the season the maximum and minimum wage was increased to £12 and £7 respectively. It would rise again over the coming years but the retain and transfer system remained until 1964.

Bibliography

Liverpool Daily Post, Liverpool Echo, Liverpool Evening Express, Liverpool Football Echo, The Daily Mirror, The Times, The New York Times. Liverpool FC Official Minutes, 1939-43 and 1947

Paul Agnew, *Tom Finney - My Autobiography*, Headline Book Publishing, 2003
Jeff Anderson with Stephen Done, *The Official Liverpool FC Illustrated Encyclopedia*, Carlton Books 2003
Jeff Anderson with Stephen Done, *The Official Liverpool FC Illustrated History*, Carlton Books 2002
Sir Derek Birley, *Playing the game; Sport and British Society, 1910-45*, Manchester University Press, 1995
Horatio Carter, *Footballer's Progress: an autobiography*, Sporting Handbooks, 1950
Richard Cox, Grant Jarvie and Wray Vamplew, *Encyclopedia of British Sport*, ABC-CLIO Ltd, 2000
Stan Cullis, *All for the Wolves*, Rupert Hart Davis, 1960
Eric Doig and Alex Murphy, *The Essential History of Liverpool*, headline, 2003
David Downing, *Passovotchka: Moscow Dynamo in Britain 1945*, Bloomsbury Publishing, 1999
Neil Franklin, *Soccer at Home and Abroad*, Stanley paul, 1957
Jimmy Guthrie, *Soccer Rebel: The evolution of the professional footballer*, Davis Foster (Publishers), 1976
Eddie Hapgood, *Football Ambassador*, Sporting Handbooks, 1948
Nick Hayes and Jeff Hill eds., *Millions Like Us? British Culture in the Second World War*, Liverpool University Press, 1999
Jim Holden, *Stan Cullis - The Iron Manager*, Breedon Books, 2000
David R Jack, *Matt Busby - My Story*, Souvenir Press Ltd, 1957
Peter Jeffs, *The Golden Age of Football - 1946-1953*, Breedon Books, 1991
John Keith, *Billy Liddell - The Legend who carried the Kop*, Robson Books, 2004
John Keith, *Bob Paisley - Manager of the Millennium*, Robson books, 1999
John Keith and Peter Thomas, *The Daily Express A-Z Of Mersey Soccer*, Beaverbrook Newspapers 1973
Simon Kupar, *Ajax the Dutch, the war: Football in Europe during the Second World War,* Orion Books, 2003
David Kynaston, *Austerity Britain 1945-51*, Bloomsbury Publishing, 2007
Tommy Lawton, *Football is My Business*, Sporting handbooks Ltd., 1947
Billy Liddell, *My Soccer Story*, Stanley Paul, 1960
David McVay and Andy Smith, *The Complete Centre-Forward: The Authorised biography of Tommy Lawton*, Sportsbooks Ltd, 2000
Tony Matthews, *Who's Who of Liverpool*, Mainstream, 2006
David Millar, *Stanley Matthews - The Authorised Biography*, Pavilion, 1989
Stanley Mortensen, *Football is my game*, Sampson Low, 1949
Peter Oakes, *Bob Paisley - My 50 Golden Reds*, Front Page Books, 1990
Bob Paisley, *A Lifetime in Football*, Arthur Baker, 1983
Bob Paisley, *Bob Paisley's Liverpool Scrapbook*, Souvenir Press, 1979
Brian Pead, *Ee-Aye-Addio We've won the Cup*, Champion Press, 1993.
Brian Pead, *Liverpool: A Complete Record 1892-1986*, Breedon Books 1986
Brian Pead, *Liverpool Champion of Champions*, Breedon Books 1990
Sidney Pollard, *The Development of the British Economy 1914-1990*, Arnold, 1996
Anton Ripon, *Gas Masks for Goal Posts: Football in Britain during the Second World War*, Sutton Publishing Ltd, 2005
Jack Rollin, *Soccer at War 1939-45. The complete record of British football and footballers during the Second World War*, Headline Book Publishing, 2005
Jimmy Seed, *The Jimmy Seed Story*, Phoenix Sports Books, 1957
Ivan Sharpe, *Sunday Chronicle Football Annual 1946/47*, Sunday Chronicle, 1946
Tomas Taw, *Football's War and Peace. The tumultuous season of 1946/47*, Desert Island Books, 2003
N. Varley, *Golden Boy: A Biography of Wilf Mannion*, Aurum Press, 1997
Taylor, R., Ward, A., and Williams, J., *Three Sides of the Mersey: An Oral History of Everton, Liverpool and Tranmere Rovers*, Robson books, 1993
Billy Wright, *Football is my Passport*, The Sportsmans Book Club, 1959
Billy Wright, *One Hundred Caps and All That*, Soccer Book Club, 1962
David Wotherspoon, *The Mighty Mariners - The story of Marine Association Football Club*, David Wotherspoon, 1997

At the End of the Storm